# OUR FORGOTTEN PAST

## PAST

**Seven centuries of life on the land**

Edited by
Jerome Blum

Texts by
Jerome Blum
Joan Thirsk
Diedrich Saalfeld
Yves-Marie Bercé
Jacqueline Simpson
William N. Parker
Harvey Franklin

*256 illustrations*
*54 in colour*

**THAMES AND HUDSON**

Frontispiece: Peasant at Dalecarlia, Sweden, with two girls, 1909

*Editor and publisher wish to acknowledge the generous
advice given by all the authors on the selection of the
illustrations and the wording of the captions. It must
be made clear, however, that final responsibility for
these picture sections remains entirely with the publisher.*

Designed and produced by
Thames and Hudson
Managing Editor: Ian Sutton
Design: Ruth Rosenberg
Editorial: Marcy Bourne
Picture Research: Alla Weaver
Susan Johnson (chapters 8, 9)

Filmset in Great Britain by Tameside Filmsetting Limited
Monochrome origination in Great Britain by DSCI, London
Colour origination in Switzerland by Cliché Lux, Neuchâtel
Printed and bound in the Netherlands by
Royal Smeets Offset, Weert

First published in the USA in 1982 by
Thames and Hudson Inc., 500 Fifth Avenue,
New York, New York 10110
Library of Congress Catalog Card Number 81-85070

# Contents

# Introduction

In our urban and industrial society it is difficult to realize how recently it was that most people in the Western world lived on and from the land. Until far into the 19th century, and in some lands into the 20th century, the greatest part of the population lived out in the country. Much of the blame for our failure to remember the way it was – for what might be called a collective amnesia about our own past – lies with the scholars who devoted themselves to the study of the past of European and American society. Conscious always of the present and its problems, these scholars, whether historians, economists or sociologists, directed their researches and their writings to the distinctive features of urban and industrial civilization. They concerned themselves with such phenomena as the spread of industrialization, the growth of cities, the creation and rise of new social classes, the appearance and evolution of new values and new social attitudes, and the political, economic and social impact of these phenomena upon society. In doing this, they neglected the history of most of the people who ever lived.

There were, of course, a few who did study and write about the rural past. Some among these authors had a tendency to romanticize and even to idealize the peasant and his institutions. They indulged in a nostalgia for a way of life that could never be retrieved, and thought that they discerned values and harmonies in the village world that they felt were regrettably absent from their own workaday societies. Others, concerned about the declining importance of agriculture and especially about the worsening economic condition of the small farmer and the farm labourer, often allowed their ideological interests to affect their accounts and their conclusions.

In the decades since the end of World War II, however, a small but always growing number of scholars in Europe and America have turned to an intensive and objective examination of our rural past. They have written studies of villages and of provinces that utilize long-overlooked source materials and that have a depth of perception and a range of applicability that far transcend the boundaries of the local area with which they are concerned. Other have written national studies and still others have provided syntheses that disregard national and linguistic barriers and that provide a pan-European perspective. Ambitious multi-volumed series, with sections written by leading authorities, have

been launched, and new scholarly journals devoted to rural history have been established. As a consequence of all this activity, much more is now known about the centuries that form our forgotten past.

In these same decades, and increasingly in more recent years, an unfocused but unmistakable nostalgia for rural life as people imagined it once was has surfaced in all the industrial societies of the Western world. It has appeared not only among the small minority who, repelled by the urgencies and the stresses and strains of urban and industrial life, are unable to adjust, and seek to escape by a return to the land, but it has also had an impact upon a far larger number of people who long for a simpler and less structured way of life and who suspect that our rural forebears had a better time of it than we have. This nostalgia finds its reflection in the writings of some social scientists about village life in the less developed countries of our modern world. They contend that the old self-contained culture was more humane and more moral and more protective of the welfare of the villagers than are the institutions and the demands of modernization that are displacing the traditional patterns of village life. And certainly the emergence, after the end of the Second World War and the final collapse of European overseas empires, of the so called Third World nations as potent forces in world politics and economies has awakened a new and vital interest in rural matters, including our own rural past. Our awareness of these overwhelmingly rural societies and their always increasing importance in our own lives has made us realize that we, the urban and industrial societies, are the exception, and that the great mass of mankind is still made up of peasants who live on and from the land, dependent upon soil and weather and, like our forebears, living often at the very margin of subsistence.

This growing interest in rural life has persuaded the authors and publishers of this volume that it is worthwhile to produce a book for the non-specialist that presents the scholarly findings that have changed old views and old perceptions of our own rural past. Till now these findings and revisions have been published in academic monographs and professional journals that have a readership limited almost exclusively to a relatively small circle of specialists. Our book makes this knowledge available to a far wider audience.

The book deals with the history, economy and culture of rural society, in Europe from the British Isles across to Russia, and in America. Its time span extends from the late Middle Ages, when early modern society was slowly emerging out of the wreckage of medieval civilization, down into the 20th century when the urban and industrial way of life had clearly established its domination in the Western world. Each chapter of the book considers a fundamental aspect of rural life, and each is written by a scholar, whether a historian, economist, folklorist or geographer, who is an established authority. The chapters are arranged in a logical progression so that as the reader proceeds through the book he gains a rounded and realistic picture of the rural life that was once the norm in Europe and in the United States.

The book begins with a discussion of the basic units of rural life, the family and the village community. There were, of course, many local and regional variations in the structure of these units that were the building blocks of the old society, but they all bore striking similarities in their organization and function. The community was a closed or nearly closed group in which everyone knew everyone else, and in which tradition and habit provided the stability that held the community together. The community was made up of families rather than of individuals, or, more exactly, of households, for the domestic unit then usually included persons who were not kinsmen of the core family.

The villagers had a considerable amount of autonomy in the administration of their communities, but this was at the sufferance of the people who held the real power out in the countryside. These people were the nobles. They are the subject of the next chapter, which concerns itself with the nobles' ascent to their dominant position, their exclusivity and their privileges, and their role in and contribution to the hierarchical structure that provided the mechanism by which the society governed itself. The instruments and institutions by which the nobility exercised its control over the peasantry are dealt with in the third chapter. Here, the relationship between the two orders is discussed. That relationship ranged from a barely felt dependence of peasant upon lord to a serfdom that scarcely differed from chattel slavery and that in some lands ended not much more than a century ago.

Next, under the expert guidance of Dr Joan Thirsk, the reader follows the people of the villages out into their fields. Dr Thirsk tells how the villagers went about earning their livings from the land, and discusses such matters as the techniques of tillage, the layout of the fields and the crops that were raised in them. Their efforts, hampered by the vagaries of climate and, above all, by the backwardness of their farming methods and the primitive character of their implements, produced a meagre livelihood for most of Europe's rural people, as

the chapter by Dr Diedrich Saalfeld clearly demonstrates. For, as a famed scholar has observed, much of Western history since the end of the Middle Ages has been a history of want, hunger and misery, a fact that has scarcely penetrated into the modern historical consciousness.

The misery and the exploitation that was so often the lot of the European peasantry led to frequent local disturbances and sometimes to widespread and violent outbursts. As Professor Yves-Marie Bercé shows, peasant unrest was a constant of European rural history, just as labour unrest is inseparable from the modern industrial order. It had its peaks and its valleys, but it was always simmering under the surface, ready to erupt when the impositions of lord, state or church became intolerable, or when some self-seeking leader aroused the villagers with promises of freedom and land and riches, or when some wild and unfounded rumour provided the spark that was all that was needed to set the rural world aflame.

Village life, of course, was not all toil and trouble. The rural world had its rich culture. There were stories and legends, art and music and dancing and festivals. And there was the dark side, too, of magic and witchcraft and the casting of spells and superstitions and fears of the unknown. This is the world of the folklorist that is explored by Dr Jacqueline Simpson.

The next chapter deals with rural America. The antecedents of rural life in America lay in Europe, brought over by the colonists who first broke the soil of the New World. But rural life in America quickly took on a unique character and quality. Professor William N. Parker provides an overview of the American farm scene from colonial times, but focuses his chapter on the farmer of the American Middle West. He was the archetypal American farmer. He was a special breed of man, independent, innovative, politically active and suspicious of the motives of those who did not share his way of life or his view of the world.

Since the last decades of the 19th century and especially since the end of the First World War industrialization and urbanization have had a destructive impact upon the traditional patterns of rural life. In the book's concluding chapter, Professor Harvey Franklin analyzes the inability of peasant agriculture to compete with industrialized farming, and the incompatibility of the structure and demands of the modern world with the old ways.

The many illustrations that accompany and amplify the text help bring to life, or at least aid in a perception of the way people lived and help us to remember what has for so long been our forgotten past. That past is where the roots of our civilization and our own roots lie, and the more we know about those roots the more we know about ourselves.

JEROME BLUM

# 1 THE VILLAGE AND THE FAMILY

JEROME BLUM

# The village and the family

The village was once the peasant's world: indeed, in Russia the peasant called his community *mir*, the Russian word for world – and for peace. It was essentially a self-contained, a self-maintained and a self-reliant entity, remote from the outside world, an island of people living in the midst of their work place, conscious always of their collective unity. It was a community of workers – it had no leisure class. Nearly always its people led a hard life. Theirs was an existence precariously balanced on the margin of subsistence. To maintain that balance the villagers had to achieve a subtle equilibrium of their resources. That was why change could be introduced only slowly and why peasants resisted as long as they could pressures for change that came from outside the village. The old ways had proven themselves and so the villagers were faithful to them. Time and again they justified their actions by such formulae as 'from time immemorial', 'according to local custom', and similar phrases. Each village community directed the collective life of its people. The extent of the collective control varied with local circumstances but the differences were of degree and not of kind. Each community imposed regulations that limited and channelled the activities of individuals in the interest of the group, and each engaged to a greater or lesser extent in collective economic activity.

All that is gone now, erased by the transformation in European rural life that began in the 18th century. And, as so often happens with dying or newly dead institutions, the passing of the traditional village community evoked a romantic nostalgia. Over a century ago, a renowned Belgian scholar mourned the waning of the village of old which, he wrote, secured for countrymen 'the enjoyment of liberty, equality and order, and as great a degree of happiness as is compatible with human destinies'. Later writers have often shared this regret, attributing to the village way of life values and virtues that surpass those of modern industrial society. It seems more reasonable to suppose that the village community of the past, like other human institutions, had both its blessings and its shortcomings. However, for this as for every other generalization about these communities, only an assumption is possible. Definitive conclusions about village communities are difficult if not impossible because of their great number, the many differences among them and, above all else, the obscurity which veils so much of the history of rural Europe and its people.

## Kinship and co-operation

The perils of generalizations about the village community evidenced themselves from the outset of scholarly interest in the subject. German and Danish scholars of the mid-19th century concluded that in the 1st century BC Germans had practised agrarian communism, that is, collective ownership and use of the land. Convinced that organized social life had been egalitarian at its inception, these men, soon joined by like-minded scholars in other lands, sought support for their hypothesis by looking for instances of existing or recently abandoned agrarian communism. Their search revealed that agrarian communism had been or was still used in places in Europe, Asia, India and Central and South America. They assumed that this was the manner in which land had been held originally in each of these regions. It was an easy step to frame a universal law that declared that social evolution everywhere began with the communal ownership of the land.

The new 'law' was destined to enjoy only a brief life. Continued historical research showed that examples of agrarian communism presented as evidence for its antiquity actually had their origins in far more recent times. Moreover, archaeological excavations of settlements of the 1st century AD in the Netherlands, England and Denmark, and studies of primitive peoples, have shown that there is no strict temporal order of progression from collectivism to individual occupancy. The former was not the necessary preliminary step to the latter.

In the initial stages of settled cultivation in Europe, land is thought to have been held by a patriarchal family group of kinsmen living together as one household. Many hands must have been needed for the heavy task of clearing the land and preparing it for tillage. The single family unit – the nuclear family – lacked the labour resources needed for this operation and so presumably joined together with families or relatives in a co-operative effort. When the land had been made cultivable the need for co-operation no longer existed. The land of the patriarchal commune was divided among the nuclear families, with each family operating its own holding with its own labour resources. Possibly, too, natural increase within the patriarchal commune and conflicts among its members may have been factors in its disintegration.

The nuclear families joined with one another in new communes that were based not upon kinship but upon

*The sense of community that arose through the village's common system of work expressed itself in festivals and ceremonial gatherings. In this etching by Daniel Hopfer of about 1500 a banquet is laid on the left while on the right the pipers strike up for the dance.*

residence in a common neighbourhood, and so sharing common social and economic interests. In short, these were territorial communes: groupings of people who lived in the same neighbourhood. Each member household had its own separate holding and ran it as an independent operation. All members had the right to use the forests, pastures, meadows, streams and wastes that lay within the boundaries of the commune. These resources belonged to the commune and were managed by the commune as a corporate body.

New pressures and a new need for closer co-operation brought about the transition from territorial commune to village commune, from the loose organization that held together people living in the same neighbourhood to the much tighter organization and closer co-operation of people clustered together in a village. In western and central Europe the increase in population during the High Middle Ages set up a need for more food and for more land. This pressure was met by clearing new land, by converting pastures, meadows and wastes into grainland, and by the adoption of more intensive methods of cultivation that involved the rotation of fields. The holdings of individual households were thrown together and then divided into two or three open, unfenced fields and rotated every two or three years between crops, nearly always of grain, and fallow. The fields were parcelled into strips that were distributed among the households in proportion to the amount of land each had before the introduction of the new open-field system. The new system demanded

greatly increased and continuous co-operation among the holders of the strips to regulate such matters as access to the individual strips, times of ploughing, sowing, harrowing and harvesting, pasturing of cattle on the stubble of the harvested fields and on the fallow, protection of the sown fields from trespass by cattle or by unauthorized persons, and so on. In short, it required the close communal regulation of husbandry, and by extension communal regulation of the life of the village, since husbandry was the chief and in many villages the sole occupation.

In much of western Europe the transition to the open fields and their accompanying communal control occurred from the 12th to the 14th century. In eastern Europe the change became common only in the 15th and 16th centuries. Wherever it was introduced the open-field system grew gradually through the centuries, with controls increasing as time went by. The system never caught on in those parts of Europe that were unsuited for the grain production that the system emphasized. In these regions, communal bonds were much looser and much less confining than they were in the grain-producing regions of Europe.

Other developments spurred the establishment and strengthening of the village commune. To make the management of their estates more efficient many seigniors in western and central Europe made written declarations in which they defined the rights and obligations of the peasants who lived on their land. These documents, given to the village as a unit, reinforced existing communal bonds or brought about the establishment of communal organizations in villages where they did not yet exist. In eastern Europe, in the Grand Duchy of Lithuania that stretched from the shores of the Baltic to the borders of the Ottoman Empire, and in Russia, the introduction of close communal control came often at the instance of seigniors and of sovereigns who grouped the peasants into communes to make it easier to control them and to impose obligations on them.

The meadows and pastures and wastes that the villagers held in common provided an especially powerful force that impelled communal co-operation and ensured the survival of the collective spirit. The management of these resources, so vital to the economy of every household, compelled the villagers to organize and to act as a collective body. The introduction of communal responsibility for some or all of the obligations demanded of the peasant by seignior and by sovereign provided another persuasive motive for communal co-operation and control. Instead of obligations being levied on the individual householders they were imposed upon the community as a unit. It was up to the villagers to divide the obligations among the households and to pay for those of their fellows who, for whatever reason, were delinquent. This principle of joint responsibility established itself in central and eastern Europe in the 15th and 16th centuries. It became common, too, in other parts of Europe.

Finally, the propinquity of village life must have engendered a strong communal consciousness. The small size of most villages gave each settlement a familial quality, intensified by intermarriage among the villagers. They knew and shared each other's joys and sorrows. They worked together, they worshipped together, they rejoiced together in village celebrations, they met together to decide on matters of importance to the community and they had a common adversary in the person of their seignior and his officials against whom they, as a community, could present a united front.

The villagers had a name for this shared existence. They called it, in their respective tongues, 'neighbourhood' or 'neighbourliness'. Each household in the village depended upon every other household for mutual assistance. When a new dwelling had to be built or an old one repaired, when a roof needed thatching, when help was needed in an emergency, when a disaster befell a household, the villagers could count on their neighbours for help. In fact, a system of reciprocity developed, with claims and counter-claims between individual households who could call in these claims when needed. In Denmark, Norway, Ireland and other places, these acts of mutual assistance were made occasions for celebration when the work was finished, with the beneficiary of the aid expected to provide food and drink and perhaps music for dancing. The rationale that lay behind the neighbourliness was

revealed to a Russian landowner who in 1871 was exiled to his estate in Smolensk. He tried to hire villagers to repair a dam and was taken aback by the exorbitant price they demanded for the work. Then a peasant friend of his childhood told him that if he had simply invited the villagers to help they would have come 'for the sake of honour', expecting nothing except a glass of vodka. 'Today', explained the peasant, 'you need to repair the dam and you want to pay us. Tomorrow when we'll need something from you we will have to pay for it. Let us live like good neighbours. . . .' The landowner followed this counsel and soon his dam was repaired at no cost save for some vodka.

'Neighbourliness' did not mean that the village was free of discord. Far from it. Propinquity could and did lead to endless gossiping and prying, so that privacy was impossible, and it led to family feuds and to physical assaults and brutality. In some villages in England in the 16th and 17th centuries hatreds were so intense that church services could not be held because villagers refused to assemble under the same roof with their enemies, and courts were deluged with accusations of neighbour against neighbour. Conflicts often rose between the wealthier peasants who formed the village oligarchy and the other villagers who resented the restrictions imposed on them by the oligarchs in such things as the use of the commons, or inequities in the distribution of obligations or of land.

Nonetheless, despite the discontents and quarrels of communal life, the villagers apparently usually adjusted to the situation, or managed to resolve their difficulties without recourse to outside authority. Social pressures may have restrained peasants from carrying their quarrels to outsiders. Tradition also had accustomed them to keep their grievances within the community. Perhaps, too, they had learned from experience that formal complaints to outside authorities were more likely to annoy and anger these powers than to produce a desired result.

Everyone who lived in the village belonged to the community and had to abide by its rules and regulations. But residence in the village was usually a closely guarded right and the villagers made it difficult for outsiders to move in. They wanted to avoid the danger of increased pressure on the common lands, or they feared that the newcomer might be lazy or improvident and so would not contribute his share of the obligations demanded of the community. In many places the newcomer could settle only after an affirmative vote of the village assembly. In Lower Alsace he had to go through a probationary period before acceptance into membership. In villages in Austria, Switzerland, Savoy, Burgundy and Lorraine he had to pay an entry fee if he wanted to use communal resources. In Denmark he had to go through a formal ritual whose main feature was a drinking party given by the newcomer. Villages in Saxony once had the same requirement but replaced it with an entry fee.

In Lower Austria, villagers not only made it difficult for new settlers to come in but also forced people out. They drove a stake before the door of the man they wanted to expel. The target of their opprobrium lost his right to use communal resources including the village well; no one would speak to him or work for him or have anything to do with him and the members of his household. Under the pressures of this ostracism the unwanted peasant had no choice but to leave. In parts of northern France and Flanders peasants went even further in their efforts to drive out an unwelcome newcomer. They not only ostracized the man and his family but sometimes set fire to his house and outbuildings, mutilated his livestock, broke his farm tools, sowed his fields with tares and on occasion physically assaulted him. In contrast, in regions where land was plentiful and population scant, as in Russia, newcomers were welcomed. Villagers there wanted new settlers because they helped meet the heavy obligations demanded of the commune by seignior and state.

The establishment of new villages went on continuously as new lands were settled, as in 18th-century Hungary after the expulsion of the Ottoman Turks, or as old regions were resettled after they had been devastated by war or some other disaster, like 17th-century Russia after the Time of Troubles or Burgundy and Lorraine after the Thirty Years' War. Often migrating peasants carried the idea of the commune with them. That happened in Poland, where German colonists in the 13th century established communes in their new settlements; soon the indigenous Poles followed their example.

No one knows how many villages there were. France alone is said to have had about 44,000 of them on the eve of the Revolution in 1789. In Russia a survey in the 1850s of 22 provinces containing 47 per cent of the population of European Russia counted 100,348 rural settlements. These ranged from isolated farmsteads occupied by a single family to villages with more than 500 homesteads. By far the largest number of these settlements – over 53,000 of them – contained between 51 and 300 people. Over 22,000 had between 11 and 50 inhabitants. Only 5,238 rural settlements had fewer than ten people, and only 1,254 had over 2,000 inhabitants. In England the average size of villages in the late 17th century was probably 200 or even fewer, and in 19th-century England rural settlements of fewer than 100 people were still common.

### Village democracy?

Writers, as earlier suggested, have sometimes portrayed the old village community as a citadel of egalitarianism and democracy, or as a closed preserve in which peasants enjoyed a protected, humane and moral existence that vanished with the triumph of individualism over communal collectivism. The village community could, indeed, serve as a social and economic leveller, especially where the land was periodically redistributed among the villagers. In some settlements in European Russia and in Siberia in the 18th and 19th centuries the poorer villagers convinced their more prosperous neighbours to agree to introduce repartition of the village land to gain equality in holdings. In villages in Switzerland, peasants who had no livestock and so made no use of the common pastures persuaded the community to let them use part of the common land to plant crops. These and other instances of the introduction of egalitarianism, however, were very much the exception. Inequality in rural Europe began with the primitive occupation of the soil, intensified during the Middle Ages as population grew, and accelerated from the late 15th century onward as demographic changes, economic fluctuations, differences in abilities and initiative among peasants, and the consequent upward and downward movement of families over time, as well as the unceasing subdivision and parcelling of land, produced evergreater stratification in the village. This was true, albeit to a lesser degree, even in lands where periodic redistribution of the land had been introduced to gain and preserve equality. Data for Russia from the late 18th and the first half of the 19th century show a relatively large number of cotters, peasants who had only a scrap of land around their huts, and entirely landless peasants. Many of these landless people were farmhands who lived with the households of peasants who had holdings. Others were the domestic servants of their seigniors. Some peasants managed to gain

*'Piers the Pinder', a drawing from a 14-century manuscript. The pinder was an officer of a manor responsible for impounding stray animals. He carries a spade with an iron edge and blows a horn.*

larger shares than their fellows. That could happen when pieces of land fell vacant. The commune turned over this land to a prosperous villager who had a disproportionate influence in the operations of the commune and who could afford to hire landless or nearly landless peasants to work for him. In villages in the fertile black earth of the province of Kursk in the 1890s some households had as many as five allotments, while five or six had to share one allotment. In eastern Galicia, too, the wealthier peasants used their influence to get more than their fair share of the land of the village. In 18th-century Spain, peasants who were allotted plots of communal land at periodic redistributions often rented their allotments to wealthier peasants and worked as hired hands for these peasants.

As could be expected, the inequality was intensified in villages that did not periodically redistribute their land. Such villages made up by far the largest part of Europe's rural settlements. Here the uppermost stratum, socially and economically, was made up of those peasants who held what was called, by a variety of local and regional names, a 'full holding', or even several full holdings. The size of the full holding varied widely according to local custom, tradition, and topography. In Hungary its area ranged from 17 to 57 acres but the average was a little over 34 acres. In Bohemia the full holdings had about 61 acres, in White Russia about 52 acres, in Poland something over 40 acres, in the province of Lower Austria from 34 to 126 acres, in wooded and mountainous parts of the neighbouring province of Upper Austria often over 280 acres, and so on. After the stratum of peasants with full holdings, came, in descending order, peasants with three-quarters, half and quarter holdings, followed by smallholders who had less than a quarter holding, next cotters who had a hut and yard with perhaps a small vegetable garden. Then came the landless labourer who worked for the seignior or for a landholding peasant and who lodged in the home of another peasant or perhaps rented a dwelling from his employer and, finally, the farmhand or servant who lived as a member of the household of his employer. Each category had its own local or regional name. Sometimes the classification was straightforward with the peasant called full, half or quarter peasant depending upon the proportion of a full holding that he occupied, followed by cotters and, finally, the landless, called lodgers. In Haute-Maine in France there was a tripartite division into *laboreurs*, who lived comfortably from their holdings, *bordagers*, who held 12 to 24 acres and just about made ends meet, and *journaliers*, who had to work for others to earn their livings. In contrast, in Lower Saxony there were five subdivisions within the smallholder group alone. The obligation owed by the peasant to seignior, state and church was scaled according to his category.

Sometimes the rank order and status in the village depended upon the number of work animals owned by the household. That criterion was used in the canton of Zurich, in villages in the Ukraine and in the Danubian principalities of Moldavia and Wallachia. In Zurich the number of animals required to determine status differed in different parts of the canton; in one village a man might need only two work animals to be considered a full peasant, while in another he had to have four or five oxen and one or two horses. In the Danubian principalities the classification was fixed by law in 1831 into three strata: those who owned four or more oxen, those who had two oxen and those who had only one ox or none at all.

The inequality within the village increased prodigiously over time, especially after the upsurge in population that began in the middle third of the 18th century. In Saxony, peasants with full holdings had made up 49½ per cent of the population there in 1550. By 1750 that proportion had fallen to 25 per cent and by 1843 it was only 14 per cent. Meanwhile, the ratio of cotters and landless peasants went from 18 per cent in 1550 to 38 per cent in 1750 and 52 per cent in 1843. In Kurmark, the largest division of the province of Brandenburg, there were three times as many landless peasants at the end of the 18th century as there were peasants with holdings, and half of the peasants who had land were smallholders and cotters. Data for other lands show a similar preponderance of landless peasants and smallholders. For example, when at the beginning of the 18th century the Habsburgs won back all of Hungary from the Turks scarcely any of the peasants there had less than a quarter holding, and cotters and landless peasants were all but unknown. By 1848 nearly two-thirds of the country's greatly increased population were in these categories. In England the growing number of impoverished and landless peasants caused expenditures on parish poor relief to increase from less than £700,000 in 1750 to £8,000,000 in 1818. In the late 18th century 86 per cent of the peasant households in Picardy, 75 per cent in French Flanders, and 30 to 40 per cent in lower Normandy had no land.

Peasants whose holdings were too small to support them or who were landless had to find outside employment. Usually they worked as hired farm labourers for the seignior or for other peasants in their home village or in nearby settlements. Others became migrant workers. Each spring the roads of Europe came alive as thousands of peasants poured out of their villages to seek work in distant places, returning home in late autumn. Most of them found employment as farmhands but some were skilled artisans, such as carpenters and masons. Many engaged in cottage industry, spinning and weaving cloth and making wares to sell, or trade, to their neighbours or to merchants, who carried the goods to other markets. Some found work in mining, in metallurgy, in forest industries, in transport, or went out with packs to peddle small wares from village to village.

The disparities in social and economic status allowed the more prosperous peasant to gain a large measure of

control over his less fortunate neighbours. He hired
them, he rented land to them, he lent money, he advanced
or sold grain to them in times of shortage and he rented
work animals and equipment they might need to work
their own holdings; furthermore, he could refuse
employment and loans to villagers who fell out of his
favour. He was, indeed, the *coq du village*, as the French
called him. Inevitably, the wealthier peasants dominated
the community. They were the village oligarchs, whose
will prevailed in the decisions made by the community.
They often used their superior position to gain special
privileges for themselves, such as paying less than their
proper share of the community's obligations to lord and
state, or avoiding military service for their sons, or
using more of the common resources of the village than
did their neighbours, and even expropriating common
land for themselves. The plain fact was that there was
not much egalitarianism in the village community.
Those who were in the lower strata of the socio-
economic scale were at best second-class citizens in most
places.

### The village assembly

The inferior status of these people was reflected in their
exclusion from the governance of the community. In
most villages only the more prosperous peasants had
the right to participate actively in the deliberations of
the village assembly, which ruled over the communal
life of the settlement. Usually only heads of landholding
households were active members and sometimes only
the heads of households who had holdings over a
certain size. In some places, such as in Lower Saxony or
in the village of Laxton in Nottinghamshire, active
membership went with the occupancy of certain
houses in the village. Presumably these houses dated
back to the origins of the community. The exclusion of
smallholders was not universal. In villages in Hungary
and Switzerland, and doubtless elsewhere, they sometimes had the right to vote in the assembly, and in 18th-
century French villages all adult males could vote.
Women were usually excluded from active participation though there were some exceptions, such as in
some French rural communities, or in northern Russia,
where a woman could represent a household whose
male head was dead or was off working in some distant
place. In the village of Termignon in Savoy 32 of the
195 members of the village assembly were widows or
spinsters. In some manors in England all the villagers
attended the meetings of the lord's court, on other
manors only the freeholders and copyholders. In
France, unlike other lands, both seignior and parish
priest could be members of the commune, participating
in the rights of common, paying their share of the
commune's obligations, and supposedly enjoying no
special privileges, although the seignior was known
officially as 'the first inhabitant' or the 'first communer'.

The frequency of the meetings of the village assembly
varied widely. In places in Bohemia, Hungary, Holland

*Detail from a 16th-century astrological engraving by Hans Sebald Beham
illustrates the occupations over which Saturn rules. Fishing, ploughing,
drawing water, pig-killing, even the beggars and prisoners, all go to
make up the pattern of the village community.*

and Switzerland the assembly met only once a year, in
villages in Little Poland three times a year, at least ten
times a year in the Romanian village of Nerej, in the 19th
and 20th centuries, as often as every two weeks in
Russian villages that belonged to the Sheremetev
family, and even every Sunday after church in villages
in Denmark and in the Île-de-France. Elsewhere, as in
villages of north-west Germany, the assembly had no
set meeting times but convened as often as needed at the
call of the village headman.

No matter how frequently, the villagers held their
meetings on Sundays and holidays so as not to interfere
with their working time. Often the preacher announced
the meeting from the pulpit of the village church. A
drum or the church bell proclaimed the meeting after
the service; in France as the parishioners left the church
an official loudly reminded them of the meeting. In
places in Denmark and the Netherlands the villagers
assembled at the sound of a cowhorn. Elsewhere a
special symbol, such as a notched stick or a piece of
metal, or in settlements in Poland a ball, passed from
house to house to summon the villagers to a meeting.

In England the village assembly was overshadowed
by the manorial court. The lord or his steward summoned the court and presided over it. The court itself,
however, was comprised of a jury of the villagers. Over
the years the court's rulings created a body of village
law and tradition that was called the 'custom of the
manor'. The court concerned itself with the agricultural
operations of the village, appointed village officials
and admitted new members to the community. As a

'court baron' it dealt with matters relating to the custom of the manor and with disputes among the villagers; as a 'court leet' it served as a court of record trying minor offences and presenting more serious ones to the Court of Quarter Sessions. The manorial court met usually in spring and again in autumn to attend to major concerns and sat at more frequent intervals to take care of lesser matters. The villagers, for their part, had their own meetings to discuss and decide questions affecting community life, sometimes meeting simultaneously with the lord's court, and sometimes meeting separately.

In many villages the assembly met in the open air, often under a special tree, usually an oak or a linden, or in the churchyard, or on a special mound. In Russian villages any convenient open space served. In villages in Denmark and on the island of Guernsey each member of the assembly had a small rock as his own seat, with the rocks arranged in a semicircle. Perhaps, as one ethnologist suggested, the continuation of the meetings in the open reflected the ancient belief among many people that evil lurked in the close confinement of a building. Whatever the accuracy of his hypothesis, when village assemblies moved their meetings indoors they sometimes symbolically perpetuated their old meeting place. In England, for example, many manorial courts convened at their original meeting site, and then immediately adjourned to a large room to conduct their business.

In many places all members of the assembly were expected to attend the meetings, with fines levied for absences without valid reason or for tardiness. In England the size of the fine sometimes varied with the status of the absentee. At Standon in Staffordshire, where all the villagers were expected to attend the manorial court, freeholders were fined a shilling for non-attendance, leaseholders and other tenants six-pence, and cottagers only twopence. Despite the fines, villagers apparently often missed meetings, if the experience of villages in the Île-de-France can be regarded as typical: in just one of these villages attendance at seven consecutive meetings between January 1610 and December 1612 varied from a low of 9 to a high of 34.

The meetings themselves were sometimes disorderly and even riotous affairs, marked by much bickering and name-calling and occasional physical assaults. This seems to have been especially true in Russia, where the meetings lacked all pretense of formal procedure. No one presided, anyone could attend and speak, though the suffrage was limited to the heads of households, and speakers freely interrupted one another, often employing earthy epithets, so that, as an English traveller in the 1870s discovered, the meeting was frequently reduced to a 'confused, unintelligible din'. Despite this, a consensus emerged at which point the village headman or other elder came forward to take the sense of the meeting. A government report of the 1830s on villages of Russian peasants living on state-owned land found that assemblies often became drinking bouts with the outcome of the discussion determined by the person who supplied the most drinks for the voters. In other lands there seems to have been more formality but this did not always guarantee decorum. Reports from 18th-century France told of outbreaks of violence at the meetings, and of sessions at which the loudest and most pugnacious members carried the day. In villages in central Germany and in Austria communal regulations forbade the carrying of weapons at assembly meetings for fear that over-excited or intoxicated members might use them.

The day-to-day governance of the community was entrusted to officials who were either chosen by the village assembly or, in England, by the manorial court, or were appointed by the lord of the manor or his steward. Usually each village had its own officers but sometimes neighbouring small settlements joined together and had a single set of officials. The chief officer, the headman, was known by many and varied names, among them 'king' in Irish and Norwegian villages. In central and eastern Europe the office was often either hereditary or went with the occupation of a certain holding that was generally larger than the usual full-sized peasant holding. In many villages the headman served for one year or even six months, although longer terms and even life tenure were not unknown. In Ireland, for example, the 'king', who gained his office by winning the trust of his fellow villagers, served for life. In Norway and Denmark and neighbouring northwest Germany the office rotated among the heads of landholding households according to a fixed order and for a set term. In villages in Lower Austria the seignior decided when elections should be held, so that the headman served for an indeterminate term. In places in Leicestershire, in the canton of Zurich, in the valleys of the Jura mountains along the French–Swiss frontier, in Lower Saxony and in the Tyrol, the villagers chose two headmen who divided the duties of the office between themselves.

The headman, as chief executive of the village, served as the intermediary between the village and the seignior. The lord held him responsible for the governance of the community. His duties included such matters as making sure that the villagers met their obligations to the lord, maintaining order in the village and, in some settlements, enforcing religious orthodoxy. Sometimes, too, the state used him as its agent, in charge of tax collections, road and bridge maintenance and recruitment. In short, the village headman, standing between his fellow villagers and lord and state, was in the unenviable position of being the man in the middle. He not only had to carry out the orders of seignior and state, but also had to appease his village constituency. That often proved difficult. The villagers were quick to reproach the headman and even to assault him when they felt that he had failed them or had leaned too far in the direction of the seignior. Nor was it always easy to please the seignior. The headman's natural inclination would tend to be to favour his fellow peasants. The lords, of course, were aware of this and did not hesitate to bring strong pressures on the headman to keep him in line. The pressures included fines and even corporal punishment of headmen who failed to carry out their orders or whom they deemed negligent or who had been overly lenient to the villagers.

The office of village headman carried honour and status with it and often there were material rewards. In many villages the headman was excused from all or part of the dues in cash, kind and labour that he normally would have had to pay to the lord, the state, the church and the community. In some places additional land went with the office. Occasionally the headman had special privileges in the use of the common resources of the village. In central Europe he sometimes was given the right to run the village tavern. Here and there, in villages scattered from central Europe to England, he could keep all or part of certain small fines and fees that were paid by the villagers. It was possible, too, for an unscrupulous man to use the office for illicit personal gain. A Russian government report of the 1830s claimed that chiefs of villages on state-owned land kept part or all of the money paid to the community for the rental of communal land, and headmen of villages in 18th-century Poland and France were said to have been corrupt. Yet despite the licit and illicit rewards, peasants often tried to avoid the office because they were aware of the difficulties it involved. They found substitutes when they could. In France and in Russia threats of punishment often had to be used to compel peasants to take the office. The unwillingness of more prosperous peasants to serve explains why men of lesser means and stature sometimes held the office.

In most villages, a council with as few as two and as many as twelve or more members aided and advised the headman. In some settlements the headman was subordinate to the council, and there were villages where the council served as chief executive without a headman. The council could act in the name of the village assembly and so could spare that body from frequent meetings and prolonged debates. Sometimes the council supplanted the village assembly. That happened in many communities in Champagne in the late 18th century and in a number of Hungarian villages in the 18th and 19th centuries. Often the village assembly elected the council members, elsewhere the lord or his steward appointed them and sometimes the headman chose them. In still other settlements some of the councilmen were elected, some named by the lord, and some appointed by the headman. In villages in Electoral Saxony council membership was hereditary; in certain places in England all the residents served in rotation, and there were communities where the outgoing councilmen appointed their successors who were then confirmed by the village assembly. The councilmen usually served for a fixed term, but in some villages, as for example Harleston in Northumberland, or villages in Hungary and Electoral Saxony, they held the office for life.

Most villages had employees, their number and duty depending on the size of the settlement and its needs. They included members who were employed as shepherd, herdsman, watchman, midwife, smith, village clerk and schoolmaster, to name some of the more usual posts. Some of the employees were paid out of the village treasury, some were provided with a house and land, or were excused from certain obligations, or were allowed special privileges in the use of the common resources of the village, and some, like the smith and the midwife, charged a fee for their services.

## Communal life, communal land

The control over village life exercised by the community depended upon local needs and traditions and upon the extent of the autonomy allowed the community by seignior and state. Typically, the community's most active role concerned the co-ordination of the farming activities of its members. In open-field country the strips of each household lay intermingled with the strips of other households so that all farming operations had to be performed at the same time. The community, either through the decision of its assembly or by the orders of its elected officials, set the times for ploughing and sowing and all the other farming operations, decided what crops should be planted and when the harvested fields should be opened for pasturing of the villagers' livestock, who could use the common resources of the village, and how much use they could make of them. In villages that used other systems of husbandry, such as tilling a piece of land consecutively for a period of years, then allowing it to go back to brush and taking another piece of land into cultivation, the community decided what land should be tilled and for how long. The community fixed the stint, that is, the number of cattle each household could pasture on the common (though in many villages that was set by custom or by the size of the peasant's holding), organized the village's animals into a common herd tended by a shepherd or cowherd hired by the community and decided when the animals should be led up into mountain pastures and when they should be brought down.

Sometimes the community sold, exchanged or leased some of its common land. The income went into the communal coffers, or was distributed among the villagers, or was used for some special purpose such as paying for a new bell or a stained glass window for the village church. Sometimes the community had to sell land to pay off money that it owed to its lord or to the state or church. Communities in need of more land bought or rented ploughland or pasture, or by joint communal effort cleared or reclaimed land. Normally, newly acquired land lay close to the village, but, when circumstances demanded, the land could lie at a distance: mountain villages in Corsica owned land along the coast on which they pastured their cattle in winter.

The community was responsible, too, for the maintenance of internal order. Often it monitored the religious and moral life of its members, requiring them to observe the Sabbath, to attend church and take the sacraments, and it punished drunkenness, gambling, and sexual transgressions. In villages in Switzerland, Lithuania, Austria and Germany, the community had its own courts, presided over by its own officers, and could try minor offences. In other lands the community or its representatives participated in the judgments of the lord of the manor's court, whether directly, as in England and in 16th- and 17th-century Russia, where a jury of villagers served as part of the lord's court, or indirectly, as in villages of eastern Germany, where the village assembly acted in an advisory capacity.

The community took care of such public services as maintenance and repair of roads, bridges, dikes and water courses, protection against fire and maintenance of the church and rectory. The villagers themselves usually provided the labour needed for these operations, although sometimes the community hired labourers for this work. The community provided welfare services, taking care of the indigent, the sick and orphans, and appointed guardians for minors. In Norway each farmer of the parish had to board and lodge one of the village poor for a certain period of time. In England the Elizabethan Poor Law of 1601 required each parish to levy a tax on its parishioners to be used for the support of the indigent, and required that the able-bodied poor work, and that needy children serve as apprentices. Some communities supported a village school. Often the local cleric served as the teacher, holding classes in

*Some villages were able to support a school. In 1657 a Polish artist cast an unsympathetic eye on one in his native land.*

18

the parsonage, and sometimes the community hired a schoolmaster. In Denmark a royal decree of 1824 ordered every village to build a school and hire a schoolmaster. In Russia a commission in 1770 recommended the establishment of a village school for every 100 to 250 peasant households with the costs borne by the villagers, but nothing came of the proposal. In lands of central and eastern Europe the community had to send conscripts for the compulsory military service that was introduced into these lands in the 18th century. In Russia the village community had to outfit the conscripts and pay their transportation to their assigned military posts. This could amount to a considerable sum, especially in years of heavy conscription. To meet the costs that it incurred by its many activities, the community made regular levies upon its members.

Communal controls and communal authority were at their weakest when the peasants lived in isolated farmsteads or in hamlets, where they employed systems of tillage that did not require close and continuous cooperation among the farmers, and where animal husbandry was the principal occupation. These conditions were likely to prevail in mountainous regions. In those parts of Norway and Denmark where most peasants lived in hamlets or isolated farmsteads, neighbours joined together into loose groups whose main purpose was to provide help and support in times of need, and to come together at times of rejoicing, as at weddings, and of sorrow, as at funerals, where the neighbours made the coffin, carried the body to the cemetery and dug the grave. In the Carpathian mountains of eastern Galicia communal organizations barely existed. In England communal controls were far less rigorous in regions where pastoral farming predominated than in grain-producing areas. But even the loosest of communal organizations imposed certain limitations upon its members, particularly with regard to common resources, to ensure that everyone would share equitably in their use. These restrictions included such provisions as a limit on the amount of timber the commune member could take from the common woods, or the number of cattle he could graze on the common pastures, or the amount of meadowland that he could mow for hay.

The spectrum of communal authority ran from loose communities such as these, through increasing degrees of regulation to agrarian communism in which the commune held the land of the village and decided how much land each of its members should have. The Great Russian village commune, the *mir*, is the best-known example of this extreme form of communal control. First appearing in the 15th and early 16th centuries, agrarian communism had become nearly universal in the provinces of Great Russia by the 19th century. At the end of that century well over 90 per cent of all peasant land in these provinces was held by communes rather than by individuals. The households of the commune had permanent possession only of their

cottage or hut and the scrap of land around it. Each household had the right to the use of common pasture, meadow and forest, and to an allotment of ploughland. The commune, meeting in assembly, or its elected officials acting as its agents, made the allotments according to what it considered to be the needs and the labour resources of the household. When needs or labour resources changed or when new households were established the commune could redistribute land, increasing or decreasing the size of the allotments as needs dictated. Through these redistributions the commune reduced inequalities among the households of the village, checked the tendency towards the splintering of holdings through inheritance or alienation, provided land for newcomers and for newly wed couples and, most important from the viewpoint of seignior and sovereign, ensured the ability of each household to meet its obligations to lord and to state.

The frequency of the redistributions of ploughland varied. The scant data indicate that redistributions were highly exceptional in the 16th and 17th centuries. In the 18th century the practice became increasingly common and by the middle of the next century just about every commune periodically redistributed its land. Many did this after each of the eleven censuses that were carried out at irregular intervals between 1719 and 1897. Some communes made general repartitions much more frequently, such as every six years, and even annual general repartitions were not unknown. Partial redistributions were made continuously to take care of such things as the establishment of a new homestead, or a change in the number of persons in an existing homestead.

Agrarian communism did not limit itself to Great Russia. In the 18th and 19th centuries it was in use in villages in many parts of Hungary and Poland, in eastern Galicia and in Moldavia and the plainland of Bukovina, now parts of modern-day Romania. Nor was it unknown in western Europe. Villages along the Moselle River practised collective ownership for several centuries, abandoning it only in the 19th century. Widespread agrarian communism persisted in early 20th-century Spain, in Leon, on the Aragonese slope of the Pyrenees and in the province of Estramadura. In most of Sardinia land was held communally; enclosure and private landholding began only in the mid-19th century. In nearby Corsica, too, communes held the land. Individual landholding emerged only gradually in the 18th and 19th centuries and still was not complete in the second half of the 20th century.

In Denmark periodic redistribution of ploughland seems to have been general in earlier centuries and had not entirely disappeared in the 18th century. In Sweden repartition of land held in common continued up into the mid-18th century; land that lay outside the commonly held land was held permanently by individual households. In Norway repartition persisted up to 1821 when a royal decree forbade it as a hindrance to agricultural progress. In Scotland groups of families, at times including as many as twenty households, rented land jointly. Sometimes each family kept the same holding, but more frequently the families periodically, and often annually, redistributed the land among themselves. By the middle of the 19th century the practice had mostly disappeared except for villages in the more remote parts of Scotland. In 1830 a writer reported that villages in a part of County Mayo redistributed their land every three years. In the 19th century in the Austrian provinces of Carinthia, Carniola, Tyrol and Vorarlberg, many peasant villages still periodically redistributed their ploughland.

Periodic redistributions were especially common among peasants who used the extensive tillage system called runrig, or infield-outfield husbandry. They permanently tilled the infield, the land that lay close to the settlement, and for a few years tilled part of the outfield, the land that lay away from the village, and then abandoned it for another part of the outfield. The villagers decided what part of the outfield they would use and then distributed parts of it among the households. In the Highlands of Scotland redistribution often was made every year. In Sutton Coldfield, in Warwickshire, the villagers up to the early part of the 18th century redistributed outfield plots every five years. In the second half of the 19th century many of the villages of the Eifel district, which lay between the Rhine and the Belgian Ardennes, still distributed a section of their outfields each year. Often in regions where the peasants used infield-outfield husbandry, the individual households retained permanent possession of their portion of the permanently tilled infield, but in some places this land, too, was periodically redistributed: villages in Norway and Ireland continued this practice until recent times.

Equitable repartition was a difficult task. The arable land had to be divided into holdings that were as nearly as possible equal to each other in productivity and accessibility. The intimate knowledge, gained over decades and even centuries, of the land they tilled enabled the peasants to carry out the operation without the benefit of sophisticated surveying techniques or surveying instruments. They subdivided each of the fields of the village into units of equal quality, split each of these units into strips of approximately the same size and shape, and then distributed strips scattered through the fields of the village to each household. The number of strips allotted to the household was determined by criteria established by village custom, such as the number of adults, or adult males, or number of work animals in the household. There were places where the distribution was left to chance, the commune members drawing lots to determine their respective allotments. And there were villages where the parcels were distributed according to a set rotation; over time each household held every parcel in every field.

Inevitably, despite the efforts to provide an equitable distribution, some peasants ended with land of inferior quality. To compensate them the commune awarded them a greater number of strips or made them a money payment. Sometimes there was not enough land to go around and so some households were periodically excluded from the possession of holdings. That practice was followed in villages in the Austrian province of Carniola. In Russia the tax burden of the household was proportionate to the size of the holding and not to its productivity, and so peasants in the infertile soil in northern Russia who earned livelihoods in cottage and forest industries tried to get as little land as possible at the periodic repartitions.

In many parts of Europe, including regions where redistribution of ploughland was unknown, the villagers each year divided their meadows among the households as haying time drew near. The portion alloted to each household was determined by a fixed rotation of plots among the households, or by a lottery. (The villagers in one English parish felt that it was unseemly for the rector to draw a lot, and so he was always assigned the strip near the brook.) The annual redistribution of meadowland continued in many places into the 20th century and was still practised in the second half of the century in villages in Sweden and England.

In a form of tenure midway between individual possession and collective landholding the land was held by the community, but each member of the commune owned an abstract share or shares of the land. This share entitled him to the use of an amount of ploughland equal to his abstract share, but not the right to claim a specific plot or plots as his own. Presumably, the shareholders all had a common ancestor who had established a patriarchal commune. When the commune broke up each member received an abstract share of the communal land that corresponded in area or quality to his share of the family patrimony. The shareholder could sell his share to his fellow shareholders or to outsiders if the commune gave its approval. Land was held by this tenure in villages in Ireland up to the 17th century, and in the 18th and 19th centuries in community settlements along the Moselle River, in Norway, in eastern Galicia, in Poland and in different parts of Russia. The admission of outsiders into these communes diluted their familial character and spelled the end of their special tenure. Each household became the permanent occupant of a specific holding. The commune no longer claimed title to the arable land but continued its supervision of the pastures, meadows, and other resources that were still held in common. This transition occurred in northern Russia and in Poland by the end of the 18th century.

## The landlords

Everywhere the autonomy enjoyed by the community in the management of its affairs was by the sufferance of the seignior, the superior owner of the land to whom the peasants of the village owed obligations in cash, in kind or in labour services. In the lands of eastern

*A hedger and ditcher, drawn from life by Thomas Rowlandson, about 1800.*

rights of common and, by expropriation, foreclosure, and purchase, converted peasant holdings into demesne and reduced the erstwhile peasant occupants to small-holders or landless day labourers. This process was already noticeable by the 16th century in parts of England, in eastern Germany and in Burgundy, appeared in later years in other European lands and gained momentum as the years went by, especially in the era of rising prices for farm goods in the latter half of the 18th and the first part of the 19th century.

Increased involvement of the lord of the manor in the day-to-day management of his property proved to be one of the consequences of this new interest taken by the seigniors. In villages in Rhenish Prussia, in the countryside around Lübeck and in provinces of western Russia the lord or his employees assumed the leading role in the economy of the village, including supervision of the fields of the village and of the agricultural operations of the villagers. In communities in Russia, Saxony and Silesia, the headman had some of his authority taken from him, and in other villages the office, hitherto elective or hereditary, now was held by an appointee of the seignior. In England the open fields that covered much of the country's arable land were swallowed up in the great wave of enclosures, initiated by noble and gentry landowners, which began around 1760 and continued for the next sixty years. With the disappearance of the open fields and the commons the village community withered away.

## The church and the family

In France and in England, and especially in the open-field region of these two lands, the boundaries of village and parish usually coincided. In other lands of Europe this congruity between parish and village was exceptional, though in places the boundaries of surviving territorial communes were the same as those of the parish. But whether or not village and parish coincided, the community life of the village centred around the church. It was the one group social activity in which everyone joined and in which everyone shared. The church bell marked the stages in the life of each villager from baptism to funeral, and its memorial services kept alive the memory of past generations. The maintenance of the church was often the heaviest expense that rested on the community treasury. Often the village assembly met in the churchyard. In his sermons the preacher provided news and official government announcements in addition to religious teachings. In France the village assembly sometimes also served as the parish vestry, though in theory they were separate bodies, with the village priest presiding over both church and secular discussions. In England, where by the 18th century and even earlier the manorial courts had declined, the parish vestry assumed its duties and responsibilities, and became in effect the ruling body of the community. That continued until the Local Government Act of 1894 stripped the parish vestry of

Europe, where the peasants were serfs and were literally the property of the lord, the seignior's authority had scarcely any limitations. The privileges that were allowed the villagers, including the formation of a communal organization, depended entirely upon the will of their owner. In western and central Europe, custom and the laws and courts of the sovereign placed restrictions on the authority of the seigniors. Despite these restraints, the lord had considerable influence within the village community, as evidenced by such things as the lord or his steward appointing the officers of the village, presiding over the manorial court or using their influence to ensure that the village officers and council followed their suggestions and met their demands.

In any event, landowners nearly everywhere allowed their peasants much freedom in the management of their communal affairs – and thereby spared themselves time, trouble, and expense. That state of affairs continued until seigniors became more and more interested in increasing their incomes from their land. In pursuit of this goal, lords reasserted old and forgotten dues and privileges, claimed for their exclusive use land long used as commons by the villagers, introduced new crops and new techniques of cultivation, enclosed land and thereby deprived the villagers of their traditional all of its civil powers and restricted its activities to church matters.

Important as the church was, the primary focus of peasant life everywhere lay in the family, or more exactly, in the household, the members of the family plus others who lived with the family. Indeed, in many lands the word for family was rarely used. Instead, people were identified as members of a household. When the word 'family' was used, as in 16th- and 17th-century England, it included everyone living in a single house, whether related or not. The household was a tightly organized unit with all its members totally involved in the effort to make the household as nearly self-sufficient as possible. Though the land might be held in the name of the head of the household, it was the household that held the land, enjoyed the privileges and was responsible for the obligations that went with the land. The status and importance within the community of the individual peasant were dependent upon the prestige of the household to which he belonged and his position in it. People lived out their entire lives within the household, surrounded always by other people. Living arrangements allowed little or no privacy. In most peasant homes everyone lived, ate and slept in the same room, or at best there were a couple of rooms. Everyone in the house was subordinate to the will and orders of the head of the household.

It is easy to imagine the quarrels, the jealousies, the resentments, the ceaseless tension that this kind of life must have engendered. The scant evidence seems to indicate that the household was held together less by love and affection than by the need to serve economic and reproductive purposes. The excessive drinking that was so common among the peasantry of Europe from Ireland across to Russia may well have had roots in the discord and unhappiness that seems so often to have characterized pre-industrial rural household life.

The household included members of the family and live-in farmhands and servants. Going into service was a normal part of growing up just about everywhere in Europe. Boys and girls alike left home, sometimes when they were as young as six or seven, to work as servants or apprentices. Most of the time they found employment in a nearby peasant household; only rarely did they have to go further away. Nearly always they were treated like members of the family, eating, sleeping and working with the family and sharing in its leisure activities. Often the young servants remained until maturity and left only when they married (usually to other live-in servants), rented a cottage and earned their livings as day labourers. Many, however, spent their lives as live-in farmhands and servants. In Bavaria, in 1794, out of an estimated 122,000 adult male peasants of over 21, more than 50,000 were farmhands who lived with their employers. In England, from the early 16th to the mid-19th century, an estimated third or more of all households had live-in servants.

Children, whether blood relatives or servants, were by all odds the worst off among the members of the household. To people who lived constantly on the margin of subsistence, and that included a large majority of the peasantry, children were regarded as unwelcome burdens. They kept their mother from full-time employment during their earliest years and they had to be fed, clothed, and housed until they were old enough to be gainfully employed. These circumstances contributed importantly to the parental neglect that existed everywhere, which helps explain why infant and child mortality reached such extraordinary heights in pre-industrial Europe. In France one infant out of every five died before it completed its first year of life. That was the recorded rate. The real rate must have been much higher because of the unrecorded death of infants who died in the first few days or weeks of life. In the late 17th and early 18th century about half of the recorded children of French peasants died by the age of ten. In England between a quarter and a third of the children of rural peasants died before they reached the age of fifteen. Parental disinterest in their children did not always end with neglect; parents sometimes murdered their unwanted children or let them die from exposure or starvation. To the poor, who apparently rarely knew of contraception, more children only meant more wretchedness.

If the child managed to survive, its parents put it to work at the earliest possible age, either in the child's own homestead or as a servant in another household, as young as at the age of six or seven. The child was used for such work as guarding sheep or cattle, collecting firewood, or frightening away birds from the sown fields. Those who were used to guard animals, a frequent employment for children, spent long and boring hours of loneliness, interrupted only by fits of brief and furious activity if for some reason the animals were panic-stricken. Whatever their job, the children worked at it from dawn to dusk, they suffered abuse and beatings from their elders, they were the last to get fed, and they were given the poorest and the least amounts of food, and no attention was paid to their emotional needs.

In much of rural Europe the household consisted of the nuclear or conjugal family, that is, man, wife, children, and servants. In many places, however, domestic groupings followed other patterns. One variation was the so called stem family in which one married son remained living with the parents while the other children went off on their own. In another model all the sons remained, so that the household was made up of several conjugal units related by blood or marriage. In this kind of household, called the multiple family, the members lived under a single roof or in a group of dwellings and ate together, in shifts if necessary. The members held their land jointly, shared jointly in its products, and usually owned no individual property except for clothing and other personal effects. Often a household went through several types of organization, beginning as a single conjugal unit, growing larger as children came, still larger when sons married and brought their brides into the household, then shrinking back to a single conjugal unit as the children left and, finally, ending with the death of the parents and the division of their property among their heirs.

The multiple-family type of organization found its greatest use among the Slavic and Slavicized peoples of the Balkans, and in parts of Bohemia, Moravia, Silesia, Slovakia, southern Poland, Hungary, Romania and Russia. In the early 20th century, by which time the multiple-family type of organization had gone far into decline, multiple families still held an estimated 30 to 40 per cent of the land of this vast region. Elsewhere in Europe the multiple-family form had been used much less frequently, and by the 18th and 19th centuries was found only in remote and backward regions of western and central Europe.

Sometimes every household in a village was a multiple unit. In other places multiple and nuclear households lived side by side. In regions of dispersed settlement, multiple-family households, like nuclear households, lived on isolated farmsteads or in hamlets of three or four households. The multiple-family household could have as many as 80 to 100 people in it, but they usually numbered around 20 or 30, and sometimes considerably less. A mid-19th century census in the Papal States reported an average of 10 to 12 people, and in 53 multiple-family homesteads on an estate in Courland in 1797 the average was about 14 persons per household. Many multiple households lasted for at most only three generations, from founding couple through to their grandchildren. Then the household disintegrated as rivalries and discontents drove apart the third generation, who were not as closely related as their parents had been, and as increase in family size pressed on the household's resources and made their management more difficult. The members divided up the family property and set themselves up as nuclear-family households or established new multiple families.

Some multiple-family households restricted their membership to kinsmen, some took in non-family members and some were organized by friends who made an agreement of fictitious brotherhood. Generally, membership went in the male line. Daughters left on marriage to join the family of their husbands. The male members of the household chose one of their number to act as head, or automatically accorded the position to the oldest man. In some places the head made the decisions that determined the household's activities as well as the private lives of its members. In other places all members took part in making the decisions, and the head acted only as an agent who carried out their orders. Often there was a female head, too, who supervised the women of the household. Frequently she was the wife of the headman, but sometimes another woman was selected either because she was the most competent, or to prevent one married couple from having too much authority.

## Agrarian advance and communal decline

Through the centuries the village community had been able to withstand the encroachments on its authority by proprietors and by the state without suffering too much damage to communal life. But it could not survive the assaults made upon it starting in the second half of the 18th century and continuing on in the 19th and early 20th centuries. Above all, it could not withstand the demands for agricultural improvements that would produce increased yields. These demands insisted upon the transition from communalism, with its collective rights and collective controls, to individualism, with its right of private property and its freedom of action for the individual. Open fields, common pastures, communal decisions about what to plant and when to carry out farming operations, communal herds and all the other trappings of the traditional agriculture were declared incompatible with the need for a more productive agriculture needed to feed Europe's fast-growing population. The constraints imposed upon the individual by the community were viewed as obstructions to the development of a more efficient use of the land. And nearly everywhere increased efficiency was identified with the consolidation of the strips in the open fields into unified individual holdings, and with the permanent division of the common lands among the holders of the unified farms.

The passage from communal to individual agriculture moved swiftly in England, Scotland, Denmark and Sweden. Nearly all the open fields and commons in these lands had been divided into individual, independently operated farms by the second quarter of the 19th century. Old villages disappeared or dwindled into insignificance as the villagers moved to their new enclosed farms. With the waning of the village the old communal life and spirit disintegrated. In other lands of Europe the transformation was neither as rapid nor as complete; in the second half of the 20th century some of their farmland still lay divided into strips or parcels in open fields.

The intervention of the state abetted and reinforced the destructive impact of individualism upon the life of the village community. Governmental involvement in village life had long predated the drive for agricultural individualism. Increased demands made by seigniors of their peasants had persuaded governments beginning in the 16th century and continuing on into the 17th and especially in the 18th century to intervene in the lord–peasant relationship. The government feared that unless checked the demands of the seigniors would reduce the ability of the peasants to pay taxes, to provide soldiers for the army of the sovereign and to increase in their number. In order to protect the peasants from excessive exploitation by their seigniors, and in order to establish its supremacy over the lords, the state ordered the regularization of the lord–peasant relationship, often setting limits on what the seignior could ask of his peasants.

In the process, the state introduced ordinances and took actions that severely weakened the autonomy of the village community. The once-distant central government became an immediate presence in the village. In France by the middle of the 18th century the village headman had become virtually an agent of the central government, government officials audited village accounts to ensure that communal funds were not misused, in certain provinces the government prescribed the method of election of village officials, and so on. Legislation of the revolutionary governments further weakened the commune, though in many places it managed to survive on into the 19th century before it finally disappeared. In England, as mentioned earlier, the manorial courts were losing out to the king's courts, while enclosures produced a further diminution in their importance by making obsolete their role as supervisor of the open fields and commons of the village.

In other lands, too, state action weakened communal autonomy. In 18th-century Lower Saxony, for example, the government took over control of communal property and made the village headman responsible for enforcing the government's regulations. During the era of the French Revolution the short-lived Helvetic Republic integrated the Swiss village communes into new and larger political districts. In Germany and in Austria the decrees of the first half of the 19th century that freed the peasants from their servile status provided no role for the commune in carrying out the operations of the emancipation. In the Austro-Hungarian Empire the government in 1849 integrated village communities into new, large townships. The new legislation ordered that everyone in these townships had equal rights to participate in local government, unlike the old communes in which only those with holdings of over a certain size qualified as voting members of the village assembly. The government of Saxony had introduced a similar reform in 1839. And, from the second half of the 18th century onward, governments supported the introduction of agricultural reforms, encouraging and even ordering the end of open fields and commons, in the interest of increasing national wealth and power.

In contrast to central and western European governments the rulers of Russia supported the village commune, or more exactly, the land-equalizing commune. They viewed the commune as insurance against social unrest and against the creation of a landless proletariat who might trouble the peace of the realm. The law that freed the Russian serf in 1861 accorded the commune the central position in the new arrangements. The legislation vested the commune with the ownership of the land of the village and made the communes responsible for not only taxes but payments for the land awarded to the village in the emancipation operation. The government continued to support the commune until the early 20th century. Then peasant unrest and revolution persuaded the regime to abandon its commitment to the commune and, instead, to encourage individual farming by the so called Stolypin reforms of 1906–11. By 1 January 1917 nearly one-tenth of all peasant land in European Russia had been enclosed.

Communal practices did not disappear completely in western and central Europe. Common meadows and pastures and forests have continued on into our own time in some places, with their use regulated by communal agreement. They are, of course, anachronisms, vestiges of an earlier day that have somehow managed to survive and that serve to recall for us the way it once was.

---

**Unending labour** was the central fact of most people's lives until quite recent times. In the towns there could be some measure of choice and range of opportunities, but town dwellers were a tiny fraction of the population. The great majority were peasants on the land, and their days were determined by the seasons and the weather, the cycle of ploughing, sowing and harvesting and the needs of their livestock.

The agricultural dimension to medieval life is not prominent in art and literature, but it is rarely entirely absent. In the background of an altarpiece there is often a vista of fields and woods; through the windows of a courtly scene we can catch a glimpse of the labourer intent upon his task. And in one of the most popular pictorial series – the Labours of the Months – it occupies the foreground in its own right. Usually combined with the signs of the Zodiac and the ecclesiastical calendar, the Months appear in a variety of media, from the exquisite miniatures of prayerbooks to large stone reliefs on cathedral portals. One of the most original cycles is that painted in fresco on the walls of the castle of Trento, in northern Italy, between 1390 and 1407. Here, in contrast to many other examples, country life is not idealized or prettified. The peasants, as has been pointed out by an Italian critic, are real peasants; 'the work they do thins and distorts their bony faces; it makes their bodies awkward, bent, twisted; it hardens and swells their hands and bows their legs'. In this detail, illustrating July (*opposite*), the three lower figures bend forward, grasping a handful of corn in the left hand and cutting it with a sickle. The man at the far end stands up, resting his sickle over his left shoulder, while he knots stalks together to make a tie for the sheaf. The cut corn is then laid flat in bundles resting on the knotted straw, and left behind, to be tied up into sheaves and then heaped into stooks by other workers following. (1)

# The peasant's world

The village community was founded on work, but it was linked together in innumerable other ways. Kinship, religion and social codes both reinforced and expressed the sense of mutual dependence between man and man.

**Villagers** who worked together also made merry together. A detail from a landscape by Valkenborch (*above*) shows a relaxed afternoon in 17th-century rural Austria. In the background a country dance is in progress, in the foreground: a drinking party and a game of bowls. *Below:* a wedding in Hungary, 1856. The bride has just arrived – her coffer is being unloaded from the cart – and is being presented to her future parents-in-law. Gipsy musicians tune their instruments and a man prepares to dance. (2, 3)

**The community was governed** by an assembly which, in most European countries and within the varying limits imposed by landowners and the state, could take decisions affecting the internal life of the village. These assemblies are documented but very few pictures of them exist. The right to attend was usually limited to heads of households, but sometimes they were open to all male villagers, and in certain cases to women too, where there was no male head. Conventions differed in different countries, but everywhere the meetings took place on Sundays so as not to interfere with work. In early times they were held in the open air, often under a special tree, but later moved indoors. A meeting in the Canton of Berne, Switzerland, towards the end of the 19th century (*above*) is shown taking place in a school. A. P. Madsen's painting of 1887 (*below*) records a much earlier practice in a Danish village. Each member of the assembly had a stone as his own seat, arranged in a circle round the tree. (4, 5)

# The golden dream

Nostalgia for the past seems to be a constant in human history, and ever since the Greeks the pastoral tradition has painted an idyllic picture of rural life. With the advent of the Industrial Revolution the countryside came to stand for everything that was simple, happy and uncorrupted.

**A farmer's family** gives thanks for their midday meal, a painting by the German artist Theodor Schüz, 1861. The harvest is in progress. On the left, a reaper joins his comrades in the shade (their sickles stuck on the branches around). On the right, people are still binding up the sheaves. In the centre, father, mother and children stand in prayer, a baby in the mother's lap and another (twins?) in the cart behind. An older man, the grandfather, dozes against the tree. All around them, generous nature brings forth her fruits. (6)

**Gleaners** were traditionally allowed a whole day, at the end of which a bell or a shout (from the man on the left) recalled them in case they strayed on to the standing corn. In Jules Breton's painting of 1859, the women may be poor, but they are statuesque, classical and stand with heroic dignity. (7)

**Even in Russia**, at a time (1934) when mechanization was being pushed through with brutal determination, traditional art maintained the myth of the idyllic village. This lacquered papier-mâché box is a typical product of Palekh, three hundred miles north-east of Moscow. In a landscape whose black background reinforces its dream-like quality, the reapers still cut and tie their sheaves as they used to, the horse still waits, the houses are still of logs and the spires and cupolas of the Orthodox church still reign over a Christian land. (8)

29

# Available skills

**Everything that the villager needed would be made in the village, and each man was a craftsman many times over.**

**Spoon-making** (*left*): detail from a Spanish manuscript of the 16th century; raw material on the left, finished product on the right. (9)

**Cooperage** (*right*): the curved planks have been fitted together and must be secured with iron rings: two scenes from 14th-century Catalonia and 19th-century England. (12, 15)

**Candle-maker** (*left*): a 15th-century carved misericord from the church of La Trinité, Vendôme. (10).

**Spinning** (*right*), Eve's first task after the Fall. In the 15th-century miniature from southern Bohemia, Eve spins and Adam digs. A more romantic housewife – certainly with more beautiful children – appears in an Italian painting of 1823. (13, 16)

**The blacksmith** (*left*) intent upon a horseshoe; another 15th-century French misericord. (11)

**The wheelwrights:** the art of fitting the spokes, boring the exact centre of the hub and shaping the rim so that the wheel spins evenly has always demanded the most careful skill. Not entirely by chance is there such a similarity of expression between the 13th-century workman (in a window at Chartres, *right*) and his comrade of the 20th. (14, 17)

**Rope-making** (*above*): the treated fibre is held round the waist and twisted by hand, the thread being turned at a distance to provide the right tension. These two illustrations are over four hundred years apart (1399 and 1824), but both show basically the same method and in both there are heaps of raw fibre (hemp or flax) and coils of thick finished rope. (18, 19)

**Making baskets** (*below*): an ancient and essential craft, capable of many regional variations. The left-hand illustration comes from an early 19th-century *Book of Trades*. The old man photographed about 1900 was the inheritor of a tradition unchanged since the Middle Ages. (20, 21)

**When the village craftsman** wished to produce a work of beauty he showed himself an artist. The style may be that of high society adapted to humbler conditions, but the vitality, imagination and charm that these pieces display make them as valued now as more sophisticated objects. This wardrobe from Upper Bavaria is dated 1786. It is in the Rococo style fashionable some fifty years earlier, with carved and gilded arabesques, painted floral ornament and four panels illustrating the seasons. Spring is a gardener holding a flower; summer a reaper with a sheaf of corn, a rake and a sickle; autumn a man holding a vine branch and a glass of wine; and winter an old man warming his hands at the fire.

(22)

# 2 THE NOBILITY AND THE LAND

JEROME BLUM

# The nobility and the land

A remarkable network of dependence held European society together for a thousand years. The network took the form of a hierarchical structure in which people were divided into groups, or orders, as they came to be called, arranged in a descending scale of status and privilege. Each order was dependent upon and deferential to the orders above it in the hierarchy. Membership in each order was determined by neither merit nor wealth but by birth. There were some movements between the orders, but they were exceptional and unimportant perturbations of the social structure, a structure so rigid that changes in status had to be by legal act, as when a commoner was ennobled or a serf was freed. Law and custom rigorously defined membership in each order, and law and custom established the hierarchy of privileges and obligations that characterized the society. Unlike modern society, there was no common body of rights and duties shared by everyone by virtue of membership in the society. Each person occupied a fixed position in the social structure and each gave his loyalty and obedience to his superior. That was the glue that for a millennium held together the network of dependence.

During those long centuries it seemed self-evident to most Europeans that the maintenance of hierarchical distinctions and inequalities preserved peace and order and defended them from anarchy. The Parlement of Paris, made up exclusively of noblemen, expressed this conviction succinctly when in 1776 it explained that the harmony of civil society rested 'on that gradation of powers, authorities, pre-eminences and distinctions which holds each man in his place and guarantees all stations against confusion'. In that same year of 1776, a small band of colonials meeting in Philadelphia declared that 'we hold these truths to be self-evident, that all men are created equal, that they are endowed by their creator with certain inalienable rights, that among these are life, liberty and the pursuit of happiness'. In those two statements, both made in the same year, can be seen the end of an old era and the beginning of a new one.

The nobility formed the uppermost stratum of the hierarchical pyramid. Nobles were only a small fraction of Europe's population. In the latter part of the 18th century and the first half of the next century, by which time their ranks had been inflated by new creations (as will be shown later), there were perhaps 3 or 4 million nobles out of 170–190 million Europeans. Their number varied widely among the states of Europe. Estimates range from 9 per cent of the adult male population of Hungary in 1840, over 8 per cent of the population of Poland before the first partition of that land in 1772, 7–8 per cent in Spain in 1768, $1-1\frac{1}{2}$ per cent in France in 1789 on the eve of the Revolution, to 1 per cent in Russia in 1858. In England where, unlike the continent, only the eldest son, or failing sons the eldest surviving male, inherited the title there were fewer than 200 peers at the end of the 18th century. That figure, however, is misleading. The English gentry, although not recognized in law as a special privileged caste, and although it did not possess patents of nobility, was analogous to the lesser nobility of the continent. The number of the gentry is unknown, but certainly it was well into the thousands.

These relatively few people, who enjoyed rights and privileges denied to the other members of their societies, were the ruling elite of Europe. There were challenges to their supremacy from men who objected to the inequities and the injustices of the hierarchical society and there were occasional resorts to violent protest. The men at the top usually had no difficulty in putting down these attacks upon their authority. Indeed, the inequalities of status and privilege were never greater than in what turned out to be the last century of the old order. Then, at its very height, the hierarchical structure began to crumble, undermined by the new and strange forces that were destined to shape our modern world.

The persistence of the hierarchical society and of the pre-eminence of the nobility was explained in large part by the tendency of mankind to accept the existing order of things without questioning. People may have grumbled but they accepted as inevitable the existence of the nobility as a privileged caste because that was the way it had always been.

## Noble origins

In fact, that was not the way it had always been. The institutionalization of the nobility as a hereditary and legally superior order only began to emerge in the 12th century. In the early Middle Ages, from the 9th to the 11th century, the word 'noble' had been used, but it was applied liberally to outstanding men who were armed retainers of a prince, or who owned a sizable property, or who were men of wealth and power. As time went by the term became more restrictive and was used to describe men who, by virtue of their wealth or prowess or outstanding service to a ruler, were recognized as the elite of their societies. Some of these men were of humble ancestry, descendants of adventurers or of peasants, but most seemed to have come from families that owned manors. Pedigree, so important to the nobility of later centuries, counted for little or nothing in the early Middle Ages. The nobility was an open and non-hereditary status and the man who was recognized as a noble did not possess any more legal rights than did any other free person.

Despite the lack of a legally defined privileged status the nobles occupied an exalted position in their societies because of their political, economic and, above all, their military importance. The function, indeed, the purpose in life of the noble was to fight; he was before everything else a warrior. Men of the lower orders fought, too, but the noble made warfare his career. Mounted and heavily armed, he was the supreme fighting machine in an age when force and violence were parts of everyday life, and so he was the most honoured and most respected of men.

The fragmentation of political life in the early Middle Ages increased the importance of the nobility. Local rulers, in order to maintain themselves in power and to defend against attacks, devised the system that centuries later was given the name of feudalism. A hierarchy of lords and vassals was created in which each noble was dependent upon the person immediately above him in the scale. Each pledged to obey his lord and to provide him with services that were primarily, but not exclusively, military. The lord, for his part, had to protect his vassals and to provide them with the means of support so that they could serve him without being distracted by the need to support themselves and their families. To accomplish this goal the lord gave his vassals land, with broad powers over the peasants who lived on the land and who paid dues and services to the vassal. In western Europe the vassal held his fief on condition of continued service to his lord. In medieval Russia the retainers who were given land by their principals held the land permanently, retaining ownership even if they left the service of their lord.

The nobles made their homes in their fiefs, away from the courts of their sovereign. Though they gave the sovereign their allegiance, rural residence allowed them greater independence and made them less dependent upon his bounty and good will. Income, power and prestige became based increasingly upon the possession of land. The manor house in which they lived was designed as a small fortress. Set usually on a rise, it was surrounded by outbuildings, including a cookhouse, kept at a distance because of the danger of fire. A ditch or stockade or earthern rampart encircled the compound. The noble and his family, retainers and servants lived and slept together in cramped quarters on the ground floor while lookouts were posted night and day in the upper storey to warn of the approach of attackers. Important nobles used stone as the building material for

these rude castles and in the 12th and 13th centuries lesser men slowly followed their lead. The retainers who lived in the noble's household included men of humble or servile birth. After meritorious service some of these men were rewarded with fiefs of their own and won recognition as nobles. Usually their descendants belonged to the petty nobility but a few among them became founders of great and famous houses.

With the passage of time, the disorders and confusions of the early Middle Ages gave way to the more orderly arrangement of society that characterized the High Middle Ages. From the end of the 11th century, laws began to define the nature and rights and obligations of each stratum of society, and to establish the pre-eminent position accorded to the nobility. By the end of the 13th century, the process had nearly been completed. Now a noble had to be a man of high birth and possessed of land inhabited by peasants. In earlier times a man was recognized as a noble because he held a fief from a superior lord. Now a man could not hold a fief unless he was of noble birth. Now access to knighthood was restricted to those who were sons or grandsons of knights. In short, the nobles had become a hereditary caste.

A downturn in the fortunes of the nobility came in the long period of economic depression, depopulation, wars and rebellions, plagues and famines that endured in Europe from the middle of the 14th century into the second half of the 15th century. The drop in income from their lands made it increasingly difficult for nobles to live in the manner that befitted their status. Many lost everything and were reduced to poverty and anonymity. Other families were extinguished through the death in battle of sons who would have carried on the line. In Catalonia the 200 great families who formed the elite in 1414 were reduced to 10 or 12 by the end of the century. Some nobles, like the so called free knights of Germany, turned to brigandage. These infamous 'robber barons' plundered villages and preyed on the convoys that carried the wares of merchants from town to town. Great lords tried to adjust to the troubled times by a resurgence of baronial powers that historians have

*Medieval society was held together by a network of mutual obligations. Here, in the early legal document called the Mirror of the Saxons ('Sachsenspiegel'), a tenant renews his oath of fealty to his lord.*

labelled 'bastard feudalism'. Central governments became powerless or nearly so, while nobles waged war against their sovereigns and with one another for domination.

Out of this era of near anarchy the national territorial state as we know it today began to emerge in the second half of the 15th and in the 16th century. Strong monarchs, supported by most of their subjects, who wanted security and good government, put an end to the internal disorders. In the process they reduced the power of

*Peasantry, nobility and clergy: the three strata of medieval society. This drawing from the Chronicle of John of Worcester shows a bizarre nightmare of Henry I of England, who dreamed that the three estates were rising in rebellion against him.*

those of the old nobility who had survived the hard times and the civil wars. In Russia, Tsar Ivan IV carried this restraint of the nobility to its logical conclusion. He literally exterminated nearly all of the old princely families. Elsewhere, monarchs were less savage, though a number of English lords were executed by the Tudors. The aim of these sovereigns was not to destroy the old nobility but to reduce its ability to disturb the internal peace and order of the realm.

There was still unrest and discontent among some of the nobles; the struggle for predominance between monarch and nobility was to continue until the end of the old order. When the central power was weak nobles resorted to intrigues, to violence and even to banditry, as some did in France during the civil wars of the 16th and 17th centuries. But the nobility could no longer contest for power on the battlefield. The growth in the size of armies, the importance of infantry pikemen and the use of small arms and artillery made the mounted knight obsolete. As the power of the central government increased, the nobility came to realize that the crown was the source of power and prestige and wealth, and also the source of ruin for those who encountered its displeasure. So the nobility accepted royal leadership, some with enthusiasm and some because they had no viable alternative.

### Born, bred . . . or bought

At this time, too, and perhaps not coincidentally, the conviction that the nobility was a genetically superior breed of humanity made its appearance. In the Middle Ages, society had accepted the predominance of the nobility because of the importance of its function as the defender of the society. But neither the nobles nor anyone else believed that nobles were innately superior beings. The teachings of the church made it clear that everyone was equal in the sight of God. Then, starting with the end of the 15th century, the idea of the natural superiority of the nobility became almost a matter of faith, and was destined to persist for the next three hundred or more years: 'Mankind', said the 19th-century Austrian field-marshal, Prince Alfred Windischgrätz, 'begins with the barons'. The nobles thought of themselves as superior beings, endowed by virtue of their noble birth with qualities that merited the respect and the deference of lesser mortals. A consciousness of their superiority never deserted them. To ensure that it would always be recognized they followed a style of living that distinguished them from those beneath them in the social pyramid. Often their feeling of superiority to the rest of humanity led to acts of intolerable, indeed, sometimes almost unbelievable, arrogance and cruelty. The lesser orders, for their part, acquiesced in the nobility's claim to genetic superiority, admired the behaviour and way of life of the nobility and accepted their own inferiority.

The belief that noble blood made a person superior led to a great concern with genealogy and an inordinate pride in ancestry. The more distinguished the lineage the more superior the family and the more likelihood its members would gain prestige and wealth. In actuality, most noble families were of recent origin, and in many cases their founders had purchased their nobility. The sale of patents of nobility, beginning in the 16th century, was a common practice of money-hungry sovereigns. Rulers realized, too, that by bestowing titles and other honours, whether they charged for them or not, they gratified the egos and ambitions of the recipients and won support for themselves without relinquishing any of their powers. This inflation of honours, as it has been termed, was a nearly European-wide phenomenon. It was said that between the accession of Louis XIII to the throne of France, in 1610, and the outbreak of the Revolution, in 1789, every wealthy man in France was ennobled. Louis XIV in one year sold nobility to 500 people at 6,000 livres each. Between 1715 and 1789 the number of French nobles more than doubled, while the country's population rose only by about fifteen per cent. In Spain a royal decree of 1758 ordered that aspirants for the rank of hidalgo, the lowest stratum of the nobility, had to pay the crown 15,000 to 30,000 reales. In 1800 the price was raised to 50,000 reales. In England a busy trade in titles opened with the accession of James I in 1603 and, with interruptions, continued until 1648. The inflation of honours began with a great increase in knighthoods, then, in 1615, James, hard pressed for money, agreed to the sale of peerages. Between 1615 and 1628 the number of English peers increased from 81 to 126, while the number of Irish peers went up from 25 in 1602 to 105 in 1641. Sales ended in 1628, but resumed in 1641 to help meet Charles I's urgent need for money.

The Hohenzollern rulers of Prussia were not so obvious in their merchandising of nobility. They did not set a price for a patent of nobility. Instead, they levied a tax of sizable proportions on the new noble. The Swedish rulers, unlike these other monarchs, did not charge for the titles they bestowed with a liberal hand. In ten years, Queen Christina, who ruled from 1632 to 1654, sextupled the number of counts and barons. She also gave nobles so much crown land and crown revenues that the government found itself in financial difficulties. Her next two successors took back the larger part of the crown land that Christina had given away but they continued to create new nobles. The story was much the same in other lands of Europe, that is, a large increase in the number of nobles, whether through purchase of patents of nobility or by free grants of monarchs. One outstanding exception was the United Provinces, where the old noble families were strong enough to prevent new creations.

The concern with lineage and with the fame and fortune of the family explain the great importance that nobles attached to marriages and to provisions for inheritance. Each family sought to arrange marriages that would provide continuation of the male line, that would preserve and increase the family's wealth and that would ally the family to an equally important, and, if possible, a more important, family. In pursuit of these goals parents often arranged marriages and the dowry to be paid by the bride's family before the prospective bride and groom met one another. Occasionally, the son of a great family married the daughter of a rich family of the bourgeoisie or of the lesser nobility, thereby bringing new wealth into his family. Daughters of great families were not permitted to marry into families lower in the social scale.

Even more care was spent on provisions for inheritance. The family's position depended upon its property and much care was taken to ensure that succeeding generations would not squander the family patrimony and thereby condemn the family to anonymity. The possession of landed property had great symbolic importance. 'Land', wrote de Tocqueville, 'is the basis of an aristocracy which clings to the soil that supports it; for it is not by privileges alone, nor by birth, but by landed property handed down from generation to generation that an aristocracy is constituted.' To prevent the loss of their land, nobles from the 15th and 16th centuries onward entailed their property. The entail provided that the property was always to go in a certain succession, usually though not always to the eldest son, and could not be sold, divided or mortgaged. The designated heir received the income of the property but had to provide for other members of the family. All too often there was not enough money to support younger sons in a style befitting their rank, nor to provide daughters with dowries large enough to attract suitable husbands. As a result, younger children frequently remained unmarried, the sons going into the army or the clergy and the daughters remaining spinsters or entering convents.

On the continent the entail, or the *fidei commissum* as it was called, was meant to persist for all time, or until the extinction of the family, though sometimes the founder set a fixed term. In England, where the law 'abhorred a perpetuity', the usual practice, known as strict settlement, was to renew the entail with each successive generation, usually at the marriage of the eldest son and heir. The effect of the strict settlement, then, was the same as that of the *fidei commissum*. By the mid-18th century an estimated half of the land of England was held under strict settlement. The two principal exceptions to the general use of entail by nobles were Russia and Sweden. The Russian nobility from early times had divided their landed property among their heirs, thereby splitting the family patrimony into smaller pieces with each successive generation. Once wealthy families were reduced to poverty in as few as three generations. Peter the Great tried to introduce the principle of single inheritance without success. In the 19th century a few very wealthy families did entail their property. In Sweden, too, family wealth was often quickly dissipated because of the absence of primogeniture and entail.

## 'No land without a lord'

The ownership of a landed estate was, of course, not the only symbolic reminder of the superior status of the nobility. Only nobles could have coats of arms, only they could carry a sword, or decorate their hats with plumes, clothe their servants in livery, or use special seals, to list some of the external signs of their high position. To set nobles even further apart from the common herd, sumptuary legislation restricted the right to wear clothes of certain materials and eat certain foods to the nobility. Tudor England even tried to regulate sports, with archery permitted for the lower orders but tennis and bowls restricted to gentlemen with incomes of over £100 a year. Commoners sometimes adopted these signs of nobility, thereby occasioning a duel with a noble outraged by these pretensions, or more likely a thrashing by the nobleman's servants. Respectful forms of addresses had to be used when speaking to a noble, with appropriate gradations scaled according to the nobleman's rank. In Austria it was a legal offence to fail to address a nobleman as 'Your Excellency'. The noble sat in the front pew at the parish church, the service did not begin until he arrived, and he received communion before anyone else. At the theatre the nobles sat in boxes – a practice that began in Paris – or in the front seats of the orchestra. At dances and garden parties a rope separated the nobility from the commoners. Symbols of his status distinguished the nobleman from the lower orders even when he ran afoul of the law. Other men had to submit to the indignity and pain of the pillory and the lash. Only in Russia were nobles subjected to whippings, until, in 1762, an imperial decree exempted nobles from corporal punishment. And when he was condemned to the supreme penalty the noble was beheaded rather than hanged, and so spared the dishonor of being treated in the same manner as a commoner.

In theory, all nobles possessed the same privileges and were equally noble. They were supposedly *una eademque nobilitas*, one and the same nobility, as the 16th-century codifier of Hungarian feudal law put it. In reality, they were divided into many strata of wealth, status and power. These divisions had already appeared in the early Middle Ages when the institution of the nobility was in its formative stage. The growth in the importance of money, education and culture, and the increase in the number of lesser nobles, widened the gulf between the higher and the lower levels of the nobility. In every land the greatest lords formed a separate caste whose rank at court and whose access to the monarch guaranteed them high civil posts, ambassadorships and military commands. They lorded it over the rest of the nobility and showed special scorn for nobles in the lowest rank and those who were of recent creation, whom they regarded as upstart nobility.

Yet, despite the unquestioned supremacy of the great nobility, the lesser nobility, as a corporate body, from the 16th century onward won political power, wealth and prestige. The extent of the gains varied from land to land but the rise of the lesser nobility, or, more exactly, of the upper strata of the lesser nobility, was a common phenomenon. In England, self-confident and well-educated men of the gentry dominated the House of Commons and held the reins of local administration, as justices of the peace, sheriffs, and commanders of the militia. Their economic position was constantly reinforced when men who had gained wealth in trade, law or royal service entered the gentry. In Russia the great nobility had been shattered by the upheavals of the second half of the 16th century and the Time of Troubles in the first years of the next century. The lesser nobles as individuals had suffered, too, and many of their families had been wiped out. But as a corporate body the lesser nobility had triumphed. They had controlled the national assembly that in 1613 had chosen Michael Romanov to be tsar, and they became the new ruling class. In Prussia a new lesser nobility, called the Junkers, emerged in the 15th and 16th centuries and assumed social, political and economic leadership. Among their forebears had been the knights, mercenaries, land agents and adventurers, some of them men of unsavoury reputation, who had settled the German–Polish frontier. The same trend towards greater economic and political importance and prestige for the lesser nobility manifested itself in other parts of Germany, in France, in Bohemia and Moravia, in Hungary and in Poland.

Typically, the lesser nobleman lived out in the country in the midst of his land. There he immersed himself in rural life, supervising the operation of his estate, spending much time in outdoor recreations, above all the hunt, and rarely journeying beyond the borders of his local region. His rusticity made him the object of ridicule for the more sophisticated court nobility and for dramatists and novelists who addressed themselves to fashionable audiences. The provincial nobleman was often portrayed as a yokel, given to drink, and semi-literate, living in a crumbling manor house and barely getting by in a hand-to-mouth existence. The country squire was, indeed, often a man of limited knowledge, colloquial in speech, living in penury, and untutored in the social graces. But there were many provincial noblemen who confounded that stereotype. Nobles such as the Prussian Junkers, the French nobles who lived in the neighbourhood of important provincial cities, such as Toulouse, Rennes and Bordeaux, or the 'improving landlords' of England, were men of action, well-to-do if not wealthy. They were shrewd and hard-driving business-men, who were quick to take advantage of opportunities to increase the profits from their land. Nobles such as these managed to combine a mercenary and selfish attitude with a strong sense of public service and patriotic devotion.

These men formed the upper strata of the lesser nobility. At the bottom were many thousands of petty noblemen whose holdings were often no larger, and sometimes were smaller, than the holdings of their peasant neighbours, and there were many who owned no land at all. Every state had swarms of these people, many of whom lived at or below the poverty line and who could scarcely be distinguished from the peasantry. Accounts from the early 16th century onward told of their large numbers and of their poverty. They scratched a meagre living from their pieces of land, they took service as domestics or retainers in the households of wealthier nobles, they besieged the government for pensions and employment, and there were those who lived on charity. Some became brigands. Others became beggars. The intendant of Seville reported in 1760 that many noblemen begged daily in the streets, and a Prussian law of 1789 forbade army officers to beg. As time went on, some among them adopted peasant ways and peasant manners, married into peasant families and gradually sank into the peasantry. The great majority, however, clung tenaciously to their status as nobles and steadfastly maintained a distance between themselves and the roturiers and peasants among whom they lived. The petty noble ploughed his own field, but he was careful to hang the sword that only a noble could carry on a tree near the road so that the passerby would know that he was a noble.

More than pride alone made the petty noble emphasize and cling to his noble status. Valuable material privileges, established at various times from the Middle Ages onward, adhered to that status. The most important concerned land. In agricultural societies, such as Europe was until recent times, land is the single most important commodity. Those who control the land dominate the society. That was why in continental Europe the right to own rural land had often been restricted to the state, the church and the nobility, and in some jurisdictions included cities as corporate bodies and institutions such as universities and charitable foundations. The monopoly on landowning persisted in these lands until the last decades of the 18th and first half of the 19th century. Only then did it begin to break down, in itself an indication of the weakening of the ancien régime. In other lands, as in much of France, the plateauland of Switzerland, Savoy and much of western Germany, the feudal principle of *nulle terre sans seigneur*, no land without a lord, had survived. Nearly all the rural land was divided into fiefs, or seigniories. The peasant who worked the land and who held it by hereditary tenure could buy, sell, mortgage and bequeath it. In popular speech, in government reports and even in legal texts he was called the proprietor. Actually, the peasant owned only the right to the use of the land. The seignior had the superior ownership of the land, and in recognition of that ownership the peasant had to make payments to the seignior in cash, kind and sometimes in labour.

## Taxes and monopolies

Another valuable privilege of the continental nobility concerned taxation. In Hungary, Poland, Livonia, the Danubian principalities, Electoral Saxony, Denmark

*Payment of dues, two more miniatures from the 'Sachsenspiegel'. Ploughing and reaping indicate the sources of the money that is being paid.*

and in much of the kingdom of Prussia the nobles paid no taxes on land registered in the tax rolls as demesne, that is, land that the noble used for his own purposes. The rest of the land that belonged to the noble, held and worked by peasants who paid the noble a money rent or obligations in kind and labour, was registered as peasant land and was taxed. The peasants paid the tax. The nobles also often enjoyed other exemptions. In Hungary they paid no taxes, nor tariffs, nor tolls, nor tithes. This freedom from all levies was one of the three cardinal privileges (as they were called) awarded to the Magyar nobility by the Golden Bull of King Andreas II, in 1222, and retained by them until 1848. Nobles in other lands did not possess such a total exemption, but often did not have to pay tariffs and tolls.

In some lands, among them some of the states in southern and western Germany, and in the German and Slav crownlands of the Austrian monarchy, rulers had managed to compel nobles to pay taxes on their demesnes. Nearly everywhere, however, the rate for noble land was considerably less than that levied on land held by peasants. In 17th-century Bohemia, for example, the tax rate on noble land was one-seventh that on peasant land. The rate for nobles was increased in the next century but was still much lower than that for peasants. At that, noble landowners in Bohemia and other Austrian crownlands managed to avoid paying some of the taxes they should have paid. The tax assessments were based on land registers. The data in the registers came not from surveys but from statements provided by the noble landowners themselves. Apparently, many of them failed to report the full extent of their holdings. In France, too, the government had taken away some of the fiscal immunities of the nobles but they still paid less than their proportionate share of the taxes. In Russia, Catherine II in the Charter of the Nobility, which she granted in 1785, had exempted the nobility from all direct taxes. Her next two successors tried to impose taxes on the nobility but their efforts met with so much resistance that their tax legislation was repealed.

Even though the state demanded no taxes or reduced taxes from its nobles, some governments involved the nobles in their fiscal system. In the course of the 17th and 18th centuries the rulers of Denmark, Poland, Russia, the Austrian monarchy and a number of small states in eastern Germany made the lords responsible for the taxes of the peasants who lived on their land. It was left to the lord to see to it that the peasants met their full fiscal obligation to the state. If he failed in this he was responsible for whatever the shortfall was. Apparently, however, the state, at least in Russia, did not press the lords to pay up for their delinquent serfs, for enormous tax arrears piled up in that country. And some lords, or their agents, in Austria and Poland, and doubtless in other lands, used their position as tax collector to demand more from the peasants than the state asked for and to pocket the difference.

Nobles also possessed valuable economic privileges. Nearly everywhere on the continent and in Scotland the peasants who lived on the land owned by the noble had to bring their grain to the lord's mill, paying a fee that was usually a set proportion of the grain for the milling. Generally, lords leased out the mill. In western Europe the lord often required his peasants to bake their bread in his ovens and to use his press for their grapes and oil seeds, all, of course, for a fee. Another common and lucrative seigniorial monopoly concerned the manufacture and sale of alcoholic beverages. Only the lord, or the person to whom he had leased the privilege, could make and sell whisky and beer on the lord's manor. Often, too, especially though not exclusively in eastern Europe, the lord alone could open a tavern on his manor. He always turned over the operation of this enterprise to a lessee. In wine producing regions of France and in the Danubian principalities only the seigniors could sell their wine for a specified period after the vintage. In France the period was usually thirty to forty days. Only then could the peasants offer their wine to buyers. In some lands the peasants could purchase certain staples, such as salt and tobacco, and herring in White Russia and Poland, only from the lord, who often charged inflated prices for merchandise that often was of inferior quality.

Nobles in many lands had the sole right to fish in the ponds and navigable streams of their manors. This could be a profitable monopoly, especially in Catholic lands, and lords frequently leased it out. In France only seigniors could have a pigeon cote. The birds, protected from being shot or snared by the peasants, who were forbidden to take any game, fed in the fields of the peasants where they did much harm. Peasants in one district complained, in 1789, that the pigeons of their seignior were responsible for the loss of one-fifth of their crops.

In sharp contrast to their fellow nobles on the continent, the English nobility possessed none of these material privileges and monopolies. English peers could be tried only by the House of Lords, they were immune from arrest for all save certain grave offenses, they had personal access to the monarch, they monopolized the lord lieutenancies of the counties and they were free of certain civic obligations such as jury duty. These perquisites were not without significance, but they could not approach the economic value of the exemptions and the monopolies enjoyed by the noblemen of the continent.

In return for the privileges accorded to them, nobles were expected to contribute to the welfare and the protection of their societies. That, at least, was the presumption. As a document presented to the Estates held at Orleans in 1560 explained, the privileges of the nobility were given them 'not only to repulse and attack enemies, but also to help and sustain the other orders and to keep them in peace and quiet under the authority of the king'. Catherine II's Charter of the Nobility declared that the nobleman when called upon was expected 'to spare neither effort nor life itself in the service of the state', and that 'the first duty and the proper task of the nobility is to defend his country'. The Prussian Law Code of 1794 stated that 'it is incumbent upon the nobility as the first order of the state, and by the nature of its calling, to defend the state, as well as to support its external dignity and its internal organic law'.

For many noblemen these expressions of the contribution expected of them remained little more than pious hopes. They showed no interest in, nor aptitude for, the military or bureaucratic life. Yet they continued to enjoy all the prerogatives of the noble estate. Many others, however, took the role assigned to them by their societies with great seriousness, and devoted themselves to the public service. The desire for personal glory, the glamour of court life and the power and wealth that came with high office undoubtedly had much to do with their decision to serve. In every land they filled the higher ranks of the civil bureaucracy and the military, and many of the lesser posts. The army held a special attraction for them for it was as a soldier that honour and valour, so highly prized in the noble scale of values, could be most easily and publicly won. Moreover, there was a widely shared conviction that men of noble birth, accustomed as they were to command and to have others defer to them, made the best officers. It was supposed, too, that their sense of honour would make them face death and danger fearlessly, and would inspire them to serve without expectation of material reward.

## Scales of justice

There was one extremely important public service that even those nobles who avoided military or bureaucratic duty provided. Nobles represented the public authority in the rural world. In much of Europe the local seignior, or his representative, or in England the lord of the manor or some other locally important member of the gentry, was for all practical purposes the government for the people who lived on his property. The extent of the public powers of the lord varied inversely with the amount of local authority exercised by the central government. The less able or the less willing the central government was to provide adequate and appropriate services, the broader the spectrum of public services provided by the nobleman. The most usual and the most important of the local public functions provided by noblemen was the conduct of the local law court, the supervision of police activities and the maintenance of law and order. In addition, in one or another land, the noble was responsible for the care of orphaned or abandoned children, providing emergency relief for vagabonds, checking weights and measures, enforcing standards of quality in artisanal production, supervising the observance of the Sabbath, dealing with problems of public health, supervising the maintenance of roads and bridges, proclaiming and enforcing the laws of the land and, as mentioned earlier, imposing and collecting taxes from the peasants. Nobles shifted many of these functions to the village community or to the village headman and council, but the ultimate responsibility lay with the noble.

On the continent the area in which the seignior had jurisdiction usually coincided with the boundaries of his property. Often, and especially in central and western Germany there were manors with several seigniors, each of whom filled a different role and drew the income to which the role entitled him. One seignior had the superior ownership of the land, another could have the jurisdictional rights, and there could be still another who was called the patron. In medieval times peasants had put themselves under the protection of a patron and in return paid him dues and services. The need for protection had long since disappeared but the patron still demanded his payments though he did nothing. Through inheritance, purchase, gift or exchange, each of these roles, including the jurisdictional one, sometimes belonged to a number of owners, each of whom demanded the share of the revenues that corresponded to his fractional share of the seigniorial role. In Spain the crown gave or sold jurisdictional rights to nobles and wealthy commoners. By the late 18th century these men had jurisdiction over seventeen cities and one-third of the towns and villages of Spain.

In earlier times many nobles had possessed wide jurisdictional authority including the right to sentence culprits to death. As the power of the central government grew, these wide powers had been reduced. In France and Savoy a distinction was made between the high, the middle and the low justice. Other lands of western and central Europe knew only the high and the low justice. High justice, possessed only by great lords, in theory allowed the lord to try major offences and to mete out the death sentence. In practice the central government ordered that this sentence had to be reviewed by the provincial Parlement or by a royal court. The judicial powers of the nobles were greatest in the lands of central and eastern Europe where the peasants were serfs or the 'hereditary subjects' of their seigniors. The nobles of Livonia, until 1632, had the right to execute peasants who lived on their manors. In Poland, lords had that right until 1768, when a new law ordered that henceforth capital offences had to be tried in royal or city courts. Most lords had regularly transferred such cases to the royal courts, so that the new decree only confirmed the existing practice. In Prussia, the law required the manorial court to call in justices from a neighbouring city to pronounce sentence in criminal cases, a royal high court reviewed the sentence, and the king had to approve sentences of exile or execution. In Austria, almost all nobles had once had the power to administer civil justice and most of the great lords could try criminal cases and could impose the death sentence. During the reigns of Empress Maria Theresa (1740–80) and her son Joseph II (1780–90) these powers were progressively diminished. Finally, a decree of 1 September 1781 reduced all seigniorial courts to courts of first instance, limited the cases they could hear and required approval of officials of the central government for all jail sentences of more than eight days.

In Russia, Empress Elizabeth in 1760 had given lords the power to banish their serfs to Siberia. Her aim was to encourage the settlement of that land. The serf-owner

*How the scales of injustice are weighted against the peasant (bound, gagged and helpless) and in favour of the knight: an engraving by the German artist known as the Petrarca-Meister, illustrating a translation of Cicero in 1531.*

was supposed to exile his peasants only for major offences but it was left to the lord to decide whether the offence was serious enough to warrant that penalty. The mother of the novelist Ivan Turgenev sent two of her serfs to Siberia because they failed to bow to her when she passed them by when they were at work in a field. The journey to Siberia, done mainly on foot, was so long and hard that an estimated seventy-five per cent perished on the way. Once he reached Siberia the exile, if he had not been sentenced to hard labour, was given land by the government and became a state peasant. In 1765 Catherine II gave lords the right to sentence their serfs to hard labour for the Admiralty, the serf-owner to set the length of the sentence. The government rescinded this right in 1809, reputedly because of its abuse by a serf-owner who had sentenced peasants to twenty years of hard labour 'in order to moderate the impudence of their behaviour'. In the 1830s and 1840s the government curbed the punitive powers of nobles, ordering that a master could not sentence his serf to more than 40 blows with the rod or 15 with the cudgel, nor could he imprison the serf for more than two months in the manor jail. If he felt that the offence demanded more severe punishment he could sentence the culprit to a maximum of three months in a government house of correction, or assign him to hard labour with a government work gang, or send him as a recruit into the army (where the term of active duty was twenty years). More severe punishments could be inflicted only by government authorities.

In some continental lands the lords sat as judges in their own courts. As a general rule, however, the lords appointed one of their estate officials, or an officer or elder of the village community, or hired someone to serve as judge. In some sovereignties the law required the judge to have a certain amount of legal training. Great lords could afford to hire a full-time judge. Lesser nobles could neither afford nor did they need a full-time judge, so one judge often worked for a number of lords, visiting each estate periodically and receiving a modest wage from each estate owner. In central and western Europe peasants could appeal decisions of their lord's court to the courts of the government, but the process was costly, time consuming and usually futile. The officers of the higher courts were either nobles or men dependent upon the favour of nobles and so were disinclined to side with peasants against their lords. In the eastern lands there was no appeal from the decisions of the lord's court. In Russia, if a peasant dared to enter complaints with the authorities about the injustices of his masters the law ordered that he was to be beaten and he could also be sentenced to hard labour.

In compensation for his services the noble collected fines and fees from the villagers. These revenues were for some lords an important part of their income. More significantly, the public powers of the nobles, and especially their judicial powers, provided them with a valuable instrument for the preservation and expansion of their own private interests. There were expenses, however. The lord had to pay the costs of maintaining his court and his jail and the costs of investigations. Other expenses, too, could be heavy, such as having to provide emergency relief to vagabonds and sending back runaways to their proper lords. The costs, the bother, the restrictions put upon their powers and, for some, the insignificant revenues persuaded a number of nobles to relinquish their judicial authority, in France to government courts, and in Austria to larger landowners who could better afford the expense. Most nobles, however, held on tenaciously to their judicial powers, along with their other privileges and prerogatives.

The Scottish crown by grant of 'pit and gallows' had given its barons the power of life and death in their courts. After the Scottish rebellion of 1745 Parliament severely limited baronial jurisdiction to petty offences. Rural England was ruled by the justices of the peace. These men were chosen from among the more important of the local gentry. Nominally appointees of the crown, they were actually chosen by the lord lieutenant of the county, and represented local interests much more than national. In their capacity as justices of the peace they administered justice in their courts, supervised the maintenance of roads, bridges, jails and workhouses, enforced apprenticeship rules, fixed wages, licensed public houses and supervised local welfare programmes, along with carrying out many other functions. Four times each year all of the JPs in each county met in Quarter Sessions where, acting as both judges and administrators, they heard cases and also made regulations for the administration of the county, including fixing the tax rate for the support of the poor. Until 1888 the JPs, meeting in Quarter Sessions, were the local governing body of each of England's counties.

They did all this without receiving salary or fees, and without the proper staff that would have been needed for efficient administration. That would have cost money, which could only have been raised by taxes, and the justices, as the principal property owners of the county, preferred inefficient but cheap government to a more efficient but more costly one. A few among the JPs were corrupt and used their office for personal profit. Most were men of probity, wealthy enough to resist the temptation of corruption, and willing, indeed, eager to spend time and effort in the public service without reward. But they were often ignorant, without knowledge of the law and swayed by the biases and prejudices of their class. Moreover, conflict of interest was nearly a constant presence in the proceedings of their courts. As one of the chief landowners, if not the chief or even the only landowner, and principal citizen of his neighbourhood, and often its major employer, the justice of the peace could not help but be involved in some, perhaps the large majority, of the cases brought before him.

## Duty, display and debt

The possession of land and authority over the people who lived on it was the one certain source of the power, status and wealth of a nobleman. The king's counsellors and his favourites could ascend to great prestige and riches, but they were always at the mercy of royal whim and of changes in the tides of politics. Land guaranteed position and the more land owned the greater the income, the greater the security of status and the greater the pre-eminence in the society. The grandees of every country were great landowners, and the few who stood at the very summit of the nobility owned enormous amounts. An 18th-century commentator estimated that one-third of all the arable land in Spain belonged to four great noble houses. In Poland, Count Felix Potocki owned properties that covered 17,000 square kilometres. Prince Stanislaus Lubomirskii owned 25,000 square kilometres, an area equal to four-fifths of the size of Belgium. There were 31 towns and 728 villages on his properties. In the 1840s, around 700,000 people lived on the land owned by Prince Paul Anton Ester-házy, the greatest of the Hungarian magnates. His properties included 30 villages, 40 towns and 34 castles. In Russia, where, until the emancipation of the serfs in 1861, the wealth of a lord was measured not by land area but by the number of adult male serfs that he owned, about 1 per cent (1,453) of the 127,103 serf-owners in 1834 owned 33 per cent of the $10\frac{7}{10}$ million adult male serfs. Count D.N. Sheremetev, the greatest of the proprietors, owned almost 300,000 serfs of both sexes and over $1\frac{9}{10}$ million acres of land. In England great estates increased in size and number from the late 17th century, so that by 1873 just 4,217 landlords owned over half of the country.

Those who were willing to chance the vagaries of court life and royal favour could expect to be rewarded. Income from offices of state and from pensions paid by the monarch, that is, honours to which payments were attached, could be important sources of revenue for their recipients. James Hay, favourite of James I of England who made him Duke of Carlisle, was said to have spent £400,000 during his life, all of which he received from the king. From 1614 to 1617 the French crown paid out a total of 14 million livres in pensions to just nine nobles. Prince de Condé alone received 3,500,000 livres. Thirty years spent in royal service gained the count of Tavannes seven royal pensions, which in 1754 amounted to 46,900 livres. Monarchs also gave gifts of land, or in Russia of peasants, as tokens of their favour. After the Duke of Marlborough's famous victory at Blenheim in 1704, Queen Anne gave him the Royal Manor and Park of Woodstock, an estate of about 15,000 acres and reputedly worth £6,000 a year. She also announced that she was going to pay for the building of a splendid castle at Woodstock to be named after Blenheim. The munificence of Anne and other monarchs paled in comparison with that of the tsars and tsaritsas of 18th-century Russia. Between 1740 and 1801 they gave 1,304,000 adult male state peasants with their wives and children to noble landowners. Empress Catherine II alone gave away over 800,000 peasants of both sexes. Catherine lavished many of her gifts upon her lovers. Alexander Vasilchikov, a young Guards lieutenant who pleased her for twenty-two months was rewarded with 7,000 peasants, 100,000 rubles in cash, a furnished palace worth 100,000 rubles, jewellery valued at 50,000 rubles, porcelain worth another 20,000 rubles and a pension of 20,000 rubles. Others of her passing fancies received similar consideration, while those who had more lasting holds on her affections had even vaster fortunes poured upon them.

Lesser nobles often had to depend upon appointments in the bureaucracy or the army for their livelihoods. A random listing of 1,700 nobles of the Prussian provinces of Kurmark and Pomerania in 1767 showed that 1,300 of them earned their livings as army officers or as bureaucrats. In England, too, the army was a favoured way of providing for impoverished nobles or for younger sons. Among the English generals in the American War of Independence, Generals Howe and Gage were second sons of Irish viscounts, Clinton was the son of a second son of the Earl of Lincoln, and Burgoyne was the son of a younger son of a wealthy baronet. If a military career did not appeal, or if the family could not afford to purchase a commission, minor posts in government bureaux were available.

Nobles also drew income from investments in commercial enterprises, such as mines, quarries, forges, canals, land drainage projects, urban development, overseas trading companies, and distilleries and breweries. It has been suggested that these investments provided capital that may have been of significance in

*Serfdom persisted in Russia until 1861. Here a landowner takes his siesta attended by household serfs, about 1830.*

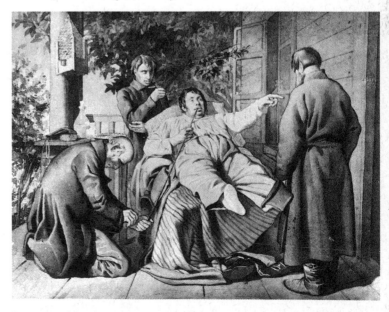

European economic development. It is, however, abundantly clear that only a minor part of total noble expenditures went for productive uses. Most European noblemen spent most of their income, and often more than their income, on consumption. The nobleman felt obliged to live in a style that befitted his station and that would win and hold the respect of his fellow nobles. He had to 'live nobly'. That meant maintaining as luxurious a life-style as possible, with a splendid house, servants, fine horses, and an open-handed hospitality to his peers. Prodigality was deemed a virtue that gave evidence of the superiority of the noble over lesser mortals, who, lacking the self-confidence of the nobleman, worried about the future and so saved and scrimped for a possible rainy day.

The higher on the social scale one ascended the more magnificent was the standard of living and the more demanding the obligations of hospitality. The Duc de Choiseul after his exile to his estate of Chanteloup in 1771, maintained an open house at all times. He had fifty-four servants in the main house, and his table was always prepared for 35–50 guests who could hunt deer in the duke's six-thousand-acre forest, or who could relax in his fine library, or stroll in his extensive formal gardens. Choiseul once explained that this style of life was not a matter of his personal taste but was an obligation for a man of his position.

Choiseul's staff at Chanteloup was small compared to the entourages of great seigniors in other lands. Some Spanish grandees had 300–500 servants, among whom were doctors and lawyers, all of whom lived with their wives and children in the household of their employer. The Duke of Alba had four hundred bedrooms in his castle but that was still not enough. In his Madrid palace alone Alba paid out 100,000 reales a month in wages to his servants. In Russia wages were no problem; the servants were serfs who lived in the household of their owner. Visitors from abroad were astounded by the number of servants, claiming that Russian nobles kept three and even five and six times as many domestics as did nobles of equal rank in other lands.

The building of new and costly residences in town and country was a major outlay. The residence was the most visible evidence of the owner's wealth and position. The more magnificent and the larger the building the greater the glory of the owner. The house became the showplace for the family's pedigree, with portraits of ancestors and coats of arms and suits of armour on display. Beginning in the mid-16th century and continuing on into the early years of the next century, nobles from England across to Poland spent great sums on the construction and furnishing of large and luxurious town houses, such as the great hôtels of Paris, or stately manor houses, such as the castles and mansions of the Danish countryside, the Elizabethan and Jacobean houses of rural England and the imposing country seats of Saxony. Another great wave of building came in the second half of the 18th century when, as in the 16th century, rising farm prices and rents increased seigniorial revenues. Over two hundred palaces were built in Hungary during the forty years of the reign of Maria Theresa, from 1740 to 1780, besides many manor houses and town residences. In other lands, too, in Silesia, Saxony, Prussia, Poland, Russia and England and the Danubian principalities, lords built luxurious manor houses and palaces with rich furnishings, and often with gardens and parks in the English style.

Less affluent nobles spent proportionately less than the grand seigniors but they, too, indulged in excessive expenditures. The result was that lords great and small piled up endless debts. The Sheremetevs, who owned more serfs and more land than any other Russian noble, consistently spent more than their enormous annual income. By 1859, Count D.N. Sheremetev owed 6 million rubles. The French Prince de Contí had an income in 1655 of 200,000 livres but managed to spend over 1 million livres. In 1741 Lord Weymouth, who had an annual income of £12,000 owed £130,000. Lesser men involved themselves accordingly. B.A. Kurakin, who had an annual income of 7,500 rubles, left debts that totalled 207,032 rubles when he died in 1764. The interest charge on his debt amounted to 12,422 rubles, or sixty-five per cent more than his annual income. Russian seigniors borrowed chiefly by mortgaging their adult male serfs with governmental credit agencies that had been established to extend credit to the nobility. By 1859, on the eve of the emancipation of the serfs, the seigniors had mortgaged two-thirds of their adult male serfs for a total of 425 million rubles. In addition, the nobles owed great amounts of money to private lenders.

Sometimes debts drove the noble into bankruptcy and he lost everything. In Silesia, for example, at the end of the 1760s over four hundred estates were put up for sale to satisfy the claims of creditors. Other nobles, however, who went bankrupt were bailed out by the crown and continued on in their profligacy. No opprobrium or disgrace attached itself to heavy debt or to bankruptcy; it was part of the accepted way of life.

In fairness to the nobility, reasons other than self-indulgence and prodigality compelled them to borrow. The heir of an estate needed cash to pay to kinsman the legacies of the deceased. Fathers had to borrow to provide dowries for their daughters. The inadequate salaries paid to lesser bureaucrats and to junior army officers meant that the only way these men could live at a scale suited to their status was to borrow. Proprietors who had suffered losses from the devastation of war had to borrow to meet the costs of reconstruction at war's end. Nor were all nobles chronically in debt; some lent money to other nobles. Moreover, by the middle of the 19th century in some lands the nobility had become much more economical and much more interested in careful management. In England by the 1880s many large estates were free or almost free from debt. It is worth noting, however, that by the mid-19th century the star of the nobility was clearly setting.

*If a nobleman had ruined himself by extravagant living and gambling he could repair his fortunes by marriage to a mercantile family. In this scene from Hogarth's 'Marriage à la Mode', the gout-crippled aristocrat, pointing to his family-tree, barters his title for a dowry.*

Perhaps this untraditional concern with prudent management gave evidence of the decline of the nobility and their adoption of bourgeois values.

Noble recreations, and above all gambling, were an important source of noble debt, especially for those who preferred to live in the capital. A skill at the gaming table, a willingness to play for high stakes and a cavalier attitude towards losses, no matter how heavy, were considered marks of elegance and breeding. Great amounts were won and lost in the course of a night's play. Other amusements included balls, often with masks that had to be worn for at least half the evening; assemblies at which people met to chat, to play cards and to flirt; theatre; concerts; and, always and everywhere, dalliance. Some nobles, especially the wealthier ones, professing boredom with country life, preferred to spend their days at court or in the capital city. Years sometimes passed between the visits of these men to their country seats. When they did go back it was often because they had been exiled from the court. In Spain, city residence was the normal pattern for the nobility, many of whom did not have country houses. They reportedly had no taste for rural life and sports, nor apparently did they have much taste for exciting city life; Spanish social life was so formal and so gloomy that Madrid was considered a hardship post for ambassadors.

### Hunting: the noble privilege

In other lands many nobles preferred country life and came only infrequently to the city. Still others spent the 'season' in the city in a constant round of social engagements, whether it was St Petersburg, Copenhagen, Bucharest, Vienna or London for the great nobility, or some provincial capital for lesser nobles. They returned to their country seats when the 'season' ended. There,

45

*Hunting was a noble's privilege that survived from feudal times, and the game laws protecting it were bitterly resented. Above: poacher caught by a gamekeeper, a French engraving. Below: a man-trap against poachers, advertised as 'humane' because it does not maim the leg.*

Humane Man Trap

drive them towards the guns in what Theodore Roosevelt, himself an ardent hunter, called 'a dismal parody upon the stern hunting life'. To preserve the game for themselves they made hunting a symbol of their noble status, and the law and custom restricted the right to hunt to the nobility. Strata were even established among the nobility in some places. In the French province of Maine and in Osnabrück in Germany large game was reserved for the great nobility. In Lower Austria the person who owned a forest did not necessarily have the right to hunt in it. Often an important noble owned that privilege, and sometimes one lord had the right to kill large game, and another only the smaller animals. In England, Parliament in 1671 forbade all freeholders with annual incomes of less than £100, which meant by far the greatest number of freeholders, from killing game, even on their own land. Later, still more restrictive legislation made it illegal for anyone who was not at least a member of the gentry or the eldest son of a gentleman to hunt, even at the invitation of the owner of the land.

The monopoly on hunting enjoyed by the nobility deprived the peasants of a valuable source of food, furs and hides. To make matters worse, the hunters in pursuit of their prey often rode through the fields of the peasants and damaged their crops. Legislation sometimes forbade hunting over sown fields or through vineyards. The hunters paid scant attention to the restrictions, for they sat as the judges in the local courts that were charged with the enforcement of these ordinances. Nor could the peasants protect their fields from the depredations of the game animals and birds that fed on the growing crops. When French peasants put up fences to keep out the animals the seigniors compelled them to take them down. In Lower Austria the peasants were allowed to erect fences but without pointed palings so that animals would not injure themselves in leaping over the fence. In some lands villagers had to keep their dogs tied up lest they run down game. Frederick II of Denmark (1559–88) forbade peasants who lived near a hunting preserve to have more than one dog, and to prevent the dog from chasing game it had to have one foreleg amputated above the knee. In many places in France, and doubtless elsewhere, peasants were forbidden to weed their fields or to mow hay at certain times of the year for fear that they would disturb nesting partridges or destroy their eggs.

The commoner who dared to hunt or trap or net birds was subject to punishment as a poacher. The penalties became more severe as the number of nobles increased and the amount of game decreased. Nowhere were the penalties more draconian than in England. Parliamentary legislation from 1770 onward ordered increasingly harsh punishment for poachers, reaching its climax in the Act of 1816. That law ordered that anyone found at night, even if only with a net, in a forest, chase or park, was to be sentenced to transportation for seven years. The severity of the law was reduced the next year

most of them filled their days with entertaining, visiting and field sports, above all hunting. From medieval times down to the early 20th century the chase had been a passion of princes and nobles. Obsessed with the sport, they hunted day after day, mounted or on foot, slaughtering untold numbers of animals and birds. Often they used beaters to flush out their quarry and to the extent that the accused had to be armed with a weapon. To catch poachers, landowners set up man-traps and spring-guns in the brush, which killed and maimed innocent persons as often as the poachers for whom the devices were intended. Judges found these contrivances legal until Parliament outlawed them in 1827.

### 'Improving landlords'

Most nobles, whether or not they spent time in the country, valued their rural properties as their country seats, and as the supplier of the income they needed to support themselves and their households. The usual noble, however, did not think of his property as a business enterprise to be operated at a profit. He used the income from his property for consumption, rather than investing it in improvements that would increase his income. Then, in the 18th century, a few nobles on the continent and a relatively large number in England adopted a new attitude towards their properties, that could be called capitalistic. These 'improving landlords', as they were called in England, introduced improved farming techniques, better implements, new crops, new field systems and improved livestock, all designed to increase the productivity and the profitability of their properties. In England they were the instigators and leaders in the enclosure movement, which transformed the face and nature of English agriculture. On the continent, where the number of 'improving landlords' was strikingly small, they were much less successful. As part of their efforts to improve agriculture these innovating nobles took a leading part in the formation of societies for the promotion of agriculture in their respective countries. Some of these organizations were destined to make important contributions through the journals they published, the model farms they established, the museums and expositions they supported and the research they sponsored.

The era of the 'improving landlord' coincided with a new enthusiasm for everything connected with agriculture that appeared among the upper orders of society. This became the rage among the stylish and was so intense that in France, where much of it centred, it came to be called *agromanie*. Writers apotheosized the peasant and hailed agriculture as the most admirable of all arts. A Swiss peasant named Jakob Gujer, best known by his nickname of Kleinjogg, or Little Jake, who transformed a debt-ridden holding into a successful farm by using improved farming methods, became an international celebrity. He was 'discovered' by a Swiss disciple of the Enlightenment, who in 1761 published a book about Kleinjogg that he called *Die Wirtschaft eines philosophischen Bauer (The Economy of a Philosophical Peasant)*, which was translated into French, Italian and English. Some of the most important men of the time made a pilgrimage, as it were, to visit Gujer and talked and wrote ecstatically about the experience. Prince Ludwig Eugen of Württemberg,

reportedly with tears in his eyes, told Kleinjogg: 'I do not come down to you, I rise up to you, for you are better than I.' Goethe, who came to call in 1775, described Kleinjogg as 'one of the most noble creatures that the earth has produced'. Rousseau wanted to meet the famed Kleinjogg but never got around to it. That did not prevent him from describing Kleinjogg in a letter of 24 December 1761 as 'wiser, more virtuous, more judicious than all the philosophers of the universe'. Actually, Kleinjogg, who was skilful in ingratiating himself with his worldly visitors, seems to have been an opinionated and generally unpleasant man. He was openly scornful of the customs and recreations and holidays of his fellow villagers because he thought they contributed to laziness and backwardness. As part of his dissent he refused to wear traditional peasant dress and instead wore a simple grey blouse held together by an unornamented iron clasp. But Gujer could do no wrong in the eyes of his bewigged, besatined and perfumed visitors, who praised his dress as evidence of his rationality and simplicity.

### A talent to survive

The history of the nobility reached a glittering climax in the 18th century. Never before had Europe seen such grandeur and display. It was an efflorescence that reflected a remarkable resurgence of the nobility nearly everywhere in Europe. Nobles revived old privileges and demanded new ones from their peasants; they reaffirmed their claim to a special position in society; and they bid for greater power for their caste in government. Their actions summoned forth criticisms and complaints, which increased as the years went by and were inspired by the ideas of equality that were winning favour, especially among the increasingly self-confident bourgeoisie. With few exceptions, nobles met these attacks with defiance, praising the merits of a hierarchical society, insisting on the natural superiority of the nobility over men of lower orders, and defending their privileged status as natural and beneficial to society.

The renaissance of noble pretensions was destined to be short lived. The 18th century turned out to be the Indian summer of the European nobility. Even during that century the nobility lost some of its privileges and some of its authority. The monopoly that it possessed on landownership in some continental countries began to crumble, with commoners able to buy landed estates. The central government clipped or ended the fiscal immunities of the lords, and interjected itself in the relationship between the seignior and the peasants who held their land from him. Meanwhile, the belief in the natural superiority of the nobility and in the hierarchical structure of society was badly shaken by the impact of the ideas of the men of the Enlightenment. Their emphasis upon reason and their conviction that society should be organized for the benefit of all its members, and not just for the ruling elite, gained ever wider acceptance.

The brilliance of the 18th century faded swiftly in the next hundred years. The nobility of Europe could not withstand the revolutions, the emancipation of the peasantry in the continental lands, the decline in the local authority that they had possessed for so long, the expansion of the suffrage, the demand for civil equality and the emergence of mass political parties. In short, it could not withstand the emergence of a new kind of world in which birth and pedigree lost their importance, shunted aside by a new scale of values that determined status by the role the individual played in the production of goods and services, and by the amount of wealth that he commanded. The special privileges, the special position before the law, the monopolies and all the preferments that the nobility had expected and enjoyed for so long, gradually withered away in one land after another.

The nobility itself, of course, did not disappear. Instead, there was a gradual dilution of its pre-eminence as the decades went by. In some lands nobles managed to hold on to their positions more successfully than in others. But in every European land their domination lessened. By the eve of World War I, nobles no longer monopolized leadership roles, though they retained an importance in government that was out of all proportion to their numbers. The expansion in the activities of the state created a demand for skilled specialists, and education and merit came to be regarded as more important than noble birth. Even the ministries of foreign affairs and the army, long the special preserves of the nobility, lost their exclusivity.

Many of the commoners who distinguished themselves in government, in the military and, to a lesser extent, in the professions and in business were rewarded with patents of nobility. Now, however, nobility no longer gave its possessor rights and privileges denied to other members of his society. Rather, it was an award given to honour men of outstanding achievement. Nobility was still prized as a social asset. The centuries-old acceptance of the superior status of the nobility was too deeply ingrained in their consciousness for Europeans to abandon the deference that they had always shown to the nobility. The socially ambitious still eagerly sought after titles. Where it was not legally available, as in France, they assumed it. In that land nobility had been abolished by formal act of the Third Republic. That meant that there was no law, as there had formerly been, that forbade the assumption of a title. Whereupon many Frenchmen started calling themselves marquis or count, or added a 'de' to their name. The number of these self-ennobled Frenchmen became so large that an *Encyclopédie de la Fausse Noblesse*, published in 1976, listed over three thousand families.

Those of the nobility who could afford it, or who married the daughters of wealthy bourgeois businessmen and bankers, became men of leisure. Others engaged in business enterprise either as investors or as active managers. Still others, who lacked the means to maintain an appropriate living style, faded into undistinguished obscurity. In some lands the nobility did indeed demonstrate what one of them has called a 'staggering instinct for survival'. But since World War I, in land after land, the tides of history have engulfed the nobility. Where it still survives it has not only lost the remnants of its privileges, or had them reduced to meaninglessness, but has lost its belief in itself, its belief in 'that instinctive sense of exclusivity which marks a hereditary aristocracy'.

---

**Landownership and nobility** became inseparably linked in the 13th century and remained so for the next three hundred years. During that time European society was rigidly stratified on the hereditary principle. With rare exceptions, land was owned by members of the noble class, who were the sons of noblemen; the sons of peasants were peasants and had no prospect of ever owning land. By the 16th century this rigidity was relaxing. With the emergence of a money economy, the rise of a mercantile middle class and the growth of cities, it became possible for men to get rich without being noble, and their natural ambition was then to step up into the class above them. When this happened it was all the more important for them, lacking the qualification of noble birth, to acquire the other hallmark of nobility: land. In England, where social mobility was greater than any of the continental countries, a large estate, a title and a high-born wife were a sufficient passport to its ranks, and by the second generation no distinction was made between old and new nobility.

This portrait of John Bridgman is an icon of the age. In the years after the Restoration of Charles II he was able to rise sufficiently to claim noble status, and his family eventually became Earls of Bradford. The painting gives special prominence to his country seat, his pedigree and (in the inscription) his *wife's* pedigree. (1)

# The noble privilege

Hunting has been an aristocratic pastime for thousands of years. Once, no one of inferior rank was allowed to hunt, and as late as the present century it preserved its links with the leisured way of life.

**The ritual of the chase,** with its special costumes, skills and ceremonies, retained courtly associations through the centuries, though gradually descending on the social scale. Strict game laws enforced its restriction to the landowners. *Above:* Gaston de Foix, in a 15th-century French miniature, sits enthroned, surrounded by huntsmen and dogs. *Above right:* Lord Grosvenor and his friends ride up for the death of the stag (by Stubbs, 1762). Thousands of similar if less elaborate portraits were commissioned, in which the attributes of field sports denote the rank of the sitter. *Right:* Sir Edward Hales (England 1744) and Anton von Perfall (Germany 1876). *Far right:* how the poor saw the game laws – a poacher is caught, brought before the proprietor and accused by an irate gamekeeper; an English painting of the early 19th century. (9–13)

**The 'improving' landlord** was a phenomenon of the 18th century. Before that, a nobleman regarded his estate as the source of his income and generally lived on it to the limit. With the rise of capitalism, some landlords, especially in England, began to treat their land as an investment, maximizing its productivity and using the profit to improve it still further. It was these men who were responsible for some of the most important technical improvements in agriculture. Thomas Coke, of Holkham Hall, Norfolk (seen in the background), succeeded in breeding sheep that set new standards for wool yields and meat value. (14)

# 3 FROM SERVITUDE TO FREEDOM

JEROME BLUM

# From servitude to freedom

For a thousand years servitude and the lack of personal freedom were the conditions of existence for most of the people of rural Europe. They belonged to that order of society known as the peasantry. Through the accident of their birth into that lowest order they were denied rights and privileges and freedoms enjoyed by the other orders. They were compelled to be dependent upon and subservient to those who were above them in the social structure and to pay them dues and services in cash, kind and labour. The extent of their dependence and subservience varied over time and among the different lands of Europe. Some escaped their bonds centuries before their fellows in other lands, and there was a minority who had never known the bonds of dependence. But even those who were called free suffered discrimination, indignities and exploitation at the hands of those who by law and custom were recognized as their superiors.

The servitude and the unfreedom of most of Europe's rural population took many forms and bore many different names. Serfdom was the most common form of unfreedom. It existed for over a millennium in one land or another, and the word serf, or an equivalent, was used for people who were scarcely distinguishable from chattel slaves to those who were nearly free. That is why it is difficult to arrive at a firm definition of this protean word. Often the serf is defined as a person who was bound to the soil, who could not be separated from it and who went with the land when it was transferred from one seignior to another. That was true, for example, in 16th- and 17th-century Russia. But at other times and places, such as Prussia or Poland in the 18th century or Russia in the 18th and early 19th century, the lord could take the peasant from the land and move him about as he wished from one piece of land to another, or convert him into a landless field-hand or factory worker or domestic servant, or sell, give, exchange or gamble him away. The definition of the serf as a man bound to the person of his lord by a bond that had nothing to do with any land held by the serf was true for certain times and places. On the other hand, in 13th-century France the 'blemish of serfdom', as the lawyers put it, adhered to a piece of land. If a free man took over a holding that was recognized as servile he became a serf but regained his freedom when he left the holding. In medieval times the payment by a peasant to a seignior of certain obligations, such as a few days annually of labour services, or a fee when his holding changed hands, or an annual payment in cash or kind as recognition of the seignior's superior ownership of the land, was sometimes regarded as proof of serfdom.

## Servitude, serfdom and slavery

Out of this welter one characteristic emerges that was common to European serfdom throughout the thousand years of its existence. A peasant was regarded as unfree if he was subject to the arbitrary will of his seignior by ties that were degrading and socially incapacitating, and which were recognized and enforced by the legal and social structure of the society. In practice, that meant that the lord had the legal jurisdiction over his serfs to the complete or partial exclusion of the central power. The serf had to have his lord's permission to leave the manor even for a short time; the lord could interfere in the private life of the serf; and the lord could demand any obligation that he wished to impose. Generally, it was the rule for these obligations to be fixed, often in minute detail, by custom or by agreement between lord and villagers. Until the last century of serfdom, when some governments set maxima for certain obligations, the lords could at will increase or decrease the services he demanded of his peasants or change their nature.

Still, no matter how extensive the power of the lord, it was not great enough to deprive the serf of his legal personality; that fact distinguished the serf from the slave. Even when serfs could be bought and sold, when their lords had the power of life and death over them, they still had certain individual rights, no matter how curtailed. The law still recognized them as persons. The slave, no matter how well off he might have been, and there were times when at least some slaves enjoyed greater social and economic advantages than did serfs, was in the eyes of the law not a person but a piece of property, a chattel of his owner.

The distinction between serf and slave was not an academic one. Slavery was a well-known, even, in some lands, a flourishing, institution in the early Middle Ages. The Domesday Inquest of England, made at the order of William the Conqueror in 1086, showed that 9 per cent of all the people counted were slaves. In some western shires the proportion reached 20 per cent or more. In the succeeding decades the slaves were given holdings and absorbed into the mass of unfree tenants. In continental lands west of the Elbe, that had already happened by the 10th century. Slavery continued, but on a greatly diminished scale, except in Spain and

Portugal. There, after the Christian reconquest, slaves continued to be used for centuries, with the supply constantly replenished by captured Moors who rebelled against their Christian rulers, by Turkish prisoners of war and, in the 16th century, by black Africans. In Russia, slaves made up an important part of the farm labour force in the Kievan era from the 9th to the 12th century and remained an integral part of the rural scene into the 16th and 17th centuries. After the fall of the Kievan federation and the decline in seigniorial direct production, slave-owners often gave their slaves holdings, as in western Europe. However, the status of the slave remained unchanged; he was still the chattel of his owner. In every other respect the slave was like other unfree peasants, save that since he was not a legally recognized person he did not pay taxes. The central government became increasingly unhappy about this until, in 1724, Peter I introduced the soul tax, a levy on every adult male, and ordered that slaves had to pay it. Thus fell the last distinction between serf and slave. In the Grand Duchy of Lithuania slavery persisted until the mid-16th century. In Moldavia and Wallachia, later to become Romania, slavery first established itself in the 15th century. The slaves were war prisoners and gipsies, with the latter so predominant that the word gipsy became a synonym for slave, and thralls not of gipsy origin came to be identified as gipsies. This slavery continued until 1855, when it was abolished by governmental edict.

The origins of serfdom in western Europe can be traced back to the troubled times of the late Roman Empire when small free tenant farmers put themselves under the protection of great landlords and slaves were given holdings and became dependent peasants. The chaos of the succeeding centuries strengthened the domination of the landlords, more and more peasants became identified as unfree and, by the 10th century, most of the peasants of western Europe were serfs. For the next two hundred years their serfdom intensified as lords assumed greater powers over the people who lived on their land. Then, by the end of the 13th century, some had gained freedom and many had won partial release from their bonds. By the 16th century, the peasants of western Europe were no longer serfs, save for a relatively small number.

This remarkable evolution occurred against a background of two great secular swings in economic life. The economic expansion of the 12th and 13th centuries persuaded most landowners to give up direct agricultural production. Instead, they rented out their land to their serfs and converted the labour obligations that the serfs owed them into payments in cash and kind. They believed that they could realize a greater gain and save themselves work and trouble by becoming rent receivers rather than producers for market. In any event, they had to make concessions to their serfs to keep them from running off to the new lands that were being opened up, and which held out inducements to attract settlers, or to the growing cities where freedom awaited newcomers. As a result of these seigniorial adjustments to the changed conditions, many serfs became hereditary tenants, still subject to their lord but freed of some burdensome obligations and with far greater personal freedom. Others won complete freedom from all the ties that bound them. Lords in continental western Europe granted charters to the village communities on their manors, which fixed the obligations the peasants had to pay. In England, surveys and documents, or rolls as the English called them, that recorded the decisions of the lord's court served the same purpose by establishing what was called the 'custom of the manor'.

Prosperity had initiated the process of freedom from serfdom. Depression continued it and carried it to completion. The economic expansion of the High Middle Ages levelled off in the first half of the 14th century and then around the middle of that century gave way to stagnation and depression that lasted for

*The Russian system, by which the serf could be alienated from the land and sold, was widely deplored as archaic and barbaric. Gustave Doré here satirizes bloated Russian landlords gambling with bundles of serfs.*

the next hundred years. The most striking aspect of that long decline was a dramatic fall in population, reflected in deserted villages and abandoned holdings everywhere in western Europe. To hold the peasants that they had, and to attract new settlers to take over the empty holdings, seigniors made continued concessions. Their efforts met only with partial success. Many peasants gained freedom by running off to a town, or by settling as leaseholders on another manor whose owner gave them freedom. Some became free men because the death tolls of the plagues that wracked Europe in the 14th century broke the continuity in the keeping of records on many manors, so that seigniors were unable to prove the servile status of their peasants. Some lords, recognizing the inevitable, decided to profit from it and sold freedom to their serfs. Peasant unrest played a part, too. Rural risings in nearly every western land increased the pressure for the ending of serfdom.

Where serfdom lingered on, it was far less onerous than it had formerly been. Most of the peasants in continental western Europe were not yet free. They still owed servile dues and obligations to the lord on whose land they lived, were subject to a greater or lesser degree, depending upon the region, to his jurisdiction and punitive authority and, as members of the peasantry, the lowest order in the hierarchical structure of their societies, were denied rights and privileges enjoyed by those above them in the social scale. In some lands, notably England and Italy, the peasants gained complete freedom, but the traces of their servitude persisted for a long time.

The same centuries during which serfdom withered away in western Europe saw its establishment in the lands of eastern Europe. To understand this paradox of early modern history it is necessary to go back to the era of colonization of the east. The little that is known about the condition of the native peasantry in the eastern lands before that time indicates a widespread use of slaves and a pronounced trend towards the loss of freedom by the peasantry. The migration of Germans across the Elbe into eastern Germany, Poland, Bohemia, Silesia, Hungary, Lithuania and Livonia that began in the 12th century reversed that trend. The sovereigns and the seigniors of the eastern lands welcomed the German colonists, who, coming from the economically more advanced west, possessed the skills needed to promote economic development and thereby increase the revenues of the princes and the landowners. To persuade the Germans to come, the princes and the seigniors held out strong inducements, which included personal freedom, free hereditary tenure of their land, low fixed rents, exemption from all payments for as much as twenty years and the organization of their villages and towns according to the 'German law' rather than according to local law and custom. The German law codes that the colonists adopted as models allowed greater freedom and autonomy than were enjoyed by the native peasants. In response to these

inducements, as well as to the pressure from the growing population west of the Elbe, thousands of Germans poured into the east where the native population was small and much land lay empty.

It was not long before the special privileges accorded to the German colonists had to be extended, in their entirety or partially, to the native peoples. The competition among landowners for peasants to settle on their land compelled them to make concessions to the native population in order to hold them or to lure them away from another lord. The result was that the peasants of these lands knew more freedom in the 13th and 14th centuries than they had known in the preceding era, and than they were to know for the next five hundred years.

Like their fellow sovereigns of the east, the Russian rulers who held sway over the princedoms of the forested tableland that lay between the Oka and Volga Rivers sought to increase the strength of their realms and aggrandize their revenues by persuading peasants to leave their homes in the Dnieper River valley and settle in their princedoms. They offered personal freedom, communal autonomy, free tenures and long exemptions from all payments, and light obligations when the exemptions ran out. Settlers came in large numbers, not only attracted by the inducements, but fleeing before the Mongol onslaught that brought about the collapse of the Kievan federation. The peasants of eastern Europe, like their fellows in the west, seemed headed in the 13th and 14th centuries towards continued improvement in their status.

## Diverging paths: serfdom in eastern Europe
During the next two hundred years, however, their paths diverged. As in the west, these centuries were filled with wars, invasions, civil strife, plagues and crop failures. As in the west, too, the economies of eastern Europe entered into an era of decline, marked by falling population, abandoned holdings, emptied villages, sinking grain prices and a shortage of peasant renters and labourers.

To combat the deterioration in their economic position, the lords of the east tried some of the same palliatives that their peers had employed in the west. They imposed ceilings to hold down the wages of labour, they borrowed heavily, and some of them became brigands. But they also adopted measures that were diametrically opposite to those used in the west, and it was precisely these measures that led to the ultimate enserfment of the eastern peasantry. Instead of reducing obligations, like the western seigniors, the lords in many eastern lands imposed new and heavier obligations. And in every eastern land from the mid-14th century onward, and especially during the course of the 15th century, legislation steadily encroached on the freedom of movement of the peasantry. By the end of the 15th century most of the villagers who lived in the great plainland between the Elbe and the Volga were far along the road to serfdom. During the next hundred years the obligations demanded of them and the restrictions on their freedom increased, until by the end of the 16th century their enserfment was just about completed.

The explanation for this great difference in the fates of the peasants of eastern and western Europe lay in the contrast between the two regions in certain critical developments. In the west, the new monarchies that emerged in the 15th and 16th centuries succeeded in establishing their supremacy over the feudal nobility. In the east, with the exception of Russia, the nobility dominated political life. The sovereigns, weakened by wars, dynastic rivalries and declining revenues, needed the support of the nobility to gain and keep their thrones. To win that support they made many concessions to the nobility, including their demands for supremacy over the cities and greater powers over their peasants. In Russia, unlike other eastern lands, a strong central power emerged in the persons of the rulers of Moscow, who in the 15th and 16th centuries finally triumphed over the princes and great nobles who had contested for power with them. Their savage ascent to the autocratic rule of the Russian land owed much to the support of the lesser nobility. In return for that support the tsars awarded the nobles wide powers over the peasants who lived on their lands.

The dominance of the eastern nobility was furthered by the decline of the towns and the urban middle class. Until the 15th century the cities of eastern Europe had thrived. Then retrogression set in, attributable to the decline of the Hanseatic League, to which many of the Baltic cities belonged; the weakening of the Teutonic order, whose members had been leaders in trade; the loss of trade, because of the depopulation, wars, invasions and domestic strife of the era; and the growing competition in the Baltic of the Dutch and the English. The travail of the cities gave the nobles the opportunity to use their increased leverage with the sovereign to break the urban monopolies on foreign and domestic trade, to prevent the cities from receiving runaway serfs, to bypass the cities by selling directly to foreign buyers, to gain tariff concessions that gave them a price advantage over city shippers and, in Poland, to set maximum prices on city-made wares.

Deprived of most of their functions by these encroachments of seigniors, the cities of eastern Europe stagnated. Meanwhile, the cities of western Europe were entering a new stage of growth in both size and importance. This difference in urban development had great significance not only for the history of the lord-peasant relationship, but for European and world history as well. It meant that the claim of the nobility of eastern Europe to predominance in all aspects of social, political and economic life was left uncontested, while the west witnessed the evolution of a vigorous bourgeoisie, who in the succeeding centuries played the major role in the ascent of western Europe to world leadership. The decline of the cities is of fundamental importance in explaining why eastern Europe remained a backward agrarian society.

The abandonment (for that is what it was) by the sovereign of the peasantry made the peasants of eastern Europe more the subjects of their seignior than of the prince. The seigniors used this public power they possessed further to restrict peasant freedom, to demand increased dues and services and to change the terms of peasant tenure. In short, by entirely legal means they established themselves as the autocrats of their villages and pressed their peasants into an abject dependence upon them.

A steady increase in seigniorial production for market accompanied these developments. In earlier times, production for market had been unimportant, demesnes had been relatively small or absent, and the lords of the east had demanded little or no labour services from their peasants. In the 15th and especially in the 16th century, lords increased the size of their demesnes, often at the expense of the holdings of peasants who were dispossessed and reduced to cotters or landless labourers. To get the work force they now needed, lords increased the labour service from as little as 1–3 or at most 6 days a year to as much as 3 and, in some places, even as much as 6 days a week.

The condition of unfreedom in which the mass of the European peasantry was held by the 16th century – serfdom in the east and servitude and inferiority in the west – was destined to persist for the next 200–300 years. There were modifications and alterations in one land or another, which improved the status in some places and worsened it in others. In its essentials, however, the status of most of the peasantry remained unchanged. Custom and law denied the great majority of Europe's peasants, often including villagers who were legally free men, freedoms and privileges possessed by people of higher status, compelled them to be subservient to and dependent upon persons in these higher status groups, and required them to render certain payments and services demanded of no other category in their societies.

*Peasants paying dues, a German woodcut of 1479. They bring farm produce, including a sheep and a goose.*

## Labour, cash and kind

The weight of the obligations demanded by the seigniors formed a spectrum, from relatively light impositions in western and parts of central Europe to an oppressive and time consuming burden in the east. The obligations were set by the seignior, or by agreement between lord and villagers, or by local custom. The result was a seemingly infinite variety of dues and services. Obligations varied not only among countries and regions but often among neighbouring villages and sometimes among peasants in the same village. In the small bishopric of Hildesheim in north-west Germany, for example, there were 138 different obligations, each with its own name. In Moravia there were 246 different dues to be paid in cash, these apart from the myriad of other obligations. Some paid their obligations in one form, some in another, most in several forms: cash, kind and labour. On the Baltic coast of Livland the peasants toiled as fishermen and paid their dues in fish. The origins of the differences in obligations often can be traced back to when the peasants were first reduced to subservience by a lord who imposed his own set of demands. Often, too, lords had allowed individual peasants to commute certain obligations for a cash sum, or had freed them voluntarily from specific dues or services. Lack of uniformity occurred, too, when manors or parts of manors were combined with other manors through purchase, inheritance, exchange or gift. The peasants on each manor, or part of a manor, continued to pay their traditional obligations.

Often, but not always, the peasant's obligations were scaled according to the amount of land that he held. Geography, availability of markets and the economic preferences of the seignior could also affect the amount and nature of the obligations. Where soil was fertile, where there were nearby markets or readily available means of transportation, the lord might decide to produce for the market, and so would demand heavy labour services from his peasants. If the soil was poor, or markets distant or inaccessible, or if the lord preferred to be a rent receiver rather than a producer for market, his peasants' obligations would be in cash and kind, with little or no labour dues.

The ebb and flow of economic life also could affect the amount and nature of the peasants' obligations. When times were good and prices rose, some lords took advantage of the favourable conditions to increase their own production for market and so increased their demand for labour services. Rising prices and higher living standards also meant an increase in the cost of living for the nobles, and to get the additional income they now needed they demanded more dues in cash and kind. Sometimes, too, when economic conditions worsened and prices fell, lords sought to bolster their declining incomes by increased market production with a consequent rise in labour services, or by turning the screws on their already over-worked peasants for more dues in cash and kind.

Despite the great diversity in dues and services there was much similarity among the principal levies paid by the peasants. Labour services were probably the most common obligation. Typically, the peasants met this obligation by working in the lord's fields, but they also worked at other tasks: construction, agricultural industries, such as distilling or beet sugar manufacture, mining and metallurgical operations, and as hunting attendants.

*A lord's peasants did not always work on farms. If there were minerals on the land they might be employed as miners. The coat of arms of the Von Randegg family, from Switzerland, includes a man in traditional miner's costume, an allusion to its major source of wealth.*

In western and central Europe, where lords as a rule were not active in market production, the obligatory labour service could be as little as 1–3 days a year, though generally it seemed to have been between 12 and 16 days, and when lords were more active in production for market as much as 52 days a year. Many lords had allowed their peasants to commute the labour obligation into an annual money payment. In the east, where, as mentioned earlier, the labour obligation rose precipitously in the 16th century, the amount of labour demanded was usually scaled to the size of the peasant's holdings, whether or not he owned draught-animals and the age and sex of the people in the peasant's household. The fairly common standard became 3 days a week, but there was nothing to prevent a lord from requiring more. In Poland, many households with full-sized holdings had to furnish their master with two workers with draught-animals 4–6 days every week. By the 17th century, lords in the western Ukraine often required 6 days a week. In Lithuania a peasant household with as little as one-quarter of a standard-sized peasant holding had to supply a man and a woman each for 3 days a week, the man working with draught-animals and the woman doing manual labour. In eastern Holstein, then part of the kingdom of Denmark, the labour obligation was possibly the heaviest in all Europe. Peasant households there with full holdings had to provide their lord with 5 workers and 8 horses every day in summer and 4 workers and 8 horses in winter. Those with half-holdings had to furnish 3 people and 4 horses daily, and so on down the scale of holdings. Even the landless peasant who earned his living as a day labourer was not overlooked. His wife had to work 60–70 days a year for the lord, spin several pounds of flax for him and had to do additional days of labour if her husband was allowed to keep a cow on the common.

Carting services were another common obligation. Peasants had to use their own animals and carts or sleds to transport goods the lord sent to market, supplies he needed for his own use and whatever else he needed to have carted. Sometimes the carting counted as part of the labour service but usually it was a separate obligation. Often the number of days of carting that the peasant had to furnish was fixed, but in some lands the lord could demand as much as he wished. The service could take the peasant away from his home for weeks at a time, frequently during the cruel weather of winter. Generally the peasant paid all the costs of his journey, though sometimes custom dictated that the lord pay all or part of the expenses incurred on the trip.

In a number of the lands of eastern Europe seigniors took children away from their homes to work for them. Each year on a specified day the children of the village were assembled and the lord or his bailiff selected the ones best suited for the lord's needs. The child, or his parents, were paid wages that were less, and often much less, than the prevailing wage for hired labour, and sometimes the child received only food and clothes for his labour, and these of the poorest quality. Usually law and custom fixed the term of service for the child: generally between two and four years. In other eastern lands, among them Mecklenburg, Pomerania, Poland and Russia, the draught of children as a separate obligation was unknown. The lords there had so much authority over their serfs that they could take anyone they wanted, child or adult, to work for them as household servants or as field-hands for as long as the lord wanted. In western Europe the draught of child labour was made only in a few places and apparently these places renounced it in time. In Bavaria, for example, the practice had been outlawed in the 16th and 17th centuries, had been reinstated in 1756 and was finally banned permanently in 1801, just seven years before the emancipation decree that freed the peasants of Bavaria.

In western Europe the principal obligations of most peasants were an annual payment by villagers with hereditary tenures in recognition of the superior ownership of the land by the seignior, a fee levied when hereditary holdings were transferred by inheritance or sale and the tithe. The annual payment, or *cens* as it was called in French-speaking lands, was paid in cash or kind, or in both forms. The amount had been set in earlier times as a perpetual and unchangeable charge either in cash or as a percentage of the peasant's crop. When demanded in cash, it was usually a negligible and always decreasing burden because of the falling value of money. When demanded in kind it could be an onerous obligation if the peasant had to pay, as he did in places in France and north-west Germany, $\frac{1}{3}$–$\frac{1}{4}$ of his crop. For most peasants, however, the payment averaged around $\frac{1}{12}$ of his produce, a not inconsiderable but bearable burden.

The fee seigniors levied for transfer of a hereditary holding was sometimes only a token payment to signify recognition of the lord's superior ownership of the holding. It might be a fowl, or some jugs of wine, or a pair of gloves, or a few small coins. Far more often the seigniors imposed heavy charges. When the holding changed hands on the death of its occupant the lord took the best of the dead man's work animals or the second best, and in addition charged a heavy cash payment. Sometimes it was a year's income from the holding, or half or twice the annual income, or a percentage of the value of the holding ranging from $1\frac{1}{4}$ to 10 per cent, and exceptionally as much as 20 per cent. The fee charged when holdings changed hands by sale tended to be even larger. In most of eastern Europe, hereditary peasant tenure was uncommon and lords did not usually demand fees when these holdings were transferred.

The tithe was by far the most common of the major obligations of the peasants of western Europe. All land, including that held by nobles, the church and burghers, carried a tithe, though in France nobles and churchmen often were tithed at a lower rate. The tithe had originally been intended for the support of the church and the needy, but over the centuries that purpose had often been subverted. Now laymen owned many tithes and much of the tithe revenue that did go to the church went to wealthy prelates and monasteries. The parish priests and the needy stood at the tail end of the line and often received little. The products on which the tithe was collected depended upon local custom. The introduction of new crops or the addition of hitherto untilled land to the arable could set off heated controversies between tithepayer and titheowner as to whether the tithe had to be paid on the new crop or on the produce raised on the new ploughland.

The tithe on occasion equalled the one-tenth that the word suggests. More often it varied, in places even among the fields of a single parish. Some tithepayers had commuted all or part of the obligation into an annual money payment, but typically it remained a payment in kind. In a few fortunate places it was as little as $\frac{1}{30}$, or a little over 3 per cent, of the tithed produce. In France it frequently added up to $7\frac{1}{10}$–9 per cent of the gross crop. Given the low yields of the era, with harvests often not being more than three and four

times the seed planted, the tithe could amount to from $\frac{1}{7}$ of the net crop on good soil to $\frac{1}{3}$ on poor soil. The Hungarian peasant had to pay two tithes, one to the church and one to his lord. He had to give to the church $\frac{1}{10}$ of his grain crop and his lambs, kids and bees, and to his lord he gave $\frac{1}{9}$ of everything he raised except for the products of his garden and meadow. In England, Arthur Young, his country's outstanding agricultural writer of the 18th century, said that the tithe was 'the greatest burthen that yet remains on the agriculture of the kingdom'. In the Parliamentary acts of enclosure of the 18th and early 19th century clerical and lay tithe-owners received 15–20 per cent of the land of a parish, and in some instances even more, to compensate them for the loss of their tithes. In contrast to these heavy payments, in most of eastern Europe the tithe was either not known or not widely demanded.

In addition to these major obligations the peasants of both east and west paid a host of lesser dues to their lords in cash and kind. These included such things as supplying the seignior with a certain number of fowl, or a set amount of eggs or butter each year, or chestnuts, or mushrooms, or a fixed amount of yarn or cloth. Nearly always these dues were not oppressive, and as the use of money became more common peasants often commuted them into a single annual cash payment.

The dues and services paid to their seigniors were only part of the burden that rested upon the peasants. They were by far the principal source of the state's tax revenues. The full or partial tax exemption of the nobility and the church and the relatively small number of townsmen meant that most of the tax income came from the peasantry. The state also required labour services from the villagers, for such work as road and bridge building and maintenance or construction of public buildings. Usually they received no pay for this work. The service could be as little as 3 or 4 days a year,

or as much as 3 days a week during the summer in 18th-century Denmark, when the state engaged in an ambitious road-building programme. Other services required by the state included the quartering of troops, furnishing transport for the military and providing relays of fresh horses and conveyances for official messengers and vehicles or for persons bearing an order from an official of the state. Finally, military conscription, introduced in a number of continental states in the 18th century, fell most heavily, and in some lands solely, on the peasantry.

Because of the great disparities in the dues and services paid by peasants, the impact of these obligations upon their incomes can only be estimated. German peasants are said to have paid between 22 and 40 per cent of their gross incomes in the 18th century. A survey in 1771 of 157 Swiss villages indicated that obligations took 29 per cent of a peasant's gross income. Economists in the 18th century calculated that the obligations of the French peasant cost him from 33 to 40 per cent of his gross product. These average figures conceal wide differences among villages, as in Lower Saxony, where the range in five villages in the late 18th and early 19th century ran from $53\frac{1}{3}$ per cent down to only 8 per cent of the gross farm product.

Though most of Europe's peasants were unfree, a sizable minority were personally free. In some lands, such as Sweden and Norway, the peasants had never lost their freedom. In others, such as the Low Countries, Italy and England, freedom had come gradually in the last centuries of the Middle Ages. Many freemen on the continent traced their free status to forebears who had settled as colonists in newly opened regions, drawn there by promises that had been kept of freedom for themselves and their descendants. Others had been freed by their seigniors, sometimes without charge and sometimes for a fee. The free peasant could come and go as he pleased and could manage his own life as he pleased. Some owned their holdings, though the number of the free peasant proprietors declined in some lands, including England, as the centuries went by. Most held their land as hereditary tenants of a seignior. They had a lifelong right to the use of the holding, and they could bequeath, mortgage or sell the use of the holding, though this usually required the lord's permission.

Law and custom called these people free, but in reality most of them lived in the shadow of a seignior. Even those who owned their own land sometimes had to pay obligations that were not demanded of property owners who belonged to higher orders of society. Those who held land by hereditary tenure had to bear many of the same burdens as their servile neighbours. Often the obligations that the unfree peasants had paid in the past continued to be demanded of their now free descendants. In England, landowners required their peasant tenants to provide carting services, and levied heavy cash fees and often the traditional 'best animal' fee when the peasant bequeathed or transferred his hereditary holding. In a manual for estate stewards, published in 1727, the author listed customary obligations that the diligent steward would find in old rolls of the manor court, and recommended that the steward should insist upon them 'to prevent their oblivion'. These obligations included furnishing teams to carry produce from the lord's fields to his barns or to haul construction materials, giving the lord every year 'two fat Capons or Turkeys' or other fowl or fish of equal value, and keeping a pair of hounds for the lord's use in the chase. In other countries, too, seigniors continued to exact servile dues and services from free peasants who lived on their land. These included the payment of fees on the transfer of holdings; the requirement to mill grain at the lord's mill (in Lowland Scotland that survived in many places until well into the 19th century); the provision of labour services, sometimes, as in Bavaria, for only 4–6 days a year, and sometimes, as in Denmark, as much as $\frac{1}{4}$ or more of the amount of the labour service required of serfs; and the payment, as in Spain, of $\frac{1}{5}$–$\frac{1}{4}$ of the harvest, to name some obligations in one or another land.

Free peasants not only often paid servile obligations but also sometimes lost all or part of their personal freedom. That happened in eastern Germany and in Denmark, where seigniorial encroachments eroded the rights of many free peasants. In England, the Act of Settlement of 1662 gave legal sanction to an established custom that severely reduced personal freedom. The act decreed that the parish in which a person wanted to settle could send him back to his native parish after forty days even if he had employment, lest at some future time he might need poor relief. A century later Adam Smith denounced the law, writing that 'it is often more difficult for a poor man to pass the artificial boundary of a parish than an arm of the sea or a ridge of high mountains'. Smith may have exaggerated the impact of the law but certainly it curtailed freedom of movement. In 1795 the law was amended so that only persons actually receiving relief could be sent back to their home parishes.

## 'Best when he is weeping'

The subservience of the peasants, whether free or unfree, and their membership in what was universally regarded as the lowest order of society was mirrored in the attitude and opinion of the rest of society. In the popular mind the peasant was seen as coarse, ignorant, gross in manner, irresponsible, lazy and generally worthless. It was widely accepted as a fact that the only way to get satisfactory work out of peasants was by stern discipline. In central and eastern Europe the free use of the whip was recommended. Popular catch phrases reflected this conviction. One of the most often quoted was a verse that went: 'rustica gens est optima flens, sed pessima gaudens', 'the peasant is best when he is weeping, but worse when he is laughing'. Laws of Italian cities of the 14th and 15th centuries described peasants as naturally inferior beings who in their relations with the rest of mankind were motivated by 'malice, vulgarity and insolence'. The peasant was regarded as a lesser and sub-human form of life, a creature more animal than human, or, as a Bavarian official put it in 1737, 'a hybrid between animal and human'. An eye-witness of a rural rising in Provence in 1752 described the peasant as 'an evil animal, cunning, a ferocious half-civilized beast; he has neither heart nor honesty'. In a famed French agricultural manual that went through nineteen editions between 1600 and 1675, the author, Oliver de Serres, explained that the landowner must be severe with his peasants because they were 'worthless wretches' of perverse character whose 'general brutishness made them stupid, careless, shameless and friendless'. Two and a half centuries later a liberal nobleman of Savoy said of the peasants there that 'in their order there is no courage, no vigour; all sorts of ills flow from this parlous state; laziness, slackness, negligence, work poorly done and done after the time that it should have been done'. Austrian and Hungarian nobles who in the 1780s opposed the agrarian reforms of Emperor Joseph II said that their peasants were lazy, drunken and irresponsible louts who worked only because of their fear of the whip, and who would not know how to use freedom if they had it. Sixty years later Russian nobles, confronted by the government's intention to emancipate the serfs, were positive that if freed the peasants, being naturally indolent and irresponsible, would stop working and so bring the entire economy to a halt. They argued that with the controlling hand of the seignior removed the peasants' innate lack of discipline would bring on peasant risings of hitherto unequalled proportions. Literature and art presented the same picture of the peasant. From the Middle Ages on, the rustic, when he

was noticed at all, was portrayed as dirty, deceitful and brutish, degraded by nature and function, and much given to drunkenness, revelry and lechery.

In light of this attitude it is scarcely surprising that the maltreatment and cruelties visited upon peasants by their superiors went unnoticed and uncriticized. Some lords actually boasted of the outrages they had committed against their peasants. Visitors to 19th-century Russia told of listening to people of fashion and prominence chat about whippings they had ordered for their serfs, and of hearing a nobleman pridefully telling an appreciative group at his club about how he had sentenced three of his serfs to nearly triple the legally prescribed number of blows with the cane. Only the worst kind of excesses, such as those committed in the mid-18th century by Dar'ia Saltykov, who tortured scores of her peasants to death for petty or imagined offences, brought official action. In the Saltykov case the authorities after much delay began an investigation in 1762 that dragged on for six years. Finally Mde Saltykov was stripped of her noble rank, pilloried for one hour in Moscow and sentenced to spend the rest of her life in a convent. In contrast, the serfs who at her command had aided in torturing her victims were beaten with the knout and then condemned to a life of hard labour in Siberia.

Dar'ia Saltykov and others like her were psychopaths. Without doubt, however, thoughtless and unconscious cruelty was omnipresent. There were a few men of the upper orders who were more understanding. In an often quoted description of the French peasantry, Jean de la Bruyère, in 1689, wrote that peasants 'spare other men the pain of sowing, of cultivating and of reaping in order to live, and they deserve not to lack the bread they have sown'. In the latter decades of the old order some realized that the blame for the misery and ignorance and brutishmess of peasant life lay not with the peasant himself but with the social and economic order in which he lived. A German agriculturist of the 18th century explained that 'the more industrious the poor peasant the more miserable; for almost everyone wants to refresh himself from his sweat and fatten himself from his blood; he is thereby beaten down, discouraged, and in the end becomes slothful because he realizes that he is more tormented and more ill treated than a beast of burden'.

The long centuries of their lowly status, the condescension at best and the far more usual disdain and contempt that was their lot, left their mark upon the peasantry. They were ignorant, superstitious and uncooperative. They accepted the stamp of inferiority pressed upon them and seemed without pride and self-respect. The squalor and filth in which so many of them lived reflected not only their poverty but also their apathy and sloth. Even those men of the upper orders who wanted to help were put off by the appearance and behaviour of the peasants and by what seemed to be the hopelessness of their situation. A Danish publicist

*Landowners in Russia had greater powers over their serfs than elsewhere, and there was little to prevent cases of sadistic cruelty. These drawings by a foreign visitor show two methods of torture used in the 18th century.*

who favoured reform said, in 1763, that conservatives who argued that education would spoil the peasants were probably right. The peasant's life, he wrote, was 'so miserable that it is easy to believe that only a certain degree of stupidity and insensitiveness can render their condition bearable, and that the happiness of the peasant, if he still enjoys any, would cease as soon as he should be deprived of his two principal consolations, ignorance and brandy'. An English diplomat in the Danubian principalities in 1820 said much the same thing of the peasants there. 'Accustomed to the state of servitude', he wrote, 'which to others might appear intolerable, they are unable to form hopes for a better condition; the habitual depression of their minds had become a sort of natural stupor and apathy, which renders them equally indifferent to the enjoyments of life, and insensible to happiness, as to the pains of anguish and affliction.'

Peasants found in alcohol release from the hopelessness of their lives, from the realization that the future held nothing better for them and their children. Men, women and often children drank heavily and incessantly. In central and eastern Europe the seigniors, who had the monopoly on the manufacture and sale of spirits, and who owned the village inn, profited from, and so sometimes encouraged, the addiction of their peasants. Some Polish lords even paid their hired labourers in scrip that was redeemable only at the village tavern. Contemporaries frequently commented on the endless drinking and its destructive results. An official Prussian publication, in 1790, in an account of the poverty and misery that afflicted the peasants of upper Silesia, reported: 'Brandy or the mere thought of it transports these people from laziness, sluggishness and slackness to lightheartedness, happiness, and exuberance. . . . Brandy is everything to these people; the infant, the aged, the maiden, the wife, everyone, all drink it; they drink in the morning, the evening, at noon and at midnight; they drink whenever they can get it.' A Swedish visitor in 18th-century England marvelled at the capacity of the villagers and wondered how men who barely earned enough to feed their families could spend so much money for drink.

Of course, not all peasants lived in grinding poverty and in an alcoholic haze. Villages had their rich and their poor and sometimes the gap between the extremes was surprisingly large. There were prosperous peasants scattered throughout Europe and a few were extremely wealthy, like the serf millionaires of Russia, who owned factories and trading companies. These people were the rare exceptions. The peasant counted as prosperous was nearly always wealthy only in comparison with the abject poverty of his neighbours. In the Beauvaisis in north-west France a man who owned a plough and a team of horses was considered well-to-do. Most peasants lived out their lives on the margin of subsistence and when famine or other troubles came they had no reserves to carry them through the bad times. The records tell of the starvation, disease, death, brigandage and vagabondage that marked those evil times and of how peasants tried to keep alive by eating tree bark and flour made of acorns.

The lowly condition of the peasantry was compounded by the fact that most of them were politically powerless. Save for a few countries or provinces, the peasants, whether free or unfree, had no voice in their governments and so had no way of improving their status through political action. Unlike the other orders of society, most peasants had no established institutions through which they could express their political, social and economic interests and demands, or through which they could influence the policies of their rulers at the provincial and national levels. The few lands where they did have a voice included Norway, Sweden and, in Austria, the provinces of Tyrol and Vorarlberg, where the peasants were free. Here they had their own estates to which they sent representatives and which met with other estates of the society. In the rural cantons of Switzerland the free peasantry dominated the cantonal assemblies. In some parts of France, peasants had been allowed on occasion to participate in choosing delegates to the States General, which had met last in 1614. When the States General were next convened, 175 years later, on what proved to be the eve of the French Revolution, representatives of the Third Estate were selected through indirect elections in which the heads of all peasant households were allowed to participate. In England anyone who had a freehold that produced an income of forty shillings a year could vote for the two 'knights of the shire', who represented the county in Parliament. The vast majority of the English peasantry could not meet this qualification for the suffrage.

Though peasants were excluded from active participation in the political process they were very much involved in it as passive participants in an old political conflict. That conflict was between monarchs and the nobility. The monarchs had managed to strip the nobility of much of its political power as a corporate entity but the nobility retained its claim to special privileges and retained and broadened its claim to the land, labour, dues, and subservience of the peasants who lived on its land. That displeased the monarchs, because, as long as the peasants were dependent upon their seigniors, the monarch was not truly sovereign over all who lived in his realm. Nor was it only a matter of governance. The fiscal and military interests of the throne were involved, too. The seigniors had first claim upon the labour of their peasants and upon their payments in cash and kind. Already in the 16th century the lords in some lands had greatly increased the obligations of their peasants, and in the succeeding centuries, and especially in the second half of the 18th century, they continued to squeeze more in cash, kind and labour out of the peasants. In addition, they often took land away from the peasants by expropriation, foreclosure or purchase and added it to their own demesnes. In

*Sweden was one of the four countries in which the peasantry were represented in the legislature. In a medal of 1789 the farthest figure stands for the Fourth Estate.*

Denmark the number of manors remained about the same from the 16th to the 18th century but the total area of their demesnes nearly doubled between 1525 and 1744. In the course of the 18th century, 4,000–6,000 peasant holdings in Mecklenburg and an equal number in Pomerania were swallowed up by seigniors. In France seigniors during the 18th century appropriated land on which dues were unpaid and took over common land for their exclusive use. In most of France, in many parts of Germany and in places in Switzerland seigniors had the right to buy for themselves, within a specified time period, a hereditary peasant holding on their manor that the occupant had already sold to someone else. The time period ran from as little as forty days to thirty years, depending upon local custom. The price that the lord paid was the same as that paid by the purchaser, except that in certain places in Germany the seignior paid a lower fixed price. In other lands, too, lords absorbed peasant holdings, dispossessing their occupants and reducing them to smallholders or landless labourers.

Actions such as these were damaging to the interests of the monarch. When lords took over peasant land the throne lost revenue, because lords paid either no taxes or reduced taxes on demesne land. The ejection of the peasants from their holdings impoverished them and so reduced the taxes and the services they could afford to render to the state. The imposition of more obligations had the same deleterious effect. Rulers feared, too, that an impoverished and landless peasantry would retard the growth of population, which was a cardinal aim of their policy. They wanted more subjects because that meant more taxpayers, more workers and larger markets

to stimulate economic life, and more recruits for their armies. The rulers depended, too, on the peasantry for important public services. They knew that a people reduced to pauperdom by seigniorial exactions could not afford to continue providing these services at the level desired by the government.

Rulers had early recognized the threat to their best interests posed by seigniorial control over the peasants and the land, and had tried to place restrictions on it. Their early efforts, however, had been sporadic, piecemeal and not rigorously enforced. The Tudor rulers of England had been the first to attempt this when they tried to curb the engrossment of peasant land by landlords when they enclosed the fields of their manors. Their policy did not end enclosure nor the 'letting down of houses of husbandry', as the contemporary expression described the eviction of peasants from their holdings, though it served as a partial check. The Stuart rulers continued the policy in the 17th century but its effectiveness weakened as opposition to royal absolutism grew stronger. Significantly, the last serious attempt to restrain seigniorial engrossment came during the eleven years, from 1629 to 1640, when Charles I ruled England without Parliament. After the restoration of the monarchy in 1660 the policy flickered out, and in the next century the government actively encouraged enclosure. For now the landowning class dominated English national politics as it never had before. The result was the great enclosure movement that by 1820 had transformed English agriculture.

In contrast to the failed effort at absolutism in England, rulers of continental lands established and magnified their claim to absolute power in the 17th and 18th centuries. Nonetheless, law, tradition and the power of the nobility hampered them in their efforts to protect the peasantry from expropriation and excessive seigniorial exploitation. Their efforts met with only limited success so they decided to try another tactic. They introduced reforms in the status and tenure of the peasants who lived on the lands that belonged to the state and the crown. In some lands these peasants made up a large part of the rural population. The rulers hoped that the beneficial effects of these reforms in improving the efficiency of the peasants, and thereby the profits of the seigniors, would persuade private landowners to adopt them. That would bring about improvement in the condition of the peasantry without compulsion and without invading the property rights of the seigniors. The attempt to introduce reform by emulation was tried in the course of the 18th and 19th centuries in the duchy of Lorraine, in Prussia, Austria, Denmark, France and Russia. But very few private landowners chose to follow the example of their sovereign.

Rulers did not limit their efforts at reform to their own peasants. They issued decrees designed to reduce the authority of seigniors over their peasants. Their legislation produced no significant improvements, except for Austria and the two petty states of Savoy and

Baden. In Savoy and Baden, respectively, decrees of 1771 and 1783 ordered the end of the dependency of the peasants upon their seigniors. In Austria, Empress Maria Theresa had issued legislation that limited the powers of the seigniors, and the decrees of her son, Joseph II, removed many of the galling restrictions on peasant freedom, though the peasants remained the 'hereditary subjects', as they were called, of their seigniors, who still had much authority over them. Elsewhere, the royal intent to improve the condition of the peasantry was subverted by nobles and bureaucrats so that the peasants found themselves no better off, and in some places worse off, such as in the Baltic provinces of Russia or in the Danubian principalities.

### Dawning hope

Though these attempts at reform by the monarchs of the continent accomplished little they were of much significance. They were the first major assaults on the privileges of the seigniors, and the assault came at the command of the sovereigns. The sovereigns thereby let their societies know that the existing relationship between lord and peasant was not acceptable. The insistence of the sovereigns upon reform marked the inception, and nearly everywhere was the principal moving force, in the process that led to the emancipation of the peasantry of the continent.

The obstacles to the completion of that process were too great for the monarchs to accomplish it unaided. Fortunately for the peasantry the efforts of the monarchs coincided with a new era in economic life; with the appearance among a small but influential group of noblemen of a new interest in a more efficient and more profitable agriculture; with the widening acceptance of new ideas about the equality of man and the injustices of privilege; and with a wave of restlessness and rebellion among the peasants. The upturn in economic life began in the second quarter of the 18th century, ending a long era of secular stagnation and regression that reached back in some lands to the 1620s. Economic activity took on new vigour and continued to move forward until the second decade of the next century. A rise in prices accompanied the economic revival and not unexpectedly served to arouse a new interest in agriculture and in its improvement. There was much talk and much writing in every land about a more efficient agriculture, and a small number of landowners, among them some great proprietors, introduced improvements on their land. On the continent, however, the great majority of lords and peasants continued to follow the traditional methods, unlike contemporary England, where agricultural improvements won wide acceptance. Nonetheless, the efforts of the improvers, despite their limited impact in their own time, had major long-range effects. For the first time, great landowners, leaders in their societies, recognized the retardation of agriculture and the need for reforms, especially in the status and tenure of the peasantry. They argued that the persistence of the traditional lord–peasant relationship worked against the economic interests of both lord and peasant and had severely damaging effects upon the welfare of the state. Their personal influence, and their sponsorship of societies for the improvement of agriculture, agricultural journals, schools and model farms, persuaded an always growing number of seigniors to view their manors as sources of income rather than as sources of status and privilege, and to look with favour upon reforms that would increase productivity.

Meanwhile, ideologies that attacked the hierarchical ordering of society, and particularly the privileges of the nobility, began to win attention and support. At first only a few were attracted, but these few included a disproportionate number of those who occupied high places in the social order or who were the leading intellectual and literary figures of their time. In their criticisms they voiced the concepts of individual freedom, human rights and equality that had been loosed in Europe by the men of the Enlightenment of the 18th century. When the Enlightenment gave way to a new era its liberating ideas lived on into the next century and continued to inspire the moulders of opinion. Most of the critics were from the bourgeoisie but many were noblemen. In Denmark the small group of great proprietors who dominated the government in the 18th century agreed on the need of agrarian reform. In France noble deputies in the National Assembly proposed the abolition of seigniorial rights on the famous night of 4 August 1789. In the Austrian monarchy, nobles in the 1830s and 1840s submitted proposals to the throne for the reform of the lord–peasant relationship. These noble supporters of reform were inspired variously by the fear of peasant revolt, by the realization that reform was in their economic interest and by idealism.

The ideas of freedom and equality took fire with the outbreak of the great French Revolution in 1789. Thousands of Europeans, inspired by the events in Paris, adopted the principles of the Revolution. Yet, remarkably enough, the French Revolution retarded the liberation of the European peasantry. The Revolution aroused the fears of the ruling elites, who believed that any concession to the demands of liberals and reformers would be taken as signs of weakness and would only lead to further demands. Those who proposed reforms were identified with revolution, regicide and the overthrow of governments. The successes of the Revolution fed the fires of reaction and gave the signal for increased repression and for the strengthening of opposition to reforms. Thomas Malthus, who visited Denmark in 1799, wrote that it was fortunate that the emancipation of the Danish peasants had been in 1788. 'Had the measure been delayed a little longer', he wrote in his journal, 'probably it would never have taken place; as the government would not have ventured upon it, after the popular commotion in France.' In Austria the shock of the

Revolution dissipated the spirit of reform that had been introduced by Emperor Joseph II, which was already under heavy attack from the Austrian and Hungarian nobility.

The defenders of the traditional order repeatedly stressed their belief in the natural superiority of the nobility over the rest of mankind. They spoke of their concern for the welfare of their peasants and claimed that only under their aegis could the peasant be a useful member of society. They prophecied certain catastrophe if the peasant, lazy and irresponsible creature that he was, was freed from his dependent status. They charged, too, that the reform of the lord–peasant relationship against the wishes of the seignior violated the right of private property. In their opinion their privileges and prerogatives were an integral part of their property, and they warned that state interference with their authority over their peasants would serve as precedent for the violation of other kinds of property.

Rural unrest was another element in the mix, out of which came freedom for the peasantry. Most peasants most of the time accepted their inferior position and their oppression without overt protest. But every once in a while they would decide that they had had enough and must resist. Usually the outburst involved only a few individuals or perhaps a village. At other times whole regions would be convulsed by mass discontent and disturbances. Nearly always the protest assumed a non-violent form, such as refusal to render additional obligations, or flight to some frontier or to a city. And sometimes a trivial incident, or an unfounded rumour, or the imposition of some new obligation, would ignite a mass uprising. Then the peasants, driven by some blind fury, seized their scythes, pitchforks and axes and poured out of their villages to beat or murder their lord and his officials and to pillage the homes and burn the records of their oppressors. Nearly always the disturbances were easily contained or burned themselves out in a short time. The odds were all against the peasants, who lacked the organization, the weapons and the leadership needed to triumph. With rare exception their protests, whether violent or of a more passive nature, gained them little or nothing. But the constant undercurrent of peasant unrest, and several major uprisings, finally penetrated into the consciousness of men of the ruling orders and awakened them to the threat that peasant unrest presented to the social order. Many were already leaning in the direction of reform. Rural unrest helped to convince them that freedom for the peasant could no longer be delayed.

Reforming princes, economic developments, new ideologies and rural unrest prepared the way. The advent of the decrees of the late 18th and the 19th century that freed the peasants had been heralded long before they became realities. Yet it sometimes took a catastrophic event to precipitate out the decree of emancipation. The outbreak of the French Revolution and the 'Great Fear', the rural revolt that inflamed so much of France in the summer of 1789, quickly persuaded the French government to issue laws designed to end the dependency of the peasantry. The victorious armies of the Revolution and of Napoleon freed the peasants in the lands that they conquered and made part of the French Empire. The crushing defeat of Prussia in 1806 at the hands of Napoleon's legions dispelled any doubts that the rulers of Prussia still harboured about the need for reform, above all, reform in the lord–peasant relationship. Similarly, the Russian defeat in the Crimean War in 1855 revealed such dangerous weaknesses in the structure of the state and society that reform, and especially the abolition of serfdom, could no longer be avoided. The revolutions that engulfed so much of the continent in 1848 had direct and immediate influence in freeing the peasants of central Europe. Those still held in servile status, such as the peasants of Austria and Hungary, the Danubian principalities and some of the smaller German states, saw revolution as an opportunity to get rid of their bonds. Peasants in Prussia and a number of other German states wanted to bring to a conclusion the emancipation process that had started in their lands decades earlier but that still left many peasants unfree. So the peasants joined with the bourgeois liberals and the democrats who had touched off the revolutions. The 'bourgeois revolutions' of 1848 were also peasant revolutions, and the peasants were far more successful in achieving their goals than were their bourgeois allies. Hard-pressed governments quickly gave in to the demands of the peasants, whereupon the peasants withdrew from the revolutions, and with their withdrawal the revolutions foundered.

### The process of freedom

Nearly a hundred years elapsed between the first emancipation decree, issued in Savoy in 1771, and the last ones, in Russia in 1861 and in Romania, the erstwhile Danubian principalities, in 1864. There were great differences among the many decrees and in the legislation issued simultaneously, or in later years, to implement the initial decrees. But they all contained certain common provisions. Each one of them granted personal freedom to the peasants, though in some lands the law ordered that the peasants had to wait for a specified period before they could exercise that freedom in order to give the seigniors time to adjust to the new conditions. Along with personal freedom the legislation gave peasants equality with all other subjects before the law, granted them freedom of movement and freedom of choice of occupation, and abolished the hierarchical system of fixed social orders, each with its own rights and duties, to which men had been bound by their birth.

The freeing of the peasantry from their servitude, and their acquisition of civil equality, demanded the restructuring of many of the institutions of social and political life. Law codes, courts, police, military conscription,

The emancipation of Russian serfs finally came in 1861. Here, in a newspaper illustration, happy peasants are shown hailing their 'Liberator Tsar', Alexander II.

fiscal policies and the legislative and administrative apparatus of local and national government all had to be recast. In a few lands the process of renovation went swiftly, in most it required long years. Indeed, in most lands the decree hailed as the law that freed the peasantry did not really end their servile status. Despite the ringing declarations of freedom, much of the old servitude remained. The decrees deserve their fame because they represented the breakthrough, and readied the way for the later legislation that completed the task. There was, however, nearly always a hiatus, sometimes of many years, before the remnants of servitude disappeared, and, indeed, before all the peasants were declared legally free. The opposition and the foot-dragging of seigniors, the reactionary policies of governments who were determined to smother the ideological legacy of the French Revolution and the political powerlessness of the peasantry all helped to explain the lag. The number of years that elapsed between the date of the initial decree of emancipation and the legislation that finally ended all service obligations and service tenures varied greatly: in Savoy 21 years, in Baden 65 years, in Denmark 73 years, in Prussia 43 years and in Poland 57 years.

Indemnification to the seigniors for their loss in dues, services and land was another common feature of the emancipation legislation. In most lands a distinction was made between those dues and services that had their origin in the servile relationship of peasants to their lord, and those obligations that rose out of the peasants' occupation of land belonging to the seignior. The former, called personal obligations, were abolished without indemnification, while indemnification was ordered for the latter, called real obligations. It was difficult to draw the line between these two categories of obligations and the effort led to much confusion and to bitter disputes. Generally, the law ordered that the peasant had to pay the full amount of the indemnification, though in a few lands the state paid a sizable share. The usual procedure was for the state to advance the full amount of the indemnification to the seignior in the form of specially issued government bonds, and to have the peasants pay back the state in annual installments that included interest and amortization, stretched out over a period of time that ranged from 15 years in Romania to $56\frac{1}{2}$ years in Prussia.

Land for the freed peasants was another common though not universal feature of the emancipation process. In most cases the peasant with a holding continued in possession of his land, becoming its proprietor through the payment of indemnification. In France and Poland peasants gained land in addition to the holdings they occupied, while in Russia and Prussia many lost part of their holdings by surrendering some of it in payment of the indemnification. In the Baltic provinces of Russia the peasants had been freed without land and in Pomerania and Mecklenburg there had been what amounted to a landless emancipation. With the exceptions of Romania and Poland, peasants who were landless or nearly so before the emancipation and had earned their livings as hired labourers or domestic servants were freed without land. In Romania the emancipation decree ordered that every peasant was to get some land but the law was never fully implemented.

In Poland the government distributed small parcels of state land to about 130,000 hitherto landless peasants.

The legislation that finally ended the long-drawn-out process of emancipation did not end the social and political inferiority of the peasantry. The stroke of the lawmaker's pen could not erase centuries-old traditions and customs and the belief shared by men of all ranks in the natural superiority of the upper orders and the natural inferiority of the peasantry. Nor were the ruling elites ready to share the power and privilege that they had enjoyed for so long and regarded as their birthright. In one land or another the peasants continued to be taxed on their land at a higher rate than their erstwhile seigniors, their civil rights were hobbled by restrictions on their freedom of movement and either they were not allowed to vote or the franchise was so arranged that a small minority, made up of men from the upper social orders, had a far greater voice in elections than did the peasantry. And in a number of lands the judicial authority of the seigniors persisted for decades after the emancipation.

Despite these shortcomings the emancipation heralded an unprecedented era of freedom in the history of the peasantry. Civil equality opened up hitherto closed doors to personal advancement and to the recognition by their societies of the dignity and worth of the peasantry. Freed from dependence and servitude the peasantry emerged as a class with its own political and economic interests and programmes. That in turn brought about a remarkable change in the public image of the peasantry. Once scorned and mocked, the peasants now were wooed by political leaders of the right and left, and learned scholars and littérateurs celebrated the peasantry, extolled the virtues of village life and pictured the peasant as the preserver of the special quality of the nation.

Many of those who championed the peasant way of life were inspired by their fears of the progress of industrialization. They saw the peasantry as a bulwark against the changes they saw happening, which they disliked. But, of course, they could not stay these changes. In some countries the introduction of the new techniques in production and organization proceeded at a more rapid rate than in others, but rural society in every land ultimately felt its effects. Millions of peasants moved to the growing cities and industrialized regions of their own countries, or migrated to overseas lands. By 1914 many parts of Europe had seen a change from a predominantly rural to a predominantly urban population. This great rural exodus, this flight from the land, was possible because now the peasant was free to come and go as he pleased and to pursue freely his own self-interest. The exodus was possible, too, because now the growth of industry and transportation opened up new opportunities for the people of the villages. Now they could travel by train and ship to places far and near to seek a new start in life, freed at last from the bonds that had held their forebears for so many centuries.

---

**That man is born free**, in Rousseau's famous phrase, would have sounded strangely paradoxical to the ears of a medieval peasant, for it was precisely his birth that made him unfree. In his own village, as we saw in the first chapter, he might enjoy a measure of independence, taking his part in a largely self-contained community. But outside that community he was the victim of crippling legal handicaps, bound to his lord's estate, bound to accept his lord as his judge, bound to perform whatever tasks his lord saw fit to impose. In most parts of Europe these included a stipulated number of days working in the lord's fields. A 15th-century miniature (*opposite*) from Pierre de Crescens's treatise, *Le Livre des profits Champestres*, epitomizes the rural situation. The seignior sits at his desk on a dais, ledgers and books beside him. Before him, a group of his peasants are assembled to hear his orders for the day. Most of them carry their tools – an interesting array of 15th-century equipment, including sickles and sythes – and raise their hands in token of obedience. The man in the centre, evidently the foreman, doffs his hat.

The social history of the European countryside consists essentially of the peasants' emancipation from such servitude. Through the replacement of a landed by a commercial elite, through the achievement of political rights by the common people, the whole structure of life on the land was changed. By the 16th century, the peasants of western Europe were no longer legally serfs, but they were in danger of falling into an economic serfdom that was almost as bad. (1)

# From serfdom to service

**The financial revolution at the end of the Middle Ages initiated changes that were to affect the whole of society. Gradually, payment rather than obligation became the controlling factor in the villages as well as the towns.**

**Servitude to money** was in practice as heavy as servitude to a lord. These German farm workers of the 16th century are no doubt legally free; they can come and go as they please; but they have no choice in their way of life and are still liable to taxes that the higher classes do not have to pay.

The picture was painted in 1530 to illustrate the labour of the month of August, and it may usefully be compared to other such calendar pictures of a century or so earlier (p. 104–5). The sense of industrialization is stronger. The man by the door, perhaps an overseer, is more like a modern estate manager than the lord's officer on a feudal farm. And he has obviously just sold a sack of corn to the customer on the right: that is, the farm is no longer merely self-supporting but is a profit-making business.

Farming technique, on the other hand, has not changed very much. Corn is pulled down with rakes from the storage spaces on the left and beaten with traditional flails on the threshing floor. In the left foreground is a vessel to hold the corn, which is being removed in sacks for winnowing and grinding. (6)

Head of a peasant by Lucas Cranach, Germany *c.* 1520. (7)

The Netherlands, 16th century; by M. van Cleve. (8)

The Netherlands, 17th century; by Adriaen Brouwer. (9)

The Netherlands, *c.* 1564; by Pieter Bruegel. (10)

# The face of toil

**By the upper classes the peasants were viewed with a mixture of fear and disgust, believed to be by nature brutish and degenerate, and treated often with heartless cruelty.**

**The countryman in art** often reflects the contemptuous verdict of polite society, most often – curiously enough – in liberal Holland. But equally often he is portrayed with compassion and respect, and in the 18th and 19th centuries may even be idealized as a man close to nature and unsullied by urban civilization. At the end of the 19th century, the camera arrived to capture the features of real country people, marked by long labour and the open air.

The Netherlands, 17th century;
by B. G. Cuyp. (11)

Scotland, c. 1780; by David Allan. (14)

France, 1888; by Vincent van Gogh. (17)

The Netherlands, 16th century;
by Pieter Aertsen. (12)

France, 17th century; by Louis Le Nain. (15)

Sweden, 1909; photograph (18)

Spain, 17th century; by Velazquez. (13)

Scotland, c. 1900; photograph. (16)

Italy, c. 1900; photograph (19)

**A new world** in which peasants and workers would unite to achieve political and economic freedom was a dream of the early socialists. G. Pelizza's painting *The Fourth Estate* was provoked by the agricultural crisis that affected Italy in the 1890s. The setting is Pellizza's own district of Volpedo, and he used the local peasants as his models. 'A crowd of people, workers of the soil', he wrote, 'who are intelligent, strong, robust, united, advances like a torrent, overthrowing every obstacle in its path, thirsty for justice.' How far peasant values could really survive in an industrial society is the theme of the last chapter of this book. (20)

# 4 THE RURAL ECONOMY

## JOAN THIRSK

# The rural economy

Man's first necessities in life are food, clothing, fire and shelter, and until the mid-15th century, when this survey begins, the majority of Europe's inhabitants were content if these basic needs were met. The weather was fickle, their health and strength to work did not normally last beyond their middle forties. If they followed a certain routine of labour on the land through the seasons, however, and if the weather held fair, the land could be expected to yield an adequate food supply.

Because of the great differences between the climates of southern and northern Europe, the range of food-stuffs entering into the countryman's diet varied greatly: bread in southern Italy was made from wheat, but in northern England from oats, and in northern Germany from rye. Innumerable different sorts of beans and peas made pottage, and were sometimes mixed in bread-flour to make the grain go further. In mountainous, and, indeed, all pastoral regions, where the grain harvest was small, people ate less cereal foods, made more of nuts and sometimes vegetables and had a more than ample diet of beef and mutton, milk, butter and cheese. Every district had its delicacies that were commonplace to the local inhabitants but luxuries to outsiders. Moorland country yielded additional meat from many wild birds, hare and venison; lake country yielded pike, bass and trout; fendykes yielded eels. In southern Europe, men drank wine, in the north ale, and later hopped beer; in fruit-growing country, people had a taste for cider and perry; in dairying areas they made use of milk and whey; and, especially in summer, herbs infused in water made pleasant, cooling and cheap drinks everywhere. Fuel for the winter came from timber in forest country, from peat in low-lying fenland areas and from dried cow-dung in regions without either. Bracken never took over the hillsides for it was collected and used as bedding for livestock; rushes and reeds in watery land were regularly cut back for basket-making and roofing.

## Resources of the land

Every region had a distinct set of resources on differing scales of plenty. But one rule was imposed on all. The resources of the land everywhere had to be used with the greatest economy in order to preserve the means of life from one generation to the next. This gave men a familiarity with a great variety of flavours, for berries, herbs, roots and wild flowers all had a use: to relieve a monotonous diet. The same plants had other functions also, to relieve aches and pains and cure sickness, to supply dyes for cloth, or to provide the ingredients for soaps and cleaning agents. A renewed interest nowadays in herbs and wild flowers has taken readers back to the old herbals which flourished with the appearance of cheaper printed books in the 16th century, but which distilled a much older tradition. All plants were treasured, for all were expected to have some use for man or his animals. Thus, *elecampane*, which is now almost extinct, once grew freely in Kentish woods in England, its root being used for chest complaints, and as an infusion with honey for easing whooping cough. In Germany, the same plant was candied for stomach disorders, and was alleged to cure sheep scab. Holly leaves, now used only for Christmas decoration, were formerly widely used all over northern Europe to feed sheep and cattle, and were prized for giving the mutton a remarkably fine flavour. Elm leaves were also fed to cattle, which they savoured more than oats; and their nutritional value is now known to equal or exceed that of the best meadow hay. A single plant could have many different purposes, like tournesole (*chrozophora tinctoria*), which was used as a red and blue dye for cloth, and also to colour jellies, wines, meats and confections. Privet berries, which are hardly noticed these days when hedges are so promptly trimmed, were once used in dyeing and tanning, and, against much shrill outcry in the 17th century, to colour vinegar. The resourceful use of all wild plants brought variety into diet throughout the four seasons of the year.

The fact remains that grain and livestock were the prime foods of European man and large tracts were devoted to the production of both. But this had to be done in harmonious combination in order to conserve the resources of the land into the future. This was achieved by a respect for traditions, handed down from the past, obedience to precepts on how 'to keep the land in good heart' and a willingness within families and within the whole local community to co-operate in a reasonable partition of assets among all. In submitting to these constraints, people in all European countries arrived at farming practices which had so many similarities from region to region that they have come to be seen as a 'system'. The arable land was generally a compact area close to the centre of the village or hamlet; the meadowland was another compact piece of low-land, best situated alongside a river; year-round grazing pastures and rough wasteland lay mostly beyond these more carefully tended grounds, and provided feeding for livestock as well as wood for house repairs and fuel, and minerals and building materials such as sand, stone, lime and, in some places, even coal.

For the convenience of working it, the ploughland had to be near the farmhouse. When first laid out, it may have been usual for single families to cultivate whole fields over which they had sole possession, but successive generations, dividing, bequeathing, buying and borrowing smaller parcels to suit their changing needs, soon turned the arable into a collection of intermingled strips, each peasant holding a scattered selection in different sectors of the fields. Some historians believe that the scattered distribution was a deliberate choice from the outset. Whatever its origins, it became for many a deliberate preference after generations of experience in working it. The seeming disorder was made perfectly workable by a set of rules, enforced in manorial courts, to which all members of the village community adhered by common agreement. They cropped the arable land in accordance with a rotation; most commonly this meant a sequence of winter-sown grain (wheat and/or rye), spring-sown crops (barley and oats) followed by a year of fallow. On less fertile soils the fallow was necessary in alternate years; on more fertile soils it might be reduced to one year in every four. But everywhere it was indispensable for resting the ground and cleansing the soil of weeds, and since the same land continued under the plough for generations, the long-term consideration of maintaining fertility was paramount. After harvest each summer, and in the fallow year, the grain-stubble and the meadows after mowing were grazed in common by the livestock of the whole village. Again, village rules laid down the dates when grazing started and when it ended. In contrast, the more extensive common pastures were available for grazing the whole year round, and, to ensure that these and the fields, hedges, roads and watercourses were kept in order and that no encroachments escaped notice, the community appointed and paid its common shepherd, common cowherd and field reeves. These officials were chosen annually at manorial or village meetings, and all but the poorest and incapable took their turn to serve. In this way most people acquired some salutary experience of having to enforce the law as well as having to abide by it.

Since every village and hamlet was a self-governing community in managing its lands, the outline given here of the so called 'system' of common-field farming differed in detail in a thousand ways from one end of Europe to the other. Each community framed its by-laws according to the amount of land it possessed, and to the needs of its population: a moorland or heathland community might have 20,000 acres of common grassland at the disposal of 20 families, whereas the same sized community in a more fertile and intensively cultivated lowland parish had to make do with 200 acres. The quantity of land for growing cereals varied

similarly. The rules had to meet different circumstances but could always be changed, and were changed. As populations grew or shrank, the stint of animals that families might graze on the common lands was adjusted, in proportion to the size of their holdings, and when men became aware of new crops that might be introduced into the standard rotation, practical necessity persuaded communities gradually to adopt them. The introduction of beans and peas into many English field rotations in the later Middle Ages was one such innovation.

The most remarkable fact about common-field systems was their longevity. They persisted for at least six hundred years, and one English village – Laxton in Nottinghamshire – still retains its common fields and governing manorial court. Even when the system had outlived its usefulness, and enclosed ring-fenced farms showed themselves better able to produce the quantity of foodstuffs needed to feed the growing population, it died a long slow death. The distrust of change was not irrational. Enclosed farms could be worked more flexibly and efficiently, but they weakened co-operative effort, they deprived people of the companionship of daily work and gossip alongside their neighbours. After enclosure, social bonds in the community were no longer held together by the routine of communal toil, and, if they were not to snap entirely, they had to be strengthened in other ways. The social, as well as the economic, foundation of rural life was torn down and had to be rebuilt when common-field farming gave way to enclosures.

In the mid-15th century some kind of common-field system prevailed over a great part of Europe. But it did not hold sway everywhere. Much individual effort had also been put into the colonization of derelict land – assarting as it was called – in outlying portions of individual parishes, and in wilder tracts of stubborn, difficult terrain such as heavy oak forest, fenlands and marshlands. The result of individual initiative of this kind was that most farms, even in common-field communities, had some privately enclosed land, which was free of all community restraints, and which the peasant used as he pleased. In fen, marsh and forest, many isolated farms had come into existence, where farmers cultivated their land wholly independently from the main village centres. Experience gained by such individualists in the unfettered, free use of land was eventually to lead to the overthrow of farming regulated by communal decisions. But both ways of living had advantages and disadvantages, and these revealed themselves in a different guise as external circumstances changed. A defender of common-field farming could say with truth that it inhibited the creation of dust bowls by ensuring that land was kept in heart from generation to generation; the ruthless exploitation of land for the growing of speculative crops was checked, and the negligent farmer was disciplined by his fellows. In a bad winter of food or

*Ploughing and threshing in 15th-century Italy. Although the plough was to develop from the primitive type shown here, the agricultural routine remained very largely unchanged for the next three hundred years.*

fodder shortage, moreover, scarce resources could be pooled by common consent. A critic of the system could say with equal truth that it was harder to introduce new ways of farming or new crops, and, if larger populations started to demand much more food than before, or wanted different foodstuffs, the changes could not occur swiftly or smoothly. Such arguments were hardly heard in the 15th century, however. Alternative systems of farming were as yet few in number, and most adhered to old traditions. The weightiest preferences lay with common-field systems, under which a sharing of resources in good and bad times was possible.

## Arable versus pasture

In such distant, unfamiliar circumstances, it is difficult to measure the hard relentless toil of arable farming against the less strenuous work but tougher living conditions of pasture farmers. But the differences went very deep. Ploughing and cultivation were brought within men's capacities by their working with smaller units of land: the single plough strip in a common field varied between a half and one acre in size, its length being about twenty times its breadth. This was a good working size for several reasons: it could be ploughed in one day; it was easy to ensure effective drainage between the strips; and manure could be evenly distributed. Grain farming meant very strenuous work at certain seasons of the year, but in the slack months men had more leisurely days and at nightfall villagers spent much time gossiping with their neighbours in inns and alehouses. Pasture farming meant a much lonelier life, punctuated by more casual but also no doubt more festive meetings with their fellow men whenever shepherds or drovers plodded considerable distances to graze their livestock or to sell them at markets and fairs. In some circles the pastoral life was regarded contemptuously. It was thought to breed a lazy population, which spent its days sauntering after cattle. Shepherds were commonly spoken of as weaklings, in contrast with the strong-muscled ploughmen, who were

the mainstay of the army. But it is not clear how this prejudice, which was very strong in England, squared with the fact that the Swiss were pastoralists of a high order, and yet supplied thousands of mercenaries to swell Europe's armies in the 16th and 17th centuries.

It remained true, nevertheless, that pasture farmers followed a different life from grain farmers. Living often in lonely settlements, they had to be self-reliant. They were generally thought to be more pensive, more inclined to take up unorthodox religions, more unruly and difficult to govern. Grain farmers, on the other hand, lived in villages where they were under the eye of authority. The manorial lord might himself live in the village, and, if not, the parson did. Either or both were links in a long chain connecting local communities with the central government of church and state. Villages were thus more disciplined societies, but also more deferential with less independence of outlook.

Unaccustomed tensions were introduced into farming communities, notably from the 16th century onward, when a multitude of new crops appeared on the scene, and new commercial opportunities, and different combinations of farming speciality, forced themselves upon the attention of farmers. The stimulus behind these developments lay in changing rates of population growth, which obliged men to alter their use of land, and then to alter their whole attitude to farming systems generally. We can illustrate this most readily by considering two sharp changes of direction that occurred between 1250 and 1500, and yet a third time after 1500.

When populations grew rapidly in the 12th and 13th centuries, the production of staple foods had to be increased. On some of the older cultivated lands – in the Netherlands, for example, and near such populous centres as Cologne – this was achieved by the growing of leguminous crops such as beans and peas in the fallow year. These fixed nitrogen in the soil and improved the yields of subsequent grain crops. In addition, many new holdings were carved out of virgin soil by land-hungry peasants, intakes were made in forests and fenland was diked and drained, in order to create more land for desperately needed bread grains. When populations were drastically thinned all over Europe at the time of the Black Death in the mid-14th century, basic needs for corn and livestock suddenly reverted to a much lower level, and much marginal land had to be abandoned. This might touch some communities quite lightly, obliging them to allow a few hundred acres of tilled land to return to pasture or woodland. But it could devastate others. Southern Italy suffered grievously from depopulated and abandoned land, its problems being exacerbated by soil exhaustion and erosion that had occurred in earlier centuries when unduly congested populations had pressed too hard upon the natural resources. A similarly melancholy picture of deserted lands and empty villages met the eye in less fertile areas of northern Europe. Marginal lands were not worth cultivating when so much better land was lying idle, awaiting tenants. Thus hundreds of villages in England were deserted at this time, never to be repopulated. The platforms of peasant houses and the sunken road to the church assumed a cover of grass in the 15th century that has lain undisturbed ever since.

Now that a shortage of people, rather than land, had supervened (and this was to last throughout the 15th century) the existence of many vacant farms gave to the fortunate survivors an unaccustomed degree of choice between holdings. It enabled peasants to take land from lords on much more favourable terms than hitherto. Some chose to join a village community, taking up land that had been brought into a fair condition of fertility by centuries of tillage. Many vacant holdings, even though they consisted of scattered lands in old established villages, were quickly taken up again. But some preferred the independent life on ring-fenced farms, and cheerfully proceeded to colonize new land at the cost of great and arduous labour. Now the two systems of farming, one under communal rules, and the other outside them, coexisted over an even more extended territory, and, of course, they invited continual comparison.

The diminution of population, which gave to the surviving peasantry a new bargaining strength, profoundly altered the relations of landlords and labourers. Landowners and large farmers could not pay the high wages now demanded in conditions of scarcity. On their own farms, therefore, they were obliged to turn to less labour intensive farming systems. Many gentlemen and monastic houses in England converted their arable fields to pastures, and enclosed whatever land they could consolidate. They made the best of a bad job by keeping sheep, work that demanded no more than two or three shepherds and their boys. Such a change in land use met their personal situation admirably, for sheep kept the grass short, enriched the soil with their droppings and provided fine fleeces for the expanding cloth industry.

Thus gentlemen turned a catastrophe to advantage; and, incidentally, they recognized the economic argument in favour of enclosures for pasture. For them, at this particular juncture, it outweighed all arguments in favour of common fields. Within the peasant class self-interest led in different directions. Some used their food surpluses to feed their own families better than before; the 15th century is thought to have been a great age for meat eating. Others living around certain continental towns, where industrial output was expanding, and where middle- and upper-class city dwellers were enjoying a high standard of life, began to cater for their sophisticated demands for variety and quality. People who wanted, and could pay for, delicacies were served by peasants from rural areas in Tuscany, Liguria, Venetia and upper Italy, who developed systems of remarkably intensive cultivation. While continuing to produce their traditional crops of grain, olives and vines, they pioneered crops originally introduced into Sicily and southern Italy by Greeks or Arabs from the Levant. A market in new foodstuffs was built on the basis of rice, buckwheat, sugar-cane, vegetables, lemons, oranges and more ordinary orchard fruits. Employment in industry was further assisted by the peasants' readiness to grow industrial crops like cotton, hemp and flax, dye-crops like woad, madder and saffron, and mulberries for feeding silkworms. On the lower Rhine, particularly between Mainz and Bingen, and in Alsace, gardens and orchards of fruit and nut trees provoked astonished admiration as early as 1240. By the late 15th century these special crops had become highly profitable business enterprises. The humanist, Johannes Butzbach, claimed acquaintance with a peasant in 1496 who had earned thirty Guldern at the market in Mainz by selling cherries – a sum representing the income to be expected from a modest estate of the knightly class.

## Enclosure movements

Thus the demands expressed by a smaller, but more choosy, population persuaded peasants in districts of lively commerce to diversify crops, and reduce grain output, while gentlemen and larger farmers increased their grassland in order to benefit from less labour intensive livestock systems. These many different farming expedients had been facilitated, of course, by the spread of enclosure. They were regarded rather differently, however, after 1500, when a fresh surge in population revived the demand for basic foodstuffs and a move back to corn growing became imperative. In England, especially, men suddenly realized with a shock how much farmland had been put under grass, and how many peasant holdings had been swallowed up in large sheep farms in the previous century. Sheep had devoured men, as Sir Thomas More expressed it in his *Utopia*. A great outcry against greedy sheep farmers broke out; extensive sheep walks were seen as an insult and injury to those who desperately wanted a few acres on which to grow corn to feed their families. Every effort was made by the English government to stop further conversion of arable land to pasture, and, as land was turned back from grass to corn growing, the arguments in favour of common-field farming gained ground against enclosure. It was generally recognized that common fields fostered grain growing; it was also well understood that, when land was divided into small parcels, it gave a chance to the smallest peasant to build up a holding gradually, by acquiring strips piecemeal here and there. In other words, common-field farming was generally regarded, and officially recognized by government, as giving a living to larger numbers of ordinary husbandmen, whereas enclosures plainly gave the advantage to larger farmers and gentlemen by allowing them to amalgamate increasing quantities of land into large units. Needless to say, this official opinion did not persuade all men.

A deep conflict of viewpoint had thus been introduced into rural communities which could not easily be resolved, for both sides could marshal reasonable arguments in their favour. Strong feelings on one side led to some individuals enclosing land, regardless of the hurt they inflicted when they deprived their neighbours of common grazing. Strong resentment at those injuries led neighbours to take up bills, halberds and pitchforks, to tear down the hedges of newly made closes, drive in their cattle, and tread down newly sown crops. Yet, again and again, as grain prices fluctuated in the 16th century, individuals possessing enclosed lands demonstrated how much more quickly they could seize advantage and change course. For example, grain prices in England slumped very suddenly in 1583 and 1584, and arable farmers in southern England found themselves unable to pay their rent. Many people laid hands on a few enclosed pieces of ground, and turned to the highly profitable business of growing woad for the sake of its blue dye. The switch was so sudden and dramatic that the government feared that corn supplies would be insufficient, and totally banned the growing of the crop. But when it listened to the arguments for and against woad, it discovered that this plant provided much employment for the poor in the summer months. Indeed, it was a more labour intensive crop than grain. So the total ban on woad was relaxed in favour of a control over its acreage. Then when grain prices improved, even those controls were lifted, and woad became a commonplace crop in certain rotations. In this case enclosures had revealed their usefulness in allowing individuals to try out an unfamiliar but beneficial crop quickly. On the other hand, not all innovations, were advantageous. Men might cut down trees, divert water courses, and cause ecological changes that halved the value of their farms, injured their landlords' interests and prejudiced their neighbours, all for the sake of a new crop or system that proved worthless. This was one of the arguments used against the growing of tobacco in England in 1619.

Circumstances in the 16th century set up competition on a new scale among different systems of husbandry, while encouraging ingenious men to devise an increasing number of alternatives. A lively ferment of ideas stirred agricultural routines, especially where markets promised a ready sale for produce. Use of such ideas can be seen in the migration of drainage engineers from Italy to France and Holland, and then to England, offering to drain drowned polders and fenlands and turn them into corn land. Success came very slowly, but the continual striving reflected courage and determination, and in every decade more experience accumulated. The Italians had gained the first experience of land drainage when they laid out rice fields in the Po valley in Lombardy at the end of the 15th century. In 1534 the Orators of Brescia spoke sadly of their trials and tribulations, of the expense of drainage and of the uncertainty of success; hesitations slowed their achieve-

ments but did not end them. When economic incentives exerted much greater force, from the 16th century onward, the lower Rhone valley in France underwent drainage in the early decades, and the pools near Narbonne in 1558. In Holland, efforts at turning inundated marsh land into dry ground were on the heroic scale, and it is remarkable how closely they followed the incentive of rising grain prices. It is reckoned that about 3,700 acres of new land were reclaimed in Holland on average each year between 1540 and 1564, and again between 1590 and 1614 (war in the Netherlands explains the interval between these dates). The Dutch example, more than any other, persuaded English adventurers to follow suit. With a fine disregard for the existing pastoral economies of the English fenlands, adventurers moved in with their Dutch experts to drain large areas in the Isle of Axholme and around the Wash, turning these regions over to an arable farming system that yielded far more grain than hitherto. They also included in their rotations a new crop – coleseed – an important source of oil for industrial purposes and fodder for cattle.

The same pressing need for more corn changed land use in many forest areas also. The transformations were often less spectacular, for they were achieved by many small encroachments, as men cleared small areas of degraded woodland, first for use as pasture, then as convertible arable/grasslands. By this means men gradually upgraded land, by using local resources that they could exploit with their own family labour. Glimpses of such efforts make one realize that our soils are truly man made to an extent we can never fully appreciate. Seaweed, seashells, town rubbish, soot and industrial waste – whatever was reasonably accessible was carted on to the land to improve fertility.

## Markets, trade and transport

The improvement of agricultural land in the 16th century was not, of course, a uniform process throughout the European continent. Contemporaries regularly complained of obstinate, stick-in-the-mud peasants who carried on in the ways of their forefathers. To many, the well-tried familiar ways that assured subsistence were enough. The urge to produce more affected only those farmers in regions where a market was assured, prices encouraged extra effort, and men saw ways of spending the money they earned. These conditions were met only in the vicinity of prosperous towns – towns, moreover, that lay on rivers or near a coastal port where produce could readily be transported to more distant markets. The whole of the Netherlands was advantageously placed in this regard. It had a large industrial population of consumers who relied on other producers for their foodstuffs; it had a series of coastal ports that traded regularly eastward to Poland and Russia, north to Scandinavia, east to England and south to the Mediterranean. It is not surprising, therefore, that its agriculture was more advanced than any other in

Europe. Other larger countries had patches of highly commercialized agricultural production in a sea of average to poor standards. The lower Rhineland has already been mentioned. Westphalia was another. In England, Norfolk was the outstanding example of a remarkably highly organized county, growing corn on the light lands to feed a large population of handicraftsmen in the woodland and pastoral areas of the country, 'none of them', it was stated in 1631, 'ordinarily having any corn but from the market'. The rest of its grain was exported from the many havens and seaports round the coast to Lincolnshire, Yorkshire, Newcastle and London, and overseas to the Netherlands. The facilities that permitted this trade in foodstuffs encouraged imports of consumer goods, which further propelled the wheels of trade. These incentives were missing from regions without good roads or lacking a boisterous trade in nearby towns. The north-west of England, for example, suffered noticeably from this isolation until the later 17th century.

Agricultural improvement was patchy, but over Europe as a whole corn production rose remarkably between 1600 and 1640, so much so that it outstripped need. The increase of population which had stimulated all this effort began to fall away after about 1620, and grain prices began to sag as supply exceeded demand. A new era opened up, which was to last for over a hundred years, when grain yielded little profit to the farmer; yet he had to grow it. Harvest failure from time to time was a constant reminder of the precarious nature of food supplies. As a vehement defender of corn growing, in the common fields of the English Midlands, argued in 1611: 'admit thou hadst thine own will in turning commons into pastures, and tilled fields into closing for thy cattle, where in the end would be thy bread without ploughing and seed time?' Corn remained a basic necessity, but it no longer yielded the rewards that had stimulated corn at the expense of woodland and grass for over a hundred years.

## The age of improvement

Nevertheless, collapsing grain prices inaugurated a remarkably innovative age in European agriculture. It is usually labelled a period of crisis and depression, lasting from 1650 to 1750, and certainly for corn farmers who persisted with the same routine this was a fair description. The century was punctuated with many epidemics. Wars were another serious check to development, especially the Thirty Years' War from 1618 to 1648, and the Civil War in England from 1642 to 1648. But most calamities have some constructive consequences: they cause such devastation, and pose such problems of survival, that people are spurred into unusually energetic action to repair their losses. This was certainly the case in England. Sir Richard Weston, a cavalier driven abroad in the 1640s by the confiscation of his estate, went in careful search of farming experience in Brabant and Flanders that would help him to

*Potatoes were introduced from the New World during the 16th century and soon became a staple food, especially in Ireland. Gerard's 'Herbal' illustrated the 'Battata Virginiana' in 1597.*

turn to better use the sandy heaths on his Surrey estate at home. His travels opened his eyes to new arable rotations that were far more profitable than the wheat, barley and peas that an English farmer took for granted. On a journey across heathy land between Antwerp and Ghent, Weston saw nothing but rye, oats and French wheat (buckwheat). His first reaction was to criticize the Flemish for growing such inferior grains; he was startled when the whole system and its economic merits were explained to him. He learned that this was some of the most profitable land in the kingdom; it bore flax, which was worth four or five times the best corn, then turnips, which were similarly far more valuable than grain, then oats, undersown with clover which was mown three times in a year, and maintained a good pasture for four to five years. An acre of flax, turnips and clover combined was worth £58, whereas a single acre of barley, wheat or meadow was worth only £19. He returned to write a very influential account of clover growing, which was widely circulated among gentlemen in the 1650s, and gave the crop so much publicity that it established itself firmly in English farming practice by the mid-1660s.

This was only one of many positive lessons that men learned in the midst of the misery of war. German farmers in the Pfalz learned to grow tobacco from Spanish mercenaries in the 1590s, the English soldiery were made aware of the uses of potatoes when they campaigned in Ireland with Cromwell in the early 1650s. Moreover, the movement of soldiers who were also peasants over large distances spread new knowledge in countless unrecorded ways; it brought men to realize how many derelict areas of land awaited improvement, and how many farming systems other than the familiar corn–livestock routines were available to them.

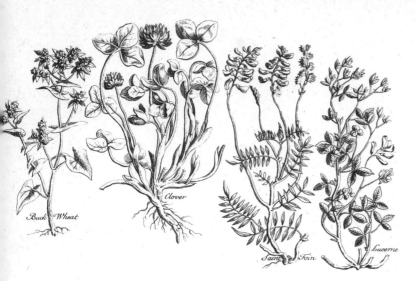

*Productivity was increased in the 18th century by the cultivation of special cereals and grasses. Thomas Hale's 'Complete Body of Husbandry', 1756, included fine engravings of buckwheat, clover, sainfoin and lucerne.*

In commercial farming areas travel strengthened the opinion that most advantage now lay decisively with enclosed farmlands where the cultivation needs of new crops could be met without asking a whole community to alter its communally agreed rotations. Travel and personal observation, together with the publication of increasingly authoritative books, did much to spread experience of special crops and new breeds of livestock through the continent. Some of the most influential migrations were French systems of gardening, with the use of elaborate cloches and bell glasses; French and German systems of forest administration; procedures for cultivating dye crops used in the lower Rhineland and in Holland; the Spanish breed of merino sheep; Italian and Arabian breeds of horses; and Dutch rabbits. Men learned that vines were dressed differently in Italy, France and Germany, and that the Russians had a way of storing grain successfully for seven years. Exchanges resulted in the introduction of a winnowing fan from China to Holland, and thence to Scotland. Dutch ploughs were brought into the fens of Lincolnshire, and Dutch drill ploughs into north-east Kent. Italian threshing rollers of 16th-century or possibly earlier origin, were introduced into 18th-century France, Austria, the Netherlands, Denmark and Sweden.

The alternatives or supplements to mainstream corn–livestock farming, introduced by foreigners into England, were many and varied between 1520 and 1620. A Dutchman supervised the growing of madder in Appledore, Kent. Frenchmen grew hops in Kent, woad in Hampshire and sold mulberry trees from Languedoc to gentlemen in Cheshire and Lancashire. Religious refugees from Holland practised vegetable gardening in Sandwich, Kent, and Frenchmen set up market gardens at St Martin-in-the-Fields in London. It is no flight of fancy to stand in Trafalgar Square today and visualize an orderly market garden on the site, with asparagus, cauliflowers, cabbages, radishes, carrots, lettuce, onions, spinach and artichokes, and a total of 1,240 bell glasses distributed along the rows to bring on early crops. Such was the garden of Robert Gascoine, clearly of French origin, lying somewhere in the parish of St Martin-in-the-Fields in 1718.

Many different combinations of crop and animal husbandry were adopted in the century between 1650 and 1750, the choice depending on the resources of different regions, and of different social classes. Most of these await a full explanation of the complex circumstances that favoured one choice rather than another. But in general terms one can see why landowners turned their attention to the planting and better management of woodlands, to fish farming, to deer keeping, to rabbit warrens and to duck decoys – enterprises that did not demand much expenditure on labour and made better use of hitherto neglected land. These choices yielded delicacies for the table, provided gifts for friends and even left something over for sale at the market. Gentlemen also kept fine vegetable gardens and orchards for household use. These were not commercial enterprises for them, but represented an economy in household expenditure since it saved them buying at the market. Farmers of moderate means maintained their corn–cattle systems, but added other crops like hops, fruit and nut trees which yielded a larger margin of profit. In eastern and southern England they adapted traditional rotations to accommodate such profitable crops as coleseed, weld (a yellow dye plant), turnips and canary grass (the seed of which was used to feed caged birds, and was a speciality of north-east Kent). In Midland England many farmers adopted systems of convertible husbandry, and, by sowing sainfoin, lucerne and clover, greatly improved the feeding values of their pastures, in order to maintain more dairy cows or fat bullocks. Butter and cheese, in particular, played a far larger role in food markets than hitherto. Poor men on suitable land turned to vegetable growing, to tobacco, flax and hemp, exploiting the advantages they had in a plentiful supply of family labour, and making a virtue of their small acreages by meticulous cultivation.

On the continent of Europe the alternatives to mainstream corn farming were equally ingenious, and suited some regions and classes better than others. In the Mediterranean region farmers laid out more vineyards and olive groves. In Languedoc, where woad cultivation had been ruined by the religious wars in the 16th century (so encouraging the growth of woad in England), farmers took up maize cultivation. In Normandy they developed sainfoin to feed horses and dairy cattle; thus the origins of Normandy butter go back a very long way. Further north on the island of Schowen, in Zealand, Holland, they made a great success of madder for dyes, the drying of the roots in madder stoves being brought to a very fine art. An English observer in 1758, wanting to encourage madder growing at home, understood that 'even on their worst land madder turns to better account than any other crops'. England was paying a sum of £180,000 a year for Dutch madder imports in the 1750s. With characteristic prudence, the Dutch, in the first year of planting madder, grew cabbages or dwarf kidney beans in the furrows to bring in cash during the time that the madder plants yielded nothing. In Germany, around Strasburg, farmers grew safflower for a rosy pink dye, much sought after for colouring silks. Strassburg onions also had a high reputation and seed was regularly imported into England. As for the difference in methods used by well-to-do and poor peasants, these emerge but rarely. When they do, they are impressive in showing resourcefulness and attention to detail. Advice on keeping silkworms, written in 1617, described the grand and the modest enterprises of southern Europe. Some men constructed hot-houses to hatch silkworms. An oven was placed at one or both ends of a building, and heat was directed through it by piling up earthen pots, like flower pots, with their bottoms facing the fire and their mouths facing into the house. Branches of rosemary or thyme, roses or other sweet herbs were put into the pots, to moderate the heat, but also because 'sweet smells are very agreeable and pleasing to the worms'. But the poorest peasant could also keep silkworms in far more modest quarters. He did not aspire to specially built hot-houses, but simply used the warmth of his living room; and to hatch the worms he carried the worm seed around in the warm pockets of his own clothing.

### New uses for old fields

These undertakings do not exhaust the ingenuity of men in devising ways of making a living when the conventional routines of grain–livestock farming failed to yield a profit. But if farmers failed to grasp alternatives, the dereliction of land was grievous to behold. This failure occurred in Tuscany and in Campagna south of Rome, where many farmers abandoned their land entirely in the 18th century. But various systems of pasture farming proved more than satisfactory. In Spanish Castile, men turned to Merino sheep production (though the sheep flocks were no longer moved large distances to exploit different seasonal grazings), and Merino wool found a far bigger market in Europe than English wool, which hitherto had won most favour. As an English report observed in 1622, in a painful analysis of England's decline, Spanish wool was 'excellent good, without dust or sand, but pure and clean; dear in show by reason of tucking, but cheap in truth'. Dairying became a major commercial enterprise, probably because the purchasing power of poor urban and rural populations was improving in the late 17th and early 18th centuries. This shift to dairying occurred in Denmark when the large-scale meat pro-

duction of the 16th century was hit by falling demand in the first half of the 17th century. The farming community turned to cheese- and butter-making. In Oldenburg and East Friesland, where dairying was an old tradition, Frisian cattle were already noted for their excellence as milkers (though they were not always black in colour). Conditions in the 17th century simply intensified specialization by encouraging the selection of cattle for milk rather than meat, until the black Frisian milking cow predominated. In England the expansion of dairying was most noticeable in the counties of the west Midlands, in Warwickshire, north Shropshire, Cheshire and Gloucestershire, where dairymen had growing industrial or trading populations on their doorstep, in the Black Country and in Bristol. Alternatively they could send their wares by coastal vessel to London. In parts of Northumberland, Durham and north Yorkshire, too, butter became a valued commercial export to Holland in the later 17th century. This was cheap butter that ordinary Dutchmen put on their own tables, while reserving their higher quality product for export.

This discrimination between the qualities of foodstuffs, and also between seasonal variations of flavour, deserves emphasis, for it reflects a highly developed sense of taste among our forebears which is too often overlooked in historical surveys of the past. The range of flavours was much wider than it is today because local differences had not been ironed out by uniformity in production methods. It is true that purchasers were not protected, as we are, from buying bad quality foodstuffs. On the other hand they had the pleasure of distinguishing subtle differences of flavour. Thus St John's monastery in Bremen differentiated in its account books in the 16th century between grass butter and hay butter, hay cheese and May cheese, St James's cheese (a July cheese) and Michaelmas cheese (September cheese). Prices varied similarly: in 1629 red summer butter was one-third more expensive in Bremen than white winter butter.

Dairying was, of course, ideally suited to family farmers. The growth of the market for cheese and butter at this time undoubtedly helped the survival of small farmers in pastoral regions. They were fast fading from the scene in more specialized grain areas, driven out by low prices and the desperate need of grain growers to achieve economies of scale by cultivating larger units. More dairying also meant more pig keeping, since pigs were fed on the whey. But pork now became a more highly differentiated meat, for while country pork producers continued to fatten pigs in the traditional way, townsmen turned to fattening them on a commercial scale, feeding them on the discarded grains of starch-makers, distillers and brewers. Pig keeping on this basis had started along Thameside in London in the early 17th century, as we discover from the statement of Jacob Mead when he was prevented by monopolists from making starch for ten weeks in 1621 and, as a

*'Method of feeding pigs without waste', another illustration from Hale's 'Complete Body of Husbandry'. It was an age of new ideas, not all of which gained currency.*

result, had 'no means of feeding his two hundred pigs'. By the early 18th century, pork from distillers' grains was plentiful and cheap; it was sold in London at 1s. 6d. per stone, whereas country-fed pork cost 2s. 6d. Its cheapness gave it the advantage in markets frequented by poor townsfolk, even though people complained that it was unsuitable for salting, that its fat was soft and of inferior quality and that it kept badly.

Yet other opportunities of gain were made available in the 17th century to pasture farmers. Their animals did not occupy all their time, but left them free to engage in part-time industrial occupations. Hence the mountainous and forest regions of southern Germany specialized in woodworking and metalworking. French peasants in Languedoc lived by lace-making and knitting. Marshland areas everywhere produced flax and hemp and made linen, rope and canvas. Claylands nursed potteries. Regions possessing ironstone and coal fostered metalworking. Thus, it was in this period that the knives of Solingen and Sheffield, the locks and buckles of south Staffordshire and the woodware of Nuremberg and district maintained an international reputation. Low grain prices might be a depressing experience for the specialist corn grower but depression did not darken everyone's lives; success depended on flexibility and the knowledge of alternatives available. A Czechoslovak peasant in the early 18th century compiled an account which showed that forty per cent of his income came from fruit; a Huntingdonshire farmer in England in 1716 found profit in growing ten acres of chervil; while an Essex farmer made soap, and, furthermore, turned the soap ashes to good account – they wrought a miraculous improvement of his grassland.

Low grain prices persuaded many corn producers on second-grade soils to turn to pasture, but they did not persuade specialized grain growers on the best arable lands radically to over-turn their farming systems. Instead, they adapted them ingeniously within the existing framework. They developed more intensive methods by introducing clover and other artificial grasses into their arable rotations, whereby more livestock could be kept. When these were fed on some of the poorer grains and on barley tailings, etc., they fertilized the fields more effectively as well as yielding another income from livestock and their products. Still more valuable were the outlets found for grain in the use of barley for beer and, increasingly, for spirits. Brewing and distilling became major enterprises all over Europe in both east and west, leading to fierce competition between countries. The English government promoted sales of English corn and malt on the continent by paying bounties and relaxing customs dues. The result was that the Dutch could buy English malt cheaper than any they could make for themselves with barley brought from Poland. When spirits first found favour, considerable quantities of French brandy made their way into England in the 17th century; then the English imposed tariffs against the French and encouraged Englishmen to distil their own. In eastern Europe landlords, rather than peasants, reaped the most advantage from distilleries, for lords usually had monopoly rights over spirit-making; indeed, in Russia and Poland, both governments strengthened and confirmed these privileges in the 18th century. Here, landowners in consequence came to depend very heavily on their income from their distilleries; the superabundance of grain had pressed this solution upon them. Thus gin and whisky drinking may be said to have saved the livelihoods of many grain farmers, though it created a serious problem among those who drowned their sorrows in it.

The inventiveness and ingenuity of European farmers were always most successful in areas where commercial markets exerted a strong influence. This was evident in the 15th and again in the 17th century. The incentive to experiment was missing from regions without good roads or which lacked a boisterous trade in nearby towns. The north-west of England, for example, suffered noticeably from this isolation until the later 17th century, but so did some regions much nearer London. Parts of the deep Weald of Kent and Sussex were set apart from the main stream of trade because traffic from London to the coast flowed more strongly in an easterly and south-easterly direction, rather than due south. Thus, the broadest channels of communication were kept open with the ports of Sandwich and Dover, and it was possible in the 18th century for cattle improvers to find, on small farms buried in the Sussex Weald, pure-bred samples of the old Sussex breed of cattle which had long since disappeared from the more commercialized, rapidly changing cornlands of the downs. William Cobbett exclaimed in wonder that such fine beasts should have their origins in the 'miserable tracts of heath and fern and bushes and sand' of Ashdown and St Leonard's Forests.

Agricultural improvement, in short, was extremely patchy, and areas of commercial agriculture coexisted with extensive regions in Europe where farming systems were still medieval. The principal obstacle in these cases was the survival of feudal systems of land tenure and privilege which burdened peasants with taxation and allowed the richer landowners to go free. Such privileges and immunities impoverished the farmers, and killed any spark of interest the gentry and nobility might have had in agricultural improvement.

### The rise of the gentleman farmer

Innovations were always risky and usually expensive; they almost invariably depended on knowledge or stimulation acquired through travel. This meant that the first pioneers of new methods of farming or new crops were educated gentlemen or merchants who had seen the world. In countries where these classes fairly shared increasing burdens of national and local taxation, they had good reason to show an interest in improving their estates and home farms. Since they possessed resources that enabled them to take risks, they could introduce practical examples of new farming methods and a fresh attitude, which, if successful and appropriate to other men's circumstances, would gradually influence a wider circle of farmers. New crops in England in the 16th and 17th centuries, such as sainfoin, tobacco and coleseed, and the improved management of woodlands and orchards, can all be traced to gentry and merchants who set an example to others. But large areas of central and eastern Europe were deprived of these beneficent economic and social influences. The great nobility in countries like Hungary, Poland and Prussia had enormous estates, owed little in taxation and took little or no interest in agriculture, while petty nobility owed little in taxes but often owned such tiny holdings that they lived at subsistence level, and were no better off than the peasantry. Thus their education, intellectual curiosity and experience of travel yielded nothing of benefit to the farming community. In such areas, systems of common-field farming persisted, and landowners' home farms were cultivated by peasants, both free and serf, on the basis of enforced labour services – a system that had long since proved so inefficient in regions of commercialized farming that it had all but disappeared by the 17th century. An Italian writer, Vincenzo Tanara, described in 1644 the cunning wiles of peasants under share-cropping systems in the Po valley, who scamped cultivations, but contrived to leave the land looking as if it had been properly ploughed. This gives us a tiny glimpse of a most compelling practical argument against feudal labour services.

Listless and indifferent lordship and an oppressed tenantry, carrying an unfair burden of taxation – these were a recipe for slovenly, unproductive agriculture, and much misery in years of bad harvest. Such conditions lay at one end of the farming spectrum, while the highly commercialized agriculture of the Dutch, under which the population depended heavily on imported grain for its staple food, lay at the other. In between lay many different systems of average farming, some striving for better yields, others content with subsistence. In general, western Europe was more productive than eastern Europe because of the commercial stimulus of more populous towns and a more lively trade which loosened the bonds of peasant servitude. But exceptions can always be found. The grain growing regions of Poland, with access to transport along the Vistula to Danzig, served western European countries, including Spain and Italy, with grain in large quantity from the second half of the 16th century onwards. Yet their feudal organization of production persisted.

Human ingenuity solved many problems of survival in the 17th and early 18th centuries, but some of those solutions did more – they also taught many lessons which bore rich fruit when populations started to rise again after 1750 and the demand for grain rose to unprecedented heights. Through men's exploration of agricultural enterprises other than grain growing they came to experiment with new implements of arable cultivation. Their ideas were tested in vegetable gardens. When market gardeners developed their intensive systems of growing vegetables by meticulous cultivation, men began to remark on their high production. They noted the economies of seed that resulted from hand-setting in rows. Farmers observed also that more widely spaced seed enabled plants to grow much larger, that regularly spaced rows greatly facilitated hoeing and that yields, in consequence, were much heavier.

### The machine takes over

From the 17th century onwards grain farmers began to experiment with implements that would enable these lessons from vegetable plots to be exploited in field cultivation. Several Englishmen were trying out seed drills in the 1650s; Andrew Yarranton, who wanted to publicize clover in the west Midlands, discussed in print in the 1660s the possibility of sowing clover seed in rows and then hoeing it. But he admitted at once that that would be impossible for a husbandman to consider, until 'some more expeditious instrument than the common hoe is found out'. Plainly, people were thinking positively about row cultivation with new tools. In north-east Kent where one speciality was canary seed to feed caged birds, family farmers by the

*A four-wheel drill plough with seed and manure hopper, which according to the caption 'was invented in the year 1745. It is so light that a man may draw it, but generally drawn by a pony or a little horse.'*

1720s had adopted two alternative methods of garden-like cultivation in the fields. Some built up sharp-tipped ridges, and sowed their seed by hand so that it would fall more surely into the furrows. Others walked along the furrows passing the seed through a kind of teapot spout. Such practices and experiments led to the construction of a horse-drawn seed drill and horse hoe by Jethro Tull in Berkshire in the early 18th century. And seed drills and horse hoes led in the end to elaborate mechanical cultivators, steam-ploughs and threshing machines, and finally to tractors and the combine harvester. Tull's name is celebrated because of the successful publicity he achieved when he wrote his book on *Horse-hoeing Husbandry* in 1731. But Tull was singular only in the degree of neurotic vexation which he felt towards his unco-operative labourers. In his opinion, they commanded excessively high wages (the purchasing power of wages was, indeed, rising) and they would not submit to his orders to set sainfoin seed by hand. This drove him to try a horse-drawn implement. Tull was far from singular in his experiments, as we have seen. In the very same years that he was experimenting with horse-drawn seed drills, they were being tried by other landowners, with far more pressing reasons to economize on labour, because they had much larger estates – men like Lord Ducie and Lord Halifax in southern England, and Lord Cathcart and Lord Stair in Scotland.

Labour-saving implements ceased to be the novel interest of a coterie around 1760 when a century of low grain prices drew to a close, and farmers who had listlessly cultivated grain crops for little profit, were encouraged to produce more. English agriculturalists were better equipped than most other European farmers to seize the maximum commercial advantage from the new situation. Enclosure was no longer obstructed by legal difficulties: the English Parliament positively assisted by allowing enclosures to be initiated by private enclosure acts. Arable rotations already in use exploited the complementary functions of grains, roots and artificial grasses, eliminating unproductive fallow years.

Implements for row cultivation promised to transfer the productivity of horticulture to the fields, while mitigating the otherwise prohibitive expenses of labour. All these factors in combination served to make English agriculture a model to landed gentlemen and farmers all over northern Europe.

The interest of foreigners in improved English farming sprang out of administrative reforms undertaken from the later 17th century, and especially in the early 18th century, in countries like Germany, Poland, Russia and the Austrian monarchy, making lords responsible for the collection and guarantee of state taxes levied on the peasants. When once this happened, landowners had to take an interest in the productivity of their farmed lands. To improve their estates they needed models, so they turned to England. The procession of European travellers visiting England built up slowly. Its beginnings in Prussia can be traced back to 1700, when a scientific society under government patronage was set up in Brandenburg, expressly to improve the arts and sciences, agriculture, industry and trade, and to unite practice with theory in order to raise the productive capacity of the nation. The Berlin Society was the only one to emerge from much grander plans, laid by Gottfried Wilhelm Leibniz, for academies in Mainz, Berlin, Petersburg, Dresden and Vienna, modelled on the Academy of Paris and the Royal Society in London. Its financial resources were meagre, coming from a monopoly of the publication of calendars, but it was a beginning. Intellectual interest in other European countries was increasingly directed to practical agricultural and commercial concerns, and, in the second half of the 18th century, many other academies and societies were set up in other German and Austrian countries. As a focus for discussion, they should not be underrated. From 1740 onwards the Prussian Society encouraged prize essays as a means of publicizing different solutions to agricultural problems. Johann Christian Schubart, who campaigned in Saxony tirelessly for farming improvement, submitted a prize essay in 1783 on clover, and used the money it earned to publish his instructions cheaply in pamphlet form. He was known as the Apostle of Clover. An anonymous Westphalian peasant wrote in 1780 from the Ebbe mountains, probably around Altena, of his experience with fodder crops. He explained his pragmatic approach thus: he was not an educated reader of theoretical treatises; rather he tried this and that, and adopted the course of farming which succeeded best in his fields. Others would have other problems; he wrestled with land and a climate not unlike that of the most barren parts of the Alps. The crop he valued most was potatoes. In his view, they had saved the lives of the mountain population of Westphalia; without them one-third would have had to emigrate or would have died in bad years. Probably this writer did not remember the famines of the Seven Years' War, which first securely established potato cultivation in Germany. But he must certainly have remembered the famine years of 1770–72, which greatly extended the crop.

This essay brings us face to face with a peasant farmer's thoroughly practical verdict on a new crop. Not only did it yield far more foodstuff than oats from the same acreage; it was a far more palatable food. Peasants tired of oat bread, eaten dry, with salt and water, he argued, whereas potatoes could be cooked in many different ways – boiled and then moistened with milk, roasted in ashes and eaten with a little butter, or eaten cold as a salad. Grated and mixed with eggs, oats and sugar, they made a rissole, which even a Spanish grandee would not recognize as potato. On this diet, he added, the peasants of Sauerland endured hard, heavy work, and yet lived as healthily as fish.

## The science of agriculture

After 1760, a steady procession of foreigners came to England to tour the kingdom and take back ideas and agricultural implements to modernize their farms and estates at home. Arthur Young, Secretary to the English Board of Agriculture, kept up a stream of correspondence with Italians, Danes, Russians, French and Germans, who used his books as guides to the improved farms and estates that were thought worth visiting while in England. Count Bernstorff, for example, reported, in August 1800, on his visit to Essex farms, and asked for an introduction to his next port of call, the Reverend Mr Close in Hampshire. In February 1798, John Reynold Forster, Professor of Natural History in the University of Halle, wrote to introduce Baron Schoen and Mr Weiss, who had come to England 'to be initiated in the principles and practise of husbandry in England'. Yet another letter, dated June 1802, reported the desire of the emperor of Russia to set up an English farm near St Petersburg, stocked with implements, cattle, seeds, workmen and dairymaids in imitation of the royal farms of George III, 'Farmer George'. After the French Revolution, Frenchmen were introduced to Young's writings in translation, particularly his *Annals of Agriculture*, on the ground

that they would help those 'whom the Revolution has hurried from the folly of idle occupations to the active and peaceable life of the husbandman'.

The traffic was not all one-way. Rather, a reciprocal exchange of ideas took place. Arthur Young himself toured France, and Francis le Rochefoucauld wrote from Altona expecting Young to visit Hamburg, Berlin and Frankfurt. Indeed, he kept a little German carriage ready, waiting for Young's use, and warned gentleman farmers round about to expect him. In Altona, Young would have been especially welcome, for three miles away at Flottbek, Caspar Voght, son of a Hamburg merchant, had set up an estate on the English model, and imported Scottish foresters and English farm managers to run it. Enormous effort was expended in levelling out rough fields, draining wet land, diverting river courses and planting hedges. Practically all the carting was done by Scottish two-wheel carts; the horse harness came from England; six different types of English plough were in use, including a Norfolk plough, a Surrey plough and an iron plough, invented by the Scotsman, James Small. The drill used was that invented by the Reverend James Cook of Lancashire in 1783; a threshing mill was brought from Scotland, and the rotations were borrowed from England. Clover was so important that Voght introduced a bunch of clover into his coat of arms. In addition, Scottish forestry skills were introduced by the migration of the Booth family from Falkirk, shipping with them a whole cargo of trees and shrubs, with which they planted 62 acres of firs, Scotch pine, and larches. This was the beginning of the tree nurseries of the Hamburg district; they throve in the damp climate of the Baltic coast between Halsenbeck and Rellingen, so reminiscent of the Scottish homeland of the original planters. In a reverse direction at this same period fruitful ideas were transmitted from Prussia to England concerning mangold and sugar-beet. As early as 1799, Herbert Marsh, later bishop of Peterborough, was sending to Arthur Young, from Leipzig, seeds of mangold, recommending the root as a crop that was never affected by caterpillar or fly, never failed and made excellent fodder for cattle. In Berlin experiments had started in 1747 and were now making decisive progress in the extraction of sugar from beet. Sugar-beet was to become a major crop first in Prussia – later all over Europe.

Rising populations needing to be fed forced the pace of agricultural change all over the European continent, in the century between 1750 and 1850. Generalized judgments made it out to be a vast territory of poor farming and poor peasants, while England was the home of an efficient agriculture. Yet, as one foreigner sourly remarked, farmers could easily have learned turnip cultivation in Holland. And two German travellers in England between 1765 and 1766, who had been too credulous in believing laudatory accounts of English farming, passed through Bedfordshire exclaiming in amazement at the amount of wasteland they saw. 'The Englishman, who allegedly uses everything, leaves places uncultivated, grazing one hundred sheep for a few months poorly on it, and using the bracken for poor man's firing.'

On the continent of Europe one could readily have found examples of rich peasants, personally free, who had secure tenures, light obligations to their lords, as well as conducting a trade or bye-employment. In the rich lowlands of Hanover an English traveller in 1817–18 noted comfortably carpeted peasant farmhouses with handsome gardens. Silesian peasants in 1806 were said to live in luxury and gluttony.

But the pessimistic judgments helped to promote decisive action. English examples, even though they were not always appropriate when transplanted, inspired radical transformations in the techniques of farming in France, Germany and countries further east. And the same princes and nobles from these backward territories, who interested themselves in agriculture, also campaigned for legal reforms that were introduced first on crown estates from the beginning of the 18th century, and gathered momentum after 1760 when they were enforced nationally. A liberation of the peasantry was effected in Hungary by the great code (the Urbarium) issued in 1767 by Maria Theresa, regulating lord–peasant relationships throughout the kingdom. Its provisions were resisted by the governing class, and not accepted by the Hungarian Diet until 1790–91, and they illustrate the pitfalls that lie athwart the path of all politicians (as well as historians) who generalize overmuch. The code was a liberating measure for the peasantry of western Hungary, but not for eastern Hungary, where the Turks had ruled with a lighter hand, and the new obligations allowed by the code were, in fact, heavier than those formerly demanded by the Turks. But, in general, the liberation of Europe's peasantry proceeded steadily: labour services were commuted into cash payments, common land was divided into enclosed fields, personal serfdom was ended by emancipation in Russia, which generally, but not always, left peasants with a family holding of land. Yet the memory of this feudal oppression survived for another two generations at least, sometimes longer. Tocqueville in 1856 thought the bitterness of the French peasantry inextinguishable, though the Revolution of 1789 had theoretically ended their exploitation sixty years before. It still coloured much peasant violence in the later 19th century, and lived again as late as 1890 in Jacques le Roy's novel of *Jacquou le Croquant*.

Technical improvements were carried across Europe by migrating populations, by the distribution of books and journals and by demonstrations of practical farming, both private and public. Albrecht Daniel Thaer, much respected as the father of improved German agriculture, wrote an extremely influential book on English farming practices, based purely on the literature that reached him in Celle, Hanover. He never

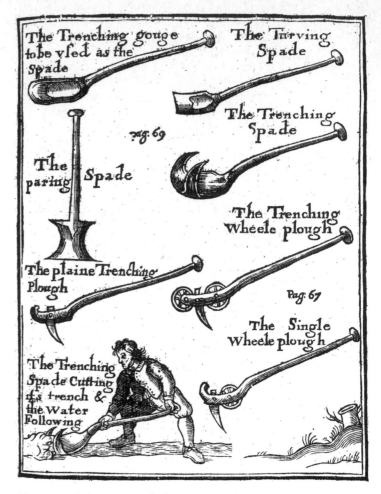

*The variety of plough forms to be found in England as early as 1653 is evident in two pages of Walter Blith's 'The English Improver Improved'.*

visited England himself. In many other cases, the details and significance of newly transmitted techniques can only be guessed at, as when we read of the swampy land of Bannat of Temeswar in Hungary being settled in 1770 by German colonists from Swabia and the Rhineland, or learn of the fine studs of horses from Holstein encountered in Hungary in 1797. Of the impact of Scottish farmers, who migrated to Dowspuda in Poland in 1816, we know more. Among other things, they taught new methods of potato cultivation and the making of Cheshire cheese. And their families stayed: Scottish names like Gowanlock and Burt were soon transformed into the more Polish-sounding names of Gowenloh and Berth.

From 1760 to 1860 the major effort in agriculture throughout Europe was put into improving the productivity of mainstream foodstuffs – grain, and other crops with a high starch content, and livestock. These were needed to provide adequate basic foods for a larger population, including many more industrial workers who were entirely dependent on bought victuals. The part-time farmer, part-time industrial worker continued to exist, and survives in large

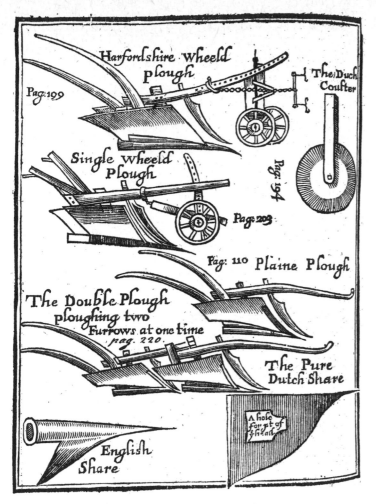

*The most advanced was the double plough, towards the bottom, which cut two furrows at a time.*

numbers today in some regions. But the countries which changed most rapidly to new farming methods were also developing their industries, thereby creating a still larger class of landless factory workers, who could not survive without paid work. This made it all the more necessary to exploit the highly productive food crops such as buckwheat, potatoes and maize. Sugar-beet, too, proved a great asset in place of expensive, imported cane sugar; it was first urgently needed during the Napoleonic Wars when the English naval blockade cut off supplies of sugar-cane from across the Atlantic. It was adopted most rapidly in Germany, but not till after 1860 did it spread widely in the Netherlands, and later still to England.

The heavy cropping of arable land obliged men to rely more heavily on artificial manures. Previously they had made do with animal manures, nitrogen-fixing legumes, with some small quantities of lime and other minerals. Around 1840, the chemists Liebig in Germany, Lawes in England and Boussingault in France devised formulae for chemical manures that started the modern fertilizer industry. Dependence on such chemical additions has today reached a point where natural resources are discarded, where much cattle manure is washed away as slurry and corn stubble is burned. Instead large sums are spent on artificial additions. This dependence is measured in some striking figures of chemical fertilizers used per unit of land, showing that in 1910–13 the Netherlands used 164 units compared with 4 in Spain and 20 in France. In 1949–50 the Netherlands used 378 units, while Hungary used 2, Yugoslavia used 6, Spain 20 and France 49. At one time the Netherlands would have been held up as the model in this survey. Now that we recognize the need to use our natural resources more prudently, and, if possible, establish a more self-sufficient cycle in agricultural routine, we look with some dismay on the dependence of agriculture on the fertilizer industry and on the use of chemicals, which are not inexhaustible.

High farming has produced high yields, but in some ways it has been profligate, and some of the more thrifty usages in our forgotten past need to be reviewed with more sympathy and understanding. Dependence nowadays on a few high yielding strains of cultivated plants and domestic animals contrasts strongly with the wide range of alternatives that were available to farmers in earlier centuries, and must prompt concern, since it destroys man's insurance against future calamities through epidemics, and against future changes of need and taste. Coleseed offers an example of a crop that has come and gone, and now returns again with its past unrecognized to serve a new use. It was first introduced into northern Europe for its oil to finish woollen textiles, to burn in lamps and for other industrial purposes. The crop was well known in the Netherlands in the mid-14th century, and spread thence to Germany and France, and in the 16th century to England. It was specially welcome because olive oil had become so expensive, but also because the waste cake was prized as cattle fodder. By the 18th century fields of coleseed were a commonplace in England from east Yorkshire throughout eastern England to Essex. The first street lighting in English towns in the 18th century would have been impossible without it. Wisbech in Cambridgeshire was one of the first to have this amenity in 1700, which, in a town of barely two thousand inhabitants, would be inexplicable if we did not also know that it had seven oil mills in 1735 crushing the seed that was grown in the neighbouring fens. Now rapeseed is returning to favour; its feared carcinogenic properties have been bred out of it by geneticists, and it is valued for margarine and cooking oil. In 1980 one quarter of a million acres of it were grown in England. But our past is so ill remembered that a journalist recently described coleseed as looking like 'a great sheet of nasty new linoleum, . . . made for Van Gogh not for Turner, . . . one of these new fangled ideas from France'. 'I'll be grateful when we're back to wheat and barley again', he wrote. Yet transported back through two centuries the same writer could have seen in 1715 one hundred and sixteen acres of rape, worth £650, on the farm of William Burkitt of Winterton in Lincolnshire. More than 150 years before that, in 1551, he would have seen the first trials with coleseed in England, around King's Lynn in Norfolk.

Many other crops apart from coleseed, that were new or in some way revitalized in Europe in the 15th to 17th centuries, receded in importance between 1760 and 1860, when the main need was to provide an adequate subsistence for all, through a plain basic diet. But after 1870, when grain poured into Europe from the Americas, and livestock products arrived in refrigerated ships from Australasia, European farmers could not compete, and once again, in favourably situated areas, farmers survived the deep depression that followed by turning to the special crops that had served so well in other bad times. Vegetable and fruit marketing was further developed, and the onion sellers of northern France began their annual trips to London and southern England. The growing of celery and other vegetables flourished in the Isle of Axholme, Lincolnshire, for despatch to the market in Sheffield.

Small farmers on the continent of Europe who existed at a very low level of productivity could not withstand the bleak economic situation in the late 19th century. Large numbers of young people from peasant areas in eastern Europe migrated to America and Canada. In the west many survived at subsistence level, and since the turn of this century have continued to survive with the help of co-operative systems which process and market their produce – these are especially well developed in France – supplemented by industrial bye-employments.

The tension between the technically efficient systems prevailing in some European regions, and the relatively simple procedures on family farms persists, but the arguments on both sides are given a new slant as men focus less exclusively on efficiency per man employed, and consider productivity per acre and the social benefits of the two different farming structures. The agricultural productivity of small holdings, judged by yields per acre, is higher than that of large farms. And the fact that they show a lower productivity per man may matter less in the future, for the advance of industrial technology poses the more urgent question, how to find work and ensure a satisfying life for men who are not needed either in industry or agriculture. Family farms can produce a good living, they keep the countryside populated, and they yield a more satisfying life than that in populous towns.

Any new policy for agriculture, whether in Europe or North America, will have to take account of this problem, and modern government can draw much instructive experience by surveying the ingenuity of farmers through many different turns of economic fortune in our forgotten past.

---

*What makes the cornfields happy, under what constellation*
*It's best to turn the soil, my friend, and train the vine*
*On the elm; the care of cattle, the management of flocks,*
*The knowledge you need for keeping frugal bees: – all this*
*I'll now begin to relate.*

**With these words** Vergil begins his celebration of rural life, *The Georgics*. It is, in fact, as well as a highly wrought literary work, a practical guide to Roman farming. Known and respected throughout the Middle Ages, it was appealed to as an authority. In this Spanish manuscript of the 15th century, the initial Q is divided into four miniature scenes which illustrate the lines quoted above: ploughing and sowing, tending cattle and exercising a horse, possibly training the vine (or planting young trees) and keeping bees.

Books, however, hardly mattered to most medieval farmers. Ploughing, sowing and reaping; the rotation of crops; animal husbandry – all these things were passed on from generation to generation, and the peasant wisely resisted most attempts to change. Even so, the situation was never entirely static. New crops were occasionally introduced, and the acreage given to old crops fluctuated with prices; the balance of arable and pastoral farming altered; breeds improved; slowly, advances were made in such areas as ploughing, planting, drainage, fertilization. In the 17th century, with increasing technical knowledge, agriculture became a science. Expertise, learned societies and modern books soon made *The Georgics* of merely academic interest. (1)

# P · VIRGILI MARONIS MAN - TVANI GEORGICORVM LIBER PRIMVS ·

HIC · VERGHES · NIT ·

## VID FACIAT LETAS SEGE - TES QVO SYDERE TERRAM ·

# Open fields

A time-traveller to the Middle Ages would see a countryside very different from that of today: instead of a patchwork of small meadows separated by hedges, he would find vast, bleak, open fields, usually three to a village, each divided into small strips.

**Medieval farming** was clearly labour intensive, not necessarily a bad thing in an economy where labour was plentiful. A French 15th-century miniature (*top*) shows five ploughing teams at work in a single field. In the German Alps, as late as 1803 (*above*), a very similar system was in operation. The scene by Wilhelm von Kobell shows a single large field in which the tasks of ploughing, harrowing and sowing are taking place simultaneously. (2, 3)

**Unique now in England**, the village of Laxton in Nottinghamshire preserves its ancient open fields and its manorial court to ensure strict observation of the community's rules. The estate map (*upper right*) is of the 17th century. The medieval pattern can persist (*right*, Neuberg, Oberpfalz), though the social system that produced it has long since vanished. In the days of manual labour, to work the land in long thin strips was as efficient as any other. (4, 5)

# The age of improvement

The 18th century marks a turning point in the history of rural life. The slow process by which independent peasant holdings were giving way to tenant farms accelerated, partly for economic reasons, partly because new technological knowledge was being brought to bear. Farming became more efficient, and, although many features of the traditional community began to disappear, country people were often more prosperous than before.

**The whole estate**, about 150 people, of the manor of Dixton in Gloucestershire is mobilized to gather the hay, in about 1730. Most of it has been cut, but near the centre a row of twenty-three men with scythes moves up the field (away from us) leaving the grass in lines (swathes) behind them. Further to the right we see the next operation: the grass is turned to dry by men and women using long rakes. It is then piled into stooks, as has been done far left and right, and is finally loaded on to haywains; there are five of them in the picture. Some groups have finished their work and are resting, and, coming away from the field in the right foreground, half a dozen men are dancing the Morris dance. In the very centre of the picture three figures on horseback may be the lord of the manor and his family – the two ladies are riding side-saddle. In the background can be seen more fields showing the ridge and furrow effect of ploughing. (6)

# The indispensable plough

After the spade, the plough has probably been the most effective agricultural instrument. Designed to turn the soil to expose the earth for a seed-bed, its component parts were established early and hardly changed until the coming of power mechanization.

**To turn the earth** the ploughshare was fitted with a mould-board, seen clearly in this miniature from Germany, about 1500. The earth was always thrown to the right, so that, when the plough returned along the next line, it was heaped up on the opposite side, creating the ridges and furrows still seen in some fields. (8)

**'Study of a Plough',** by Constable: here, several improvements have been introduced, including the adjustable coulter with four possible positions. (9)

**Simple but not primitive**, the medieval plough (*left*) consisted of a beam sometimes resting on two wheels (the land wheel larger than the furrow wheel), pulled by a horse or ox. Walking behind, the ploughman presses downwards, so that the vertical blade, the coulter, slices the earth, followed at once by the wedge-shaped ploughshare making a furrow. (7)

**'Seed-time'** (*below*), by J. F. Herring: next to the plough (which is unwheeled, although four horses pull it) goes a roller weighted with a box of stones to break up the earth. Steam-ploughing (*bottom*) was an ingenious idea that never really succeeded. The steam-engine stands at one side of the field, a pivot-wheel at the other, and the plough is propelled between them by cable. (10, 11)

# The seed and the harvest

Traditionally crops were 'rotated', often in a three-year cycle – one year winter-sown grain (wheat or rye), one year spring-sown (barley or oats), one year left fallow. The three fields of the village would be used in this way, turn and turn about.

**Winter-wheat** was sown in October (*below left*): miniature from a 15th-century Book of Hours. *Below right*: the labourer pulls the corn towards him with a hook and cuts it with a complicated sickle, which he brings down with one slashing blow; the results of each stroke lie on the ground behind him. Tying into sheaves was a skilled operation of its own. (12, 13)

**Flailing** separated the grain from the stalks. In this miniature (*above*), the sheaves are piled up from the fields on the right. Three men beat it with their heavy hinged flails, and on the left a woman removes the straw. (14)

**Haymaking** came at the end of summer and changed little with the centuries – 16th-century Flanders was like 18th-century England, seen in an earlier spread. Note how the man handles his scythe, grasping the two handles and turning his whole body from the hips. Another, behind him, sharpens his blade, while women collect the hay and load it on carts. In the left foreground, lunch lies ready. (15)

# From the good earth

The number of fruits and vegetables available was constantly increasing, as crops were introduced from other parts of Europe and from outside. The process was aided by the growing efficiency of markets, where produce from a wide area was brought together.

**Like Pomona** presiding over the fruits of the earth, a market woman painted by the 17th-century Dutch artist Joachim Beuckelaer sits surrounded by her succulent wares. Some varieties have changed slightly in three hundred years, but all are easily recognizable today – grapes, peaches and apricots (resting on a pumpkin) in front of her; squashes, pears, figs (green and black), hazel and almond nuts and blackberries on the right; broad-beans (with flowers) and cabbages in the right-hand corner; cherries, plums and peas in the foreground; and artichokes and asparagus on the extreme left. (17)

**As the towns grew,** so did their appetites. Markets had existed for centuries, but during the 18th century they became larger and more specialized. In London the piazza of Covent Garden was given over to vegetables. At first (*right*) there were merely rows of stalls; fifty years later it received a permanent stone building. (18)

**Botanical studies** go back to the Middle Ages, but it was during the 18th century that they became truly scientific. *Below:* a miniature showing barley, *c.* 1400. *Opposite right:* six examples of later illustration. Top left to bottom right: pea, onion, artichoke, rape, poppy and sunflower. (16, 19–24)

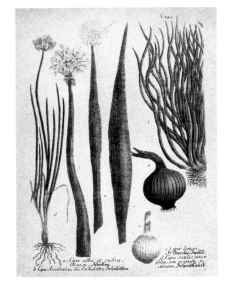

# HARVESTING MACHINERY

## THE NEW LIGHT "OPEN-BACK" STEEL FRAME BINDER

MANUFACTURED BY

R. HORNSBY & SONS LIMITED,

GRANTHAM, ENGLAND.

Sold by H. & J. Cutlack, Ely.

**Mechanization** has meant a revolution on the land. As long as man- and animal-power was the source of energy, cultivation inevitably remained basically the same; a Roman farmer would have had no difficulty settling into the routine of 18th-century England. The machine changed everything. The sheer increase in efficiency – compare, for instance, this harvester of 1892 with the first picture in the book – is only the most obvious point. The whole structure of rural life lost its purpose. As the numbers of those working the land shrank to a fraction and the products of craftsmen were superseded by those from factories, the old ties that united the village fell apart. (25)

# 5 THE STRUGGLE TO SURVIVE

DIEDRICH SAALFELD

# The struggle to survive

Any figures for the population of Europe before 1800 have to be based largely on estimates, and it is therefore not surprising that different historians have arrived at figures that vary by as much as 50 per cent. Those given by Mols and Armengaud (Table 1) can be regarded as the most accurate, though the figure for Russia is probably underestimated. Thus we can be reasonably certain that in every country of Europe up to the beginning of the 16th century the population was slowly rising at an average annual rate of less than $\frac{1}{2}$ per cent. In the 16th century the rate increased to between $\frac{1}{2}$ and 1 per cent; it dropped again in the 17th century, but rose after about 1740 to 1 per cent and over and continued to rise thereafter. In central Europe and Spain, the 17th century ended with an actual decrease in population (mostly attributable in Germany to the Thirty Years' War), and in most other countries it temporarily ceased to rise.

The natural explanation of these fluctuating phases of demographic development lies in the shifting relationship between birth-rate and death-rate in pre-industrial societies. With an average life expectancy of around 30 to 35 years, the figure for annual births was 35 to 45 per 1,000, while, under normal environmental conditions, the death-rate amounted to 35 to 40 per 1,000, giving an annual growth rate of $\frac{1}{2}$ per cent. Factors that could negate this natural increase included infectious diseases, poor harvests and (from the 14th to the 15th century in Europe) the gradual deterioration of the climate, which seems to have improved again, though slowly, in the 18th century. From time to time, serious epidemics, famines and wars could reach catastrophic proportions. The death-rate could more than double in those years. The frequently recurring 'diseases of the people' – plague, tuberculosis, cholera, dysentery, small-pox and leprosy, to name only the most widespread – claimed propor-tionately many more deaths in the closely packed large towns and crowded villages, with their inadequate hygienic arrangements, than in the sparsely settled agricultural areas. There is also a class-related pattern. The generally poorly nourished urban and rural lower classes suffered considerably more from diseases and bad harvests than the more resistant well-to-do families. The latter's prosperity, which entailed a regular, adequate supply of food and good housing and living conditions, provided a first line of defence against the sudden onset of natural disasters. The death-rate in north-west Europe dropped steeply around 1740 – and about a generation later in eastern Europe – while the birth-rate remained as high as ever. The birth-rate only fell noticeably in the last quarter of the 19th century, as the death-rate had done 100 to 150 years previously. In the middle of the present century, both settled at around 10 per 1,000, so that from this time onward population growth in Europe appears very small.

In pre-industrial society, people of all classes took it for granted that the whole rhythm of their lives would be totally dependent on the fluctuations of the environment. Birth and death were natural and everyday occurrences and were accepted as God's will. Life revolved round such events – baptisms and funerals, weddings, the sowing and harvest – and they formed the major themes of the national customs of all European peoples. After periods of widespread mortality caused by war and disease, widowed men and women quickly entered into new marriages, with the result that the number of births soon overtook the number of deaths. One often finds an unmistakable leap in population after these disasters. In the second half of the 18th century, medical knowledge grew and hygiene improved (through better education and widespread literacy), life expectancy at birth went up from 30 to 35

| Circa | France | Great Britain | Germany | Italy | Spain | Russia | Europe – Total |
|---|---|---|---|---|---|---|---|
| 1500 | 16 | 4 | 12 | 10 | 8 | 9 | 80 |
| 1600 | 19 | 7 | 16 | 13 | 10 | 14 | 105 |
| 1700 | 20 | 9 | 15 | 13 | 9 | 18 | 115 |
| 1800 | 27 | 11 | 24 | 18 | 12 | 26 | 185 |
| 1900 | 41 | 37 | 51 | 34 | 19 | 59 | 400 |

Table 1 *Population of the major countries of Europe, 1500–1900, using the pre-1914 frontiers. Figures in millions.*

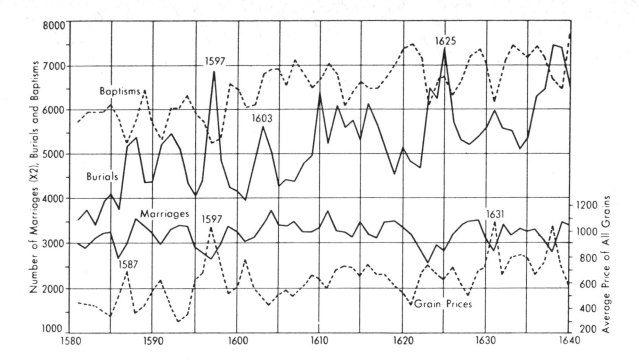

Table 2   *Grain prices, baptisms, burials and marriages in England, 1581–1640. Grain prices are adjusted one year to coincide with the year of effect (100 = average price 1450–99). The number of marriages has been multiplied by two to make it applicable to the population figures.*

years, food supplies increased, communications became more efficient – and the stage was set for the European population explosion that was to continue well into the 20th century.

The population explosion in England and western Europe had already started when Malthus wrote his *Essay on the Principle of Population* in 1798. He had observed correctly that in his time population was rising much faster than food production. Hence he concluded that an increasing deterioration of living standards could only be prevented by a conscious policy of birth control. Otherwise, epidemics or wars would lead to a really catastrophic reduction of the population and so restore the balance between demand and supply for essential foodstuffs. The lower classes would be much more severely affected than the well-to-do. For Marx, the increasing pauperization of the lower classes, who had to earn their living by manual labour, appeared unavoidable under capitalism. Both Malthus and Marx were proved wrong; technical, economic and social advances led increasingly, from the middle of the 19th century, to real economic growth, which clearly overtook the growth of the population. In the industrial countries, this brought about a marked rise in real incomes and an improvement in living standards for all classes of the population. With the knowledge we have now, the historian is bound to ask why, in previous periods of large population growth – as in the 16th century or even in the High Middle Ages – did scientific,

technical and economic advances not lead much earlier to an improvement in productivity?

Today we know that scientific knowledge and technical progress provide simply the preconditions for industrialization. These forces can only prevail after certain legal and social obstacles have been removed. In England, the way was opened for this development as early as the 16th and 17th centuries with the growth of the bourgeoisie and the relative democratization of society; on the continent it could only succeed after the liberal constitutional and social reforms of the 19th and 20th centuries.

### The social order of the pre-industrial period

In Europe, from the Middle Ages until well into the 19th century, the position of the individual and his family in the social and economic life of the village and town was determined by his political and legal rights, by property and wealth and by birth and profession. We have already seen in Chapter 2 that the most important criterion of social differentiation was therefore parentage, by which access was possible to the higher strata of society, to the material benefits of life and not least to a suitable profession. The people of the time were very conscious of this, as Benecke aptly observes: 'Before the birth of human rights in the 18th century, European society recognized as self-evident that there were basic inequalities at law between different groups of people and their dependants, according to wealth, birth and profession. Even so, early modern social structures were not rigid and caste-like but movement within them was individual and erratic: one can talk of cumulative effects but not of rational changes.'

Thus in the nation states of Europe, population was organized according to a strictly hierarchical structure. As the dominant class, the nobility constituted the First Estate. Equipped with a wide range of powers and privileges, it stood at the top of the social pyramid. It was followed by the Second Estate, the less privileged bourgeoisie, whose members had the right to live within the city walls and the special privileges of engaging in commerce and of carrying on independent businesses. The town dwellers represented a definite social stratum, in spite of clear-cut social differences within them. The whole rural population was the lowest, largest and most oppressed social group of the pre-industrial period. See Table 3 for numerical distribution of the social strata.

The clergy is not included in this table, although the church was normally placed above the nobility in the constitutions of the majority of countries in Europe. However, from the social-historical viewpoint, the position of the clergy in society was also determined by birth, though, because of their holy orders, they constituted a separate social stratum. This was itself again structured hierarchically like the rest of the society. The high ecclesiastical dignitaries and princes of the church came almost exclusively from the high nobility, and the priests came mainly from the town dwellers, rarely from the peasantry, so they may be included in these estates. Generally speaking, the clergy belonged to the higher social groups and so were among the notables in town and country.

Although the total population of Europe more than doubled between 1500 and 1800, only insignificant fluctuations took place in the mutual relationship of the three estates. So, in pre-industrial Europe four-fifths of the population belonged to the peasantry and – with a slight increase at the beginning of modern times – one-fifth to the town dwellers. In spite of its pre-eminent political and social position, the nobility only accounted for quite an insignificant figure numerically.

*Table 3  Social classification of the population of Europe, in percentages, 1500 and 1800.*

|  | 1500 | 1800 |
| --- | --- | --- |
| Landowners (nobility) | 1–2 | 1 |
| Urban | 18 | 21 |
| Rural (peasants) | 80 | 78 |
| *Classification of rural population* | | |
| Self-sufficient farmers and smallholders | 55 | 43 |
| Employed (landless or almost so) | 25 | 35 |
| Population (in millions) | 80 | 185 |

## The peasantry

As Table 3 shows, between 1500 and 1800, all classes contributed more or less equally to the growth of the population, but there were significant shifts within the three social groups. In the rural population, the proportion of villagers with little or no land rose from 30 per cent to 45 per cent, or from about $\frac{1}{4}$ to over $\frac{1}{3}$ of the population. With the stabilizing of political power and the distribution of wealth at the end of the Middle Ages, all the people living on the land – with the exception of the nobility and the leading dignitaries of church and state – were bound together as subjects of their territorial sovereign and were thus legally and politically on an equal level. It was landownership that became the most important criterion of social differentiation. As more and more people found themselves with no access to landownership or to independent participation in production, one can already speak of the beginnings, under absolutism, of a process of proletarianization. An increasing number of families were obliged to earn their living as farm hands, day labourers, farm servants or workers in cottage industry. One of the results of their exclusion from private ownership of agricultural land was that these country people no longer had a share in rights to the common land and to communal revenues. Even if they managed to become owners of houses, they remained underprivileged and thus disadvantaged inhabitants of their village. Rural poverty and mendicancy became widespread.

The rural servant lived as a member of his or her employer's household. Although these people enjoyed relatively secure working conditions and board and lodging, they lacked elementary rights enjoyed by other villagers. They had no claims on the master's family, either to a share of property or wealth on inheritance, or to provision in money or kind on marriage or on termination of contract. If they were able to find the capital out of their scanty wages to build or buy a small house and bring up a family, they lost their permanent employment as servants and were forced to accept a lower standard of living either as casual labourers or as industrial workers. Servants are difficult to isolate in contemporary sources as they were counted as part of the employer's household. In eastern Europe, which had a high proportion of large estates, they can be estimated at 10 to 15 per cent around 1800; in the rest of Europe, with the prevailing small- and medium-sized estate structure they remained under 10 per cent.

Altogether, in the more densely populated areas of Europe, the whole rural lower class had become the largest social group, and at the end of the 18th century already outnumbered the peasants who held land. For a member of this lower class there was virtually no hope of ever owning land, not only because land rarely changed hands but also because the peasant farmers intermarried within their own group, thus excluding newcomers. The more recognition there was of the different strata within the village, the more members of each stratum tended to marry only among themselves. Legal titles, titles to property, fixed assets and wealth were thus continually brought closer together, while for the lower social groups, access to both property and professional training was made impossible or at least incredibly difficult.

Important branches of industrial production were mainly carried on in the country, since that was where the vast majority of people lived. Here, not only agricultural but also textile production exceeded the demand of the local population; the surplus went to the towns and from there into the continental trade streams and overseas. We can fully agree with Joan Thirsk that, with the growing commercialization of the economy from the beginning of the modern era and in times of large population growth, the production of new commodities claimed a steadily increasing share of national economic resources. 'Pin-making, stocking knitting, lace-making, vegetable, hemp, flax and woad growing employed the poor on an unprecedented scale.' This list makes it clear that these were primarily consumer goods for day-to-day requirements, produced for the feeding and household needs of rural families and for the continental market. These were villagers for whom cottage industry was a full-time occupation, but for by far the majority it was a subsidiary source of income. This was particularly true of textile manufacture which, since the 16th century and especially in the 18th and at the beginning of the 19th, was the most important cottage industry. Many poor families occupied themselves with spinning and weaving wool and linen. But when the prices of wool yarn and linen fell by over 50 per cent in the 1820s, the textile cottage industry was doomed as a worthwhile sideline for the rural household, and in the course of the century was completely displaced by industrial production.

### Rural trades

As the division of labour between agriculture and industry became wider, specialized rural trades, requiring a certain mechanical aptitude and a special training, developed in the country areas. The blacksmiths, waggon-builders and wheelwrights, carpenters and joiners had established themselves very early. With the introduction of watermills and windmills, the majority of millers had settled in the country. Shippers and overseas merchants sometimes lived in coastal villages, but trade generally remained a privilege of the towns. Tailors, cobblers, tilers and barbers were to be found as independent tradesmen in the larger villages; less frequently, glaziers, coopers or village butchers, who practised their activities mostly as sidelines.

If local demand was large enough, the tradesman or artisan usually became a property owner of the village, and farming, if he did continue it, became a secondary occupation for him. The proportion of these independent tradesmen and artisans in the countryside by about 1800, allowing for differences in overall economic structure, can be reckoned as around 15 per cent of the rural population in the north-west and about 5 per cent in eastern Europe. A few of them, like the mill-owners, ship chandlers and brewers, even became fairly prosperous and, like the estate-owners, officials and clergy, rose to positions of dignity in their villages.

Though by 1800 they were in a minority, there were still many peasant families who drew their livelihoods exclusively or mainly from their holdings. This was particularly the case in Scandinavia and central Europe, where there was remarkable continuity of ownership in large- and medium-sized peasant farms from the Middle Ages right into the 20th century. On the other hand, the changeover to a money economy and the expansion of market-linked production did lead to new patterns of landownership and tended towards a concentration of land holdings. Cereal growing and sheep farming in particular were more efficient if operated on a larger scale. With bigger profits, large-scale farmers were in a position to increase their land holdings; so, too, were the nobility, the church, state and ecclesiastical institutions and the well capitalized urban bourgeoisie. The process can be observed most clearly in north-west Europe, where there were the least restrictions on transfers of land. From the end of the Middle Ages, the number of large estates increased, first in England and the North Sea coastal area and then generally in western and southern Europe. As we have already observed, a large rise in the rural lower classes occurred at the same time, and it was they who provided the labour force for the expansion of large-scale agriculture. This is a characteristic effect of the growing influx of capital and the increasing adaptation to a money and market economy in western European agriculture which has been taking place since the beginning of modern times.

In eastern Europe, unlike the west, peasants often held their land at the will of their lord, who could take it from them at any time and add it to their own demesne.

*The estates of society, a woodcut attributed to Dürer, about 1526: the peasant, the urban artisan and the nobility.*

The ownership of land must be regarded as the most important criterion of social differentiation in pre-industrial times; between 1500 and 1800 there developed a concentration of landownership in the hands of the nobility and the capitalist upper class. Among the peasantry there was a shift from the large- and medium-sized peasant farms to smallholdings, to secondary rural trades and to the landless and propertyless rural lower classes.

### The bourgeoisie

Like the rural population, the town dwellers were characterized by strongly marked distinctions in respect of wealth and property, but more important than either in determining a family's status was profession. This was itself, of course, connected with the idea of property. In pre-industrial times, a man's prosperity came preponderantly from earnings at work; only working activity enabled families to acquire property and wealth. According to the earning prospects that they offered, professions were arranged in a certain generally recognized hierarchy, and this – not simply their actual wealth – was the basis of the esteem enjoyed by individuals and families, as it still is.

In their earliest charters, towns were invariably granted the right to hold markets and their inhabitants the freedom to engage in commerce and industry. Rival trades were not permitted within the town precincts. In eastern Europe, under the dominant influence of the rulers as well as of the nobility and of the wealthy merchant towns, this remained generally the case until well into the 19th century. As we have already shown, in the rest of Europe proper, village trades engaged in making agricultural implements, and tools had already established themselves in the Middle Ages; in the same way, cottage industries using locally produced raw materials were very widespread in the countryside as sidelines. However, in general, the towns remained the centre of commercial exchange and industrial production until the establishment of liberal free trade in the 19th century.

The master's scroll and the possession of civic rights were both necessary for the practice of an independent bourgeois occupation. Civic rights and guild membership presupposed a certain level of wealth. At a lower level, commerce and industry (and also government institutions) needed workers who, without acquiring full civic rights, still had a definite place in the community. Since civic rights included independence and house-ownership, these less privileged town dwellers consisted almost exclusively of tenants and lodgers, who were legally as well as socially distinguished from the propertied bourgeoisie. In the documentary sources, which are based ultimately on tax returns, a differentiation was accordingly made between actual wealth and earnings. In this way, almost all urban households were assessed. Between the 16th and 18th centuries, around 10 to 12 per cent of urban households had no tangible

assets and so were not liable to urban taxes. Most widows' households fell into this category; they tried to earn a living through domestic services such as mending, sewing or washing and if that failed were dependent on alms or even on begging. Taking all such cases into account, one arrives at the conclusion that between $\frac{2}{5}$ and $\frac{1}{2}$ of the urban households should be included among the urban poor.

At the opposite end of the scale was the merchant community. The leading merchants and cloth dealers built up considerable profits and capital assets through long-distance trade, and, on the basis of this wealth, a great number of them acquired access to other lucrative sources of profit both within the towns and outside them. These men gained the esteem of their fellow citizens. They were entrusted with the highest civic offices. Often this involved depositing sureties, and if – as commonly happened – the town found itself unable to repay these capital sums, a civic office could become the hereditable privilege of a particular family. The family could then go on to buy a patent of nobility and acquire a coat of arms, which in turn led to further privileges. By such processes were the ranks of the old nobility swelled. The only other way of rising on the social hierarchy was to be a graduate of a university, and for these men the paths of advancement were the church and the professions. They were the clergymen, doctors and lawyers who filled the highest positions in the civil, ecclesiastical and civic administration, and in the courts of justice. Together with the patricians and the merchants, they formed the class of civic dignitaries who represented the town and the citizens politically. On the whole, their number remained small and can be reckoned as 3 to 5 per cent of the urban population.

In the capital, the royal household occupied a special position. The princely court itself, together with the leading representatives of state, church and society, constituted a closed circle. In the social hierarchy they stood above the urban community and also beyond the city's jurisdiction. Because they needed large numbers of servants and a plentiful supply of valuable products, they had a considerable and widespread effect on the entire population of the town and the surrounding countryside. The same is true of the episcopal cities and to a certain extent also of the subordinate centres of civil administration.

The great growth of population at the beginning of the modern period coincided, as we have seen, with a sharp rise in industrial production. The urban artisans, already organized into guilds, became, along with the merchants, the political and social activists in most towns. The artisans rose to become the most powerful social group and formed the urban middle class. By about 1800, $\frac{2}{5}$ to $\frac{3}{4}$ of the urban families belonged to this stratum of town society. It included a wide range of both service occupations and handicraft trades – from bookbinders, barbers, cobblers, innkeepers and carriers to clerks, letter-writers, small dealers and minor officials.

Their social position was more or less on a level with that of a master craftsman working alone or with only a few assistants. Their houses were simple and they lived on a relatively monotonous diet. The trades were organized on a small scale. One-man occupations were most common. They lived with their families and worked in their own houses; but the number of those who rented was proportionately larger in big towns than in small ones.

In the towns of the pre-industrial period, the position of the wood and metal trades (joiners, blacksmiths, locksmiths) and of the building and food trades (masons, carpenters, butchers and bakers) was relatively favourable and secure, with plenty of work. Masters invariably employed professional assistants – journeymen and apprentices – and often had several dependent workers. In general this applied to the trades requiring a special training, such as coopers, carriers, dyers, tanners and surgeons. In such households, the wife's duties were frequently lightened by the employment of a maid. Tradesmen who counted in the upper middle rank, those serving the carriage trade, or men like book-binders and goldsmiths, confectioners, butchers, inn-keepers and brewers, normally employed both skilled assistants and domestic servants, leading to more turn-over and extra income. With the increase in property and wealth, it was these families that rose in general esteem. Their way of life was not all that different from that of families in the higher public services or the academic professions, such as doctors, pharmacists, lawyers and professors. A step upward into the class above them was quite possible at this level.

While the proportion of the middle class in the towns of Europe remained relatively constant from the ending of the Middle Ages to the beginning of the industrial era, its internal structure was changing. The number of families who belonged to the petty bourgeoisie or who lived in rented lodgings rose much more sharply than the number of well-to-do families. By about 1800, dependent workers and servants who lived in their masters' households as journeymen and apprentices, clerks and servants, boys and maids were making up roughly one-fifth of the inhabitants in medium-sized and larger towns.

By the end of the 18th century these urban lower classes were often unable to put aside any savings towards the building of their own houses or earn enough to support a family. The cost of food was the yardstick in determining a living wage. We can see every class taking what measures it could to ensure that its living standard did not fall any lower. Master artisans and tradesmen jealously restricted entrance into their guilds. Peasants increasingly adopted the practice of leaving their farms to a single heir. The remaining children had either to marry into property, to renounce marriage or to expect a life of poverty and misery for themselves and their families. In lean years they could lose the means and even the will to survive. The

phenomenon which occurred in almost every country in western Europe in the 17th century, and which Roger Mols has called 'the European marriage problem', can be related primarily to man's anxiety for his daily bread. 'This', he writes, 'was the effect of a simultaneous in-crease in the average age at marriage and a reduction in the matrimonial frequency of each age group. Every-where else in the world and at other periods in history, four-fifths of the girls were married before they were twenty-five and the rest almost all ended by finding a husband. In the 17th century, western Europe began to be unique in this respect: between 10 and 15 per cent of girls remained permanently unmarried, and among those who got married, almost half did so after twenty-five years of age.'

## Living standards, 1500–1900

With the increase in population and the continued inefficiency in agricultural production, food margins for the people of Europe had narrowed. Especially in the period of transition to the industrial era – from the end of the 18th century until beyond the middle of the 19th – the living standards for the overwhelming majority of the population in every European country were grim. In order to assess the prosperity or other-wise of a population, we must take some account of the national resources – their level, their sources and the way they were utilized. This is an excellent indicator both for the state of a country's economic development and for living standards at a particular time. In under-standing the individual's economic position, it is above

*In the years before the French Revolution poverty became particularly severe, and many members of the rural population were reduced to beggary. This engraving by J. J. Boissieu was made in 1780.*

all the per capita income which is important: this defines not only the level of his personal expenditure relative to the norm but also provides the background for his expectations. For the period before detailed statistics are available (i.e. before the mid-19th century) this can only be done very approximately. All we can do is to compare what we know of wages with what we know of prices.

On this basis, it is agreed that a general improvement in living standards prevailed from the end of the 18th to the end of the 19th century, in the emerging industrial countries, particularly in England.

E. J. Hobsbaum, however, has strongly contested this price–wage comparison, because we possess no comparable data on the incomes of different population groups and can make no valid assertions concerning the variations in real incomes of different times and different places. Moreover, our knowledge is insufficient regarding both the chronic underemployment of the working population in the pre-industrial era and the cyclical unemployment of industrial workers in the 19th century. And really meaningful statements about the standard of living are only possible if other consumption patterns are taken into account – particularly expenditure on non-basic foodstuffs. But research up to now is still so scanty that our knowledge concerning regional differences and the development of consumption at different periods adds very little to the bare record of incomes. After the middle of the 19th century, the composition of private expenditure can be used as the most important indicator of living standards. Some examples of this generally little-noticed line of research are brought together in Table 4.

The representation of 19th-century working-class and bourgeois families in these figures for domestic expenditure is very limited: at best they are estimates and the selection is arbitrary. However, the summary indicates – better than a detailed description – definite trends of development in the pre-industrial period and in the Industrial Revolution. From the comparison of different periods, it appears that in Europe in the late Middle Ages and the Renaissance, relatively good living conditions predominated, compared with the periods before and after, the High Middle Ages and the pre-industrial era (mid-16th to mid-19th century). In the 14th to the 15th century, middle-class European households, e.g. master craftsmen, agricultural family farmers, skilled urban workers, spent about $\frac{3}{5}$ to $\frac{2}{3}$ of their earnings on food, of which meat was still a relatively large component. Living standards then deteriorated, reaching a low point around 1600; then came a certain improvement between 1660 and 1740; but by 1800 such a household had to spend almost $\frac{4}{5}$ of its earnings on food and had to make do more and more with a vegetable diet and with bread. The comparison of the household budgets of urban workers around 1500 in Augsburg with the expenditure pattern around 1600 in Antwerp and around 1800 in Berlin (in Table 5) makes these connections clear. Ernst Engel, working from the records of Belgian working families, drew up a scale of requirements in order of priority: according to him, food came first, then clothing, and then housing. For any remaining needs, such as heat and light, tools and equipment for work and for the household, education, health, recreation and personal services, only scanty means were available to the majority of the population.

Table 4  Private consumer spending in Europe, expressed in three different comparisons: first between urban workers in four large cities, from 1600 to 1800; second between classes, 1800 and 1850; and third between England and Germany, 1800–1913. Figures are percentages of the household budget.

| | EUROPEAN TOWNS | | | | EUROPE | | | | EUROPEAN COUNTRIES | | | |
|---|---|---|---|---|---|---|---|---|---|---|---|---|
| | 1500 | 1600 | c.1800 | | 1800 | | 1850 | | 1800 | 1850–60 | 1900–13 | 1900–13 |
| | Augsburg | Antwerp | Paris | Berlin | Workers | Middle-class | Country-population | Town-population | Prussia | Germany | | England |
| | | Urban workers | | | | | | | | | | |
| Bread and cereal products | 35 | 49 | 34 | 46 | 48 | 34 | 40 | 32 | 37 | 10 | 8 | 7 |
| Vegetable products | 6 | 7 | 6 | 12 | 10 | 9 | 12 | 12 | 10 | 9 | 8 | 6 |
| Animal products (meat) | 24 | 18 | 21 | 15 | 14 | 17 | 12 | 15 | 16 | 23 | 21 | 26 |
| Drink and luxuries | 5 | 4 | 5 | 2 | 4 | 4 | 6 | 6 | 9 | 17 | 15 | 7 |
| Total food | 70 | 78 | 66 | 75 | 76 | 64 | 70 | 65 | 72 | 59 | 52 | 46 |
| Clothing | 12 | 10 | 16 | 12 | 12 | 14 | 14 | 12 | 14 | 12 | 15 | 14 |
| Housing | 12 | 11 | 15 | 10 | 10 | 13 | 12 | 15 | 11 | 16 | 21 | 18 |
| Other | 6 | 1 | 3 | 3 | 2 | 9 | 4 | 8 | 3 | 13 | 12 | 14 |

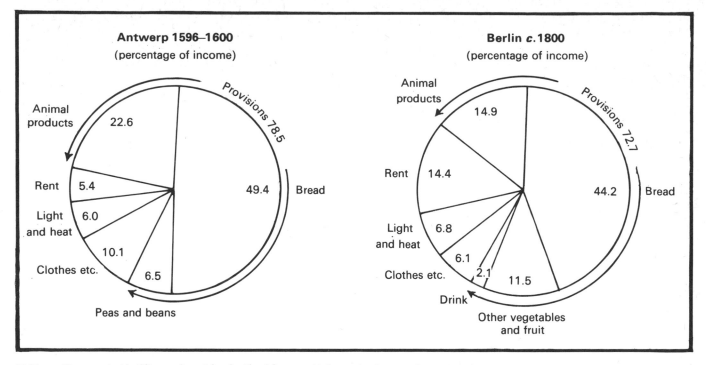

Animal products 22.6

Provisions 78.5

Rent 5.4

Light and heat 6.0

49.4 Bread

Clothes etc. 10.1

6.5

Peas and beans

Animal products 14.9

Provisions 72.7

Rent 14.4

Light and heat 6.8

44.2 Bread

Clothes etc. 6.1

2.1

Drink

11.5

Other vegetables and fruit

*Table 5   How a typical building worker with a family of five spent his income in Antwerp about 1600 and in Berlin about 1800. Figures are percentages of total income.*

Engel drew the logical conclusion, which is as valid for today as it is for the past: the poorer the family, the greater the proportion of income spent on food.

The great preoccupation of the impoverished mass of the European population in the pre-industrial period was thus to get enough food to eat, and for most of them this meant primarily bread, plus whatever vegetables were available. It is very difficult for us to imagine the lives of ordinary men and women during these centuries because there are so few hard facts to go on. One possible line of research is the so called 'corn wage', the calculation of the buying power of wages in terms of the price of cereals at any given time. This approach seems justified because during the pre-industrial period expenditure on cereals of one sort or another accounted for around 40 to 50 per cent of the earnings of families of workers, small tradesmen and rural householders. Moreover, the records of corn prices and day wages of urban workers are the fullest in all European archives and most easily interpreted; they are also comparable over longer periods and for different countries. We may also assume that the quality of bread cereals did not vary significantly.

The wage earners that we shall examine most closely are the building journeymen. These men, the masons and carpenters, were real wage labourers. They did not live in the master's household, as many other artisans did, and their services were paid for in cash. Most of them were married and so had to keep a family on their wages, unless their wives contributed to the family income by domestic or harvest work. Most of these artisans lived in villages, on account of the lower cost of living. Their place of work was usually in the towns where the greatest number of buildings and the most expensive – town houses, palaces, churches – were put up. In the country, house building was mostly the communal task of all the neighbours, with merely additional assistance from skilled building workers.

Judged by their earnings, the journeymen in the building trade belonged to the upper lower class, and their standard of living was, on the whole, similar to that of the lower middle class. But the pattern of their 'corn wages' from 1401 to 1500 and 1791 to 1850 as revealed by the documents shows very clearly the fall in real wages and the deterioration of living standards in Europe from the end of the Middle Ages to the middle of the 19th century. While in the 15th century a day's wage could buy 20–30 kilos of bread, by the beginning of the industrial era it was no more than 8–12 kilos, and in the small towns often much less. The drop in real wages reached its lowest point around 1600. The subsequent slight recovery was reversed again in most towns between 1720 and 1740 and moved slowly into a decline in real incomes until the severe famine crises of 1816/17. It was industrialization alone that brought about the end of mass poverty. After the agricultural crises of the 1820s, grain lost its outstanding importance for the majority of the European population as the most important foodstuff of the pre-industrial period. In Table 4, this can be observed from the example of Germany.

In the 1790s expenditure on cereal products still took about 40 per cent of the average family's income; in the second half of the 19th century it was not more than 10 per cent. Altogether the proportion of income spent on food and drink fell in England and the remaining western European industrial countries from about 70 per cent to less than 50 per cent within half a century.

Very little attention has been given until now to social differences in standards of living, so that only generalized observations are possible. As we have seen, in the households of the urban and rural lower classes, three-quarters and more of the total income was spent on food. But in individual cases we can never be certain whether the family income was mainly from earnings or from other resources, for instance a garden or allotment or rented land. The degree of self-sufficiency was clearly higher in the country than in the town and in eastern Europe again higher than in the west. In most of the small villages and the sparsely settled areas of eastern Europe, there was in fact a self-sufficient class below the peasant farmers: men who made their living, given the distinctly agrarian character of those extensive regions, mainly in agricultural or related activities and were thus largely supplied by natural resources. It was different in western Europe. Here, half the rural population no longer had any land to speak of and lived mainly by what they could earn at work. The assistance of wife and children was normal, as in peasant family undertakings. The earning power of the husband alone was not sufficient for the upkeep of a family; this was equally true for the families of urban lower classes. So, at the end of the 18th and the beginning of the 19th century, around half the population of Europe existed on a marginal living wage. A further third were slightly better off but could still barely support a frugal standard of living. Included here are the simple artisans, carrying on their trades by themselves, and a great number of small and middling peasants whose surpluses were largely creamed off by their overlords. This applies also to a certain extent to the large number of rural lease-holders in the north-west (where surpluses went on high rents), and still more to the peasant farmers of eastern Europe and the Balkans who still – some even well into the 20th century – were in a marked personal dependence on their landlords. West of the Elbe, however, some peasants were in a better position. In the favourable periods of the 16th and 18th centuries, provided they cultivated sufficient land with secure and favourable rights of occupancy, and with the help of their extended families and other labourers, they were able to produce surpluses that gave them a degree of material prosperity. But, on the whole, the social position both of the rural population and of the urban workers remained oppressed until the middle of the 19th century, as appears in the comparison in Table 4

between the household budgets of workers and bourgeois, around 1800, and between town and country around 1850. From this, one can also conclude that in the pre-industrial period a certain concentration of prosperous families was to be found in the towns; they gained their income mainly from commerce, money transactions and large-scale industrial production. These were the patricians, the merchants, the entrepreneurs, the bankers, the proprietors of large trade and service undertakings and the best inns, and not least the academics and the officials in the leading positions of civic, ecclesiastical and communal institutions. These more happily situated upper middle classes comprised about one-fifth of the town dwellers, and around 1800 accounted for up to three-quarters of private incomes. They needed to spend only a small part of their incomes on food and to retrench to only a small degree in the famine years. In their spaciously furnished town houses they invariably employed servants and emulated the luxury of the aristocracy with their sumptuous life-style. In the 18th century they added to the comfort of their easy lives by travelling in closed coaches, which from the 17th century increasingly replaced saddle-horses in noble and upper-middle-class households. These were used not only on business journeys but also for recreation and educational tours. Opportunities in these directions improved in the 17th and 18th centuries through the spread of cheap books and the founding of grammar schools, which supplemented the religious and classical schools. Sons of middle-class families went to the universities in increasing numbers, along with the sons of the nobility.

From the Renaissance onward, with the growing stratification of professional and family life in the towns and the rising demand for material needs, it was mainly the urban upper class who were the bearers of cultural change. This is strikingly conveyed in the appearance of the tall, spacious, richly decorated houses in the old towns, which became the political, economic and cultural centres of urban life. With the regular holding of corn, cattle and food markets, the surrounding country was also brought into the circle of the town's life and economy.

But, as we have noted in tracing the 'corn wage' graph, there was also a falling-off in living standards among the poorer classes, declining more steeply from north-west to south-east. In the still agrarian east the improvements described above did not take place, and the great mass of the rural population and the petty bourgeoisie existed on a coarse and monotonous diet, dressed in simple clothing, still largely home-made, and lived in primitive wooden houses with only a few rooms. The farmers and the urban professional middle class had a life-style which was only slightly different from that of the remainder of the subject population. Their diet was somewhat more varied: meat, fruit and vegetables appeared more often on their tables and more imported goods and hand-made and manufactured articles were to be found in their households – imported beer, coffee, chairs and furniture, handkerchiefs and bed-linen, spoons, knives and perhaps even forks, all of which came into widespread use in Europe from the 18th to the 19th century, and finally cups, plates and bowls. The small group of noble families and the urban upper classes in the cities of eastern Europe, on the other hand, followed a bourgeois life-style modelled on that of western Europe – particularly the French and the Dutch. These differences in private expenditure in the various parts of Europe cannot be presented statistically, but they can be illustrated by a brief description of the most important aspects of living – particularly of diet – in the different regions.

## Daily bread

The diet of the European population at the beginning of modern times can generally be described as simple and nourishing: it consisted chiefly of the natural products of the countryside. The population was still relatively undifferentiated and on the whole lived poorly. However, it is not easy to find records of the different types of food and how they were consumed; research so far has been concerned almost entirely with production. Thus we have relatively good information about the separate components of the diet, but little about the preparation of dishes and the meals themselves. One can make the general observation that throughout the Middle Ages until into the 17th century, they showed a strong local flavour. Whatever was cultivated in the immediate neighbourhood or could be found in the woods and fields was prepared in the kitchen. The cost of food only began to play a more important part when, in the 16th century, transport was developed for bulk supplies, which could be economically shipped over long distances on the rivers and the newly dug canals or by sea. The most economical basic food in respect of nutritional content – and given the European soil and weather conditions – was grain.

Corn, prepared in various ways, formed an essential component of all diets up to the time of industrialization, using the word corn to mean bread cereals of all kinds in different environments. In the moderately warm climatic zone of the old Roman Empire – up to the Danube in the north – it was wheat (spelt or German wheat). In the rest of western Europe, as in central and eastern Europe, there was also rye. But in the north, with its short farming season, spring wheat – especially barley mixed with oats – was the main bread cereal. These cereals were supplemented in the south by the cultivation of rice, which spread from the 15th and 16th centuries mainly through Sicily to Italy. Rice was grown in flooded fields in southern Italy and when, on account of malaria, its cultivation was forbidden in the 17th century, it was adopted in the north as an addition to the diet. Buckwheat, an immigrant from the plains of Asia, spread to southern Europe in the 16th century and then, especially on bare stretches of sandy soil and moorland, to Belgium and France. Here, until the introduction of artificial fertilizers, it formed an important supplement to the inferior yields of rye and served generally as the diet of the rural poor. From the end of the 18th century, a similar role was played by the potato, introduced from the highlands of Chile two hundred years previously, and, in Italy and the Balkans, by maize, introduced by the Spanish from Mexico and Peru.

Bread dominated the diet of ordinary men and women. From current calculations of yields, we can estimate that, in the transition period from the Middle Ages to modern times, 200–250 kilos of bread and cereal products were consumed yearly per capita in Europe. This amount is hardly conceivable to us today, when in western Europe the figure is only 80–100 kilos. Yet, with the deterioration of incomes and the purchasing power of wages it increased further to around 300 kilos from the 16th to the 19th century. The flour mixed with water, or sometimes with whey or milk and with salt added, was mainly baked into bread. In the towns, the number of bakers with their assistants – journeymen and apprentices – grew proportionately to the population. In the country, on the other hand, most of the peasant farmers had a baking oven and in the villages there was a communal bakery, at the disposal of all members of the community. Not all the flour went into bread-making. It was also used for thickening milk, soups and vegetables and, when there were no facilities for baking, it was eaten as gruel or made into noodles or flat cakes or pancakes. Cereals in one form or another were supplemented during the week with vegetables, fruit and other produce of the woods and gardens and with milk products, eggs and animal fats, less often with fish and meat. Fish, dried and pickled in barrels, was Lenten fare in Catholic Europe, but for the rest of pre-industrial Europe it appeared only rarely on the ordinary man's table. Meat, freshly slaughtered or heavily salted or smoked for keeping, was usually cooked in the stock-pot, which hung almost permanently over the open fireplace, and was eaten with bread. It was roasted only on special occasions, as the term 'Sunday roast' reminds us.

In general, meat consumption shows a markedly retrograde trend from the late Middle Ages up to the beginning of the 19th century. Estimates of around 60–100 kilos of meat per capita in 15th-century Europe are probably not excessive. The lower figure represents roughly the consumption in the country, while a town dweller's daily share of meat and meat products was around 300 grams. In the summer, the town's requirements of fresh meat could easily be met from large individual livestock holdings and from the surrounding country. On the weekly market days, young pigs and calves, lambs and sheep, game and especially poultry were offered and sold. But for winter provision, the animals – pigs, sheep, cattle – were driven into the city from greater distances. In the autumn markets, it was

*Sheep and cattle in the market of Eastcheap, London, 1598. The opposite side of the street is lined with butchers' shops.*

principally beef cattle that were bought. The purchasers were butchers, well-to-do families and households connected with large commercial undertakings, who bought for their own needs and looked after their own provisioning. Although meat production expanded further in the 16th century, in the form of increasingly specialized animal husbandry, supply could no longer keep pace with population growth; in the whole inland region of central and western Europe, livestock farming was considerably restricted by the expansion of agriculture. This was particularly true of meat production, whereas dairy farms tended to concentrate around the towns, since milk, butter and cheese had a relatively short storage life and were quickly sold in the markets.

In the 16th century, following the changed relation of supply and demand, the price of cattle and meat rose sharply. For the majority of the rural and urban lower classes, the purchase of meat and meat products became virtually impossible. At the end of the 16th century, the average annual meat consumption in Europe had fallen to about 25 kilos per capita. The same process repeated itself in the 18th century, so that around 1800 most Europeans could afford only 14–16 kilos a year. Meat consumption only recovered in the second half of the 19th century, with the rise of per capita income in the developing industrial countries of Europe, from around 20–25 kilos in 1850 to 40–50 kilos and over in the decade before the First World War.

The transition to a very unbalanced vegetable and cereal diet, and particularly the fall in the per capita consumption of meat between 1500 and 1800, confirms,

more powerfully than anything else, the fall in living standards. When, at the end of the 18th century, the steeply rising price of bread produced a crisis in the food supply, it was partly replaced by the potato. Although, from the nutritional and physiological point of view, the potato contains – per unit of weight – only a quarter of the nutrients in cereals, its bulk yield is over ten times greater; it thus gives two or three times the nutrient yield per unit of area cultivated. The potato therefore spread widely and was grown in the gardens of the landless town dwellers, smallholders and agricultural workers. It gained – and retained – the reputation of being the poor man's food, although there has always been an important place for it in the meals of the well-to-do. No other foodstuff in Europe has risen so rapidly in importance as the potato in the 19th century. In England, the average per capital annual consumption between 1795 and 1838 rose from around 60 to 100 kilos and, with certain fluctuations, remained at this level until the end of the century. For Germany, an increase from 40 to 200 kilos has been estimated in the course of the century. In the Mediterranean area, it never attained this importance; the annual per capita consumption can hardly have exceeded 30 kilos. Without question, the rapid spread of the potato helped significantly to alleviate the hunger that so sorely beset the lower classes. But in the last great European famine of 1846–47, caused by extremely adverse weather conditions, the failure of the potato harvest had effects far worse than the failure of the corn harvest; the latter shortfall could be relatively economically and rapidly made up from overseas, thanks to the longer storage life of corn and the ease by which it could be transported on the expanding traffic network of steamer and railway. In Ireland, where society was typified by the peasant smallholder living almost entirely on potatoes, the harvest failure had a more devastating effect. Of eight million rural inhabitants, one in eight is said to have been a victim of famine.

In the course of the 19th century the diet of the European population subsequently became more varied. If it was still relatively unbalanced and insufficient for a healthy life in the middle of the 19th century, industrialization in the second half of the century led to a gradual increase of per capita income and a noticeable improvement in the diet, even of the lower classes. Nutritional standards in the western industrial countries about 1900 can be described as fully adequate.

While the discrepancies grew less between the country and the town, which at this time absorbed a large influx of poor people, those between western and central Europe were becoming more marked. We gather from traveller's accounts that in eastern Europe people ate more groats and millet gruel than bread. In the only available cooking-pot, they cooked the same ever-recurring diet: barley and oats, peas and beans with different sorts of vegetables, particularly kale and turnip, which were also dried and stored for winter provisions. Variety was provided only by different seasonings – onions, herbs, fats and oil. On the occasional feast-days, this often indescribable stew might be strengthened by the addition of pickled meat. On major festivals, sheep, pigs and even oxen were roasted on the spit. The huge capacity of generally poorly fed pre-industrial people for meat, puddings, brandy or other alcoholic drink at these festivities, usually lasting several days, is legendary. In this, the inhabitants of eastern Europe around 1900 exhibited the same behaviour patterns that existed in Europe in the 17th and 18th centuries. The theologian, Sebastian Munster from Basle, in his *Kosmographia Universalis*, has vividly described this ill balanced and scanty diet. He is referring to the population of Switzerland and southern Germany, but it could apply to the whole of Europe: 'Their food is black rye bread, oat-gruel or cooked peas and beans: water and whey almost their only drink.' The meals on the bare heights of the Massif Central were even more meagre; according to La Bruyere, writing in the late 17th century, black bread and turnips were mainly eaten here and on week days there was only water to drink. In contrast, the luxurious meals on the tables of the ruling nobles and the great merchants appear rich and excessive. The food of the bourgeois in the towns presents a frugal mean between the two.

The vital need for fluids was partly met by the soups. The poorer households had to make do with water, from rain, springs or wells. It was kept in large casks or buckets, near which hung the communal scoop. As unboiled water conjured up the danger of diseases, milk remained a usual drink for the peasants of central, northern and eastern Europe until the 19th century, and, with water, served as the most important adjunct to the soups. Only the better-off people in town and country satisfied their daily fluid requirements with beer, which, for storage and taste, was strongly hopped. The less well-off families had to make do with small beer. From the 17th century, spirits became increasingly popular; it served not as a thirst-quencher but as an energizer for hard physical work; it finally became the most widespread and economical luxury of the poorer people, at male social gatherings and on festive occasions. In the warmer countries of the south, wine could be either a luxury or an everyday drink. Good wines were increasingly exported and were drunk throughout Europe at the tables of wealthy and noble families.

Durable items, rather than food, provide a more obvious illustration of regional and social variations. Next to the daily sum spent on food, the largest shares of household outgoings were accounted for by clothing and housing. In the climatic conditions of northern Europe, these were equally indispensable for survival.

## Clothing

In pre-industrial times, clothing for everyday work was made from whatever raw materials were available, that is, mostly wool and linen. Both sheep's wool and vegetable fibres were still spun privately and were made up into knitted articles or cloth – caps, gloves, stockings, waistcoats, jackets, dresses, shawls and capes, and also covers and curtains for doors and windows. The surplus was sold either through itinerant dealers or at own markets and fairs. While the weaving of linen yarn remained largely a rural occupation, until it was superseded by industrial mass-production, the making of woollen cloth since the Middle Ages had been concentrated in the towns, which in addition were importing and preparing a new raw material from the Orient: cotton. The thread thus made available was 'put out' to cottage workers to be woven into cloth on their own looms, so that the rural textile industry received a considerable boost. But in the 18th century, factory mass-production began to compete with the hand looms, and in the 19th century entirely replaced them.

The making-up of cloth into articles of clothing – suits of clothes and dresses – was undertaken by the tailors, who had multiplied in the towns since the Middle Ages as independent craftsmen. In most towns the tailors' guild was among the oldest, along with the guilds of merchants, cloth-makers and food tradesmen. Dresses, breeches, smocks, cloaks and capes were replacing the roughly prepared skins and furs that had formerly served as protection against the inclemency of the weather, though in eastern Europe and the remote rural areas these remained everyday wear much longer than in the west. In this respect, as in so many others, the towns were the pioneers of cultural progress;

buckles, leather belts and buttons took the place of the old strings and cloth-bands to fasten clothing. Stockings and shoes were coming into fashion instead of foot-wrappings and wooden clogs. Leather shoes were already widely worn in the country in the 18th century, when the peasant farmers were making more profit, though they only became common as everyday wear in the 19th century. It was also customary in those times to give leather boots to the servants employed in farmers' and tradesmens' households, with cotton shirts for the men and an apron or bonnet for the women, and perhaps a comb as a present under the Christmas tree.

In general, the higher the family income, the greater the outlay on clothing. In the higher social classes there was a definite extravagance in the women's dresses and the men's outer garments. But ever since the Middle Ages, this form of display had been liable to restrictions under civic or regal ordinances. The import of ready-made articles was deliberately limited for economic reasons, especially for the lower and middle classes. Ceremonial dress thus became the status symbol of the higher ranks of society. Thanks to the long-lasting quality of textiles, this abundant and varied display of clothing can still be admired in our museums.

### Housing

The large population increases in the 16th century and again from the 18th century onward stimulated the building trade as well as the rest of the economy. It was the established nobility and the manufacturers and tradesmen belonging to the guilds who were able to turn this to the greatest advantage and increase their wealth. The gap widened between rich and poor, between those with property and those without, and the new class distinctions found expression above all in buildings. Around the centre of the town – the town hall and the market place – were concentrated the richly decorated, multi-storeyed dwelling and business houses of the wealthy citizens and merchant princes. Outside this commercial and residential centre were the still well appointed houses of the bourgeois and finally, on the periphery of the town walls, the houses and cottages of the remaining citizens.

By the Industrial Revolution, house building could no longer keep pace with the growth of the urban population and the number of tenants and lodgers began to increase out of all proportion. The wealthy house-owners of the upper classes rarely let any part of their property to families of strangers; these mainly found accommodation in the houses of the middle classes. If the tenant practised a profession and could dispose of a relatively assured salary, he and his family might occupy a whole floor, or two floors. Single and poor people were put up in single rooms; the servants lived in the attic rooms – and often several to a room. Non-citizens and their families and people without regular jobs were not allowed into the town's residential

area, which was sometimes enclosed by fortified walls. Day labourers and unskilled workers, who were looking for occasional work in the town and were usually dependent on it, put up outside the town limits in sheds, wooden shacks and other makeshift lodgings. With the heavy increase in population, these extra-mural living quarters gradually turned into the slums of the industrial era. It was only in the urbanization process, towards the end of the 19th century, that the tenement and finally the large block of flats became the most usual type of urban housing. The result was not only a separation between work place and dwelling place but also a far-reaching and clear differentiation of settlement patterns that is generally familiar to us today.

Wood, clay, straw, stone and natural slabs were replaced increasingly by bricks, mortar and concrete. In town buildings the differentiation of spaces intended for different purposes became more clear-cut. Separate rooms were set aside for working, living and sleeping: the kitchen in particular was the housewife's domain. A typical house of the bourgeois middle class would consist of a living-room, a bedroom and the kitchen. A successful craftsman's house would also have at least one workroom, although for many the living-room also served as the work place. Further rooms were desirable for the accommodation of children and workmen, who had to sleep several to one room and often to one bed. The families of the lower classes often had to be content with one room as a dwelling or even to share it with another family.

The housing conditions of the rural population were invariably cramped. We can now gain an excellent idea about their houses through 'open air museums', where types of dwellings from different parts of the country are brought together and rebuilt. Like the medieval 'hall-house', the rural cottage often consisted even in the 17th to 18th century of only one room. The stalls and barns (that is, rooms needed for the peasant's work) were often joined to it, though the farm might also consist of several buildings for different uses. Furnishing was usually scanty. In one-room dwellings, benches were grouped round the open fireplace and the single table: the benches were not only for sitting on, but served originally for sleeping as well. Later, separate sleeping areas were usually designated – at least for the husband and wife and the younger children. As farmers' standards of living rose, the same separation of rooms according to function took place in the country as in the town, though the fireplace usually remained the focal point of the household. When beds became the norm, the benches around the walls were displaced and their number diminished. The older children and the servants still slept in spaces – sub-divided by wooden battens in the larger farms – above the stalls. Mattresses consisted of heaped-up straw or dried foliage with cloths spread on top. As bedcovers, more cloths, rarely featherbeds; these too, for the broad mass of the population, only arrived with industrialization. At mealtimes, the whole household gathered around the table, in the middle of which usually stood a soup or vegetable pot. Because by this time there were not enough benches – and no chairs – the children took their meals standing up. In most houses until the 19th century, people ate from a bowl with a wooden spoon; there were wooden boards for portions of bread, and a knife – often only a communal one – for the occasional meat.

The result of the increasing economic division of labour, from the end of the Middle Ages up to about 1800, was thus an increasing social stratification. This had a marked and obvious effect on the appearance of towns, but it made very little difference to the living conditions, the food and the clothing of the great mass of the population, who still lived in the country. True, there were changes and innovations. Sugar, coffee and tea, white bread instead of millet and oat gruel, cotton frocks and underclothes, bedsheets instead of coarse linen cloth, were indeed becoming increasingly widespread, but such things only became generally established in the second half of the 19th century. In the transition period, the wretchedness of the lower classes actually grew worse. The further rise in numbers of this class, which could not afford any professional training and so was paid the lowest wages, led to mass poverty, the overriding social problem of the 19th century.

### Mass poverty in Europe in modern times

Ever since Marx, it has been customary to attribute the mass pauperization of whole strata of the population in the 19th century to industrialization. To the historian this must seem an oversimplification. Mass poverty goes back to the social order of feudal times. Already in the Middle Ages there were symptomatic and long-lasting phases of such poverty. The movement of real wage-rates provides an impressive indicator for this phenomenon, which has been abundantly researched for the main German cities. It may be shown again comprehensively from the example of this movement in England, spread over five centuries.

In Table 6, the relation between poverty and population is clearly set out. In the late Middle Ages, real incomes had reached a position of stability; population was rising and towns were growing, but because of improved efficiency achieved by division of labour these increases were accompanied by increased production. At the end of the Middle Ages, the Black Death of 1348–50 and the subsequent recurrences of plague substantially reduced the European population – by about 40 per cent. Assets and the potential for production remained stable, so incomes improved, leading to an increased demand for industrial and for other non-basic consumer goods. Shortage of labour resulted in almost a doubling of real wage-rates. From this point on, however, population began to rise again without a corresponding improvement in efficiency, a process which operated markedly after 1520–30. The increasing self-realization of the individual led above all to a

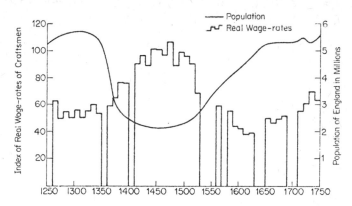

Table 6 Graph showing how the real wage-rates of craftsmen in England rose and fell in inverse proportion to the rise and fall of the population, from 1250 to 1750.

great concentration of power and capital and vigorous economic growth, but it was a growth that benefited only a minority of the population.

The development of production could not now keep pace with population increase. Prices rose steadily, so that people spoke in the 16th century of a price revolution. The purchasing power of wages and incomes diminished accordingly. The great mass of the population had to turn to cheap foodstuffs, and so was obliged to adopt an unbalanced diet of cereal and other vegetable products. This had further restrictive results; in a middle-class household in the mid-16th century, about 40 per cent of the family income was spent on bread and cereals and 20 per cent on products of animal origin; from the balance, the family had to find the cost of housing, what they needed in the way of textiles, household utensils and drink, and everything else: taxes, dues and savings for lean years.

Allowing for the devaluation of the currency, up to the end of the 16th century, real prices for foodstuffs in constant demand, such as bread, had more than doubled, and those of other foodstuffs had gone up by over 50 per cent. In contrast, wages rose by barely a half. These fluctuations in price and wage relationships meant that, with an unchanged level of food consumption, the percentage of income spent on bread went up from 40 per cent to over 60 per cent and the amount on remaining foodstuffs increased to 25 per cent. For all other requirements, barely 15 per cent remained. This was bound to lead to an obvious deterioration in living and food standards. With the increase in food prices, demand for other products fell. This was particularly noticeable in the textile industry, which represented, well into the industrial period, by far the largest non-agrarian branch of industry. The dependent and propertyless workers were again particularly badly hit by the recession, as their masters simply dismissed them when there was a drop in orders. With minor qualifications, the same applied to the remaining branches of industry and particularly to the textile cottage industry, for whose products there was no longer a market. Poverty and begging increased in a frightening way.

After a certain degree of recovery in the middle of the 17th century, to around 1740, when population growth began to slow down, this process of recession repeated itself in the second half of the 18th century and again in the 19th century after the Napoleonic Wars. With bad harvests, these ill effects were catastrophically intensified; famines and simultaneous epidemics caused the death-rate to shoot upwards.

Wilhelm Abel has convincingly reduced these variations between the needs of the consumer and the availability of goods to a pattern, and related them to economic theory. According to him, the economy of the pre-industrial era only succeeded to a very small extent in satisfying the constantly rising demand that resulted from the great growth of the population. The prices of everyday requirements, subject to constant demand, therefore rose more steeply than those of all other products: they were exceeded only by land prices and fees paid for the use of land – i.e. ground-rents. The family income had to be spent mainly on food, in order for them to get enough to eat. The prices of trade and industrial products thus always lagged behind the prices of cereals. The wages of workers who were solely dependent on their work were quite inadequate in pre-industrial times.

The first half of the 19th century saw a reversal. Harvest failures were no longer a crucial factor. Agriculture lost its function as wage-setter and price-regulator in the national economy. The lead was taken over by industry, whose production was increasingly concentrated in large-scale undertakings. With technical progress and the development of machinery, productivity of labour could be considerably increased, and from the middle of the 19th century the broad mass of the working population was involved in this increase. This emerges strikingly in the pattern of wage-rates in the last thirty years of the 19th century. The improvement in the purchasing power of wages had resulted in a restructuring of demand in the direction of more expensive goods. Thus the prices for animal products rose much more steeply than the prices for cereals. Not only the increases in real wage-rates but, to a far greater extent, the cheapening of industrial products as a result of mass-production were the decisive factors in the increased demand for these products. A rise in real income led to an improvement in the living standards of the whole population.

During the 20th century, in comparison with earlier times and with underdeveloped agrarian countries today, the living conditions of most Europeans can only be described as prosperous. Not that poverty and want have been abolished, but they are exceptions to the general rule. Generally speaking, too, rises in material standards benefit all classes of the community, and if there are still disasters and crippling set-backs, such as wars, these also – with a few special exceptions – affect everybody more or less equally. The struggle to survive, we may claim (for the moment at least), has been won.

---

**The burdens of the poor** do not occupy more than a few of the pages of history. For the ruling classes we have documents, possessions, portraits and houses; for the labouring classes – statistics. Even these are the results of prolonged and detailed research, mostly recent; and although the peasant must of necessity remain relatively undifferentiated and anonymous, we now know him rather more intimately than we did thirty or forty years ago. Such pictorial records as exist are also acquiring new life as the reality behind them is uncovered and their implications understood.

This allegory of the countryman's predicament (*opposite*) was painted about the middle of the 17th century by the Dutchman Adriaen Pietersz van de Venne. Wife and child weigh him down; they have no home and the bowl is empty of food. This was a desperate time for the peasantry of central Europe. The Thirty Years' War had ruined the economy in many regions, and in Germany the population had markedly decreased. As always after such disasters, nature seemed to compensate for her losses by a rise in the birth-rate, and, with gradually improving conditions, numbers began to rise again in consequence. But this was not necessarily to the advantage of the poor. Wealth was being stabilized in the hands of the upper and middle classes, and the poor found themselves increasingly cut off from material possessions and rights over land. As the old system of mutual dependences known as feudalism disintegrated, the disadvantages of their position became acute. From the end of the Middle Ages to the Industrial Revolution it is true to say that the living standards of ordinary people on the whole declined. (1)

# Home industries

As the economy became more commercially based, peasant families began producing goods to sell as well as to use themselves. For the majority this always remained a subsidiary source of income.

**When bread** was plentiful the excess corn could be made into alcohol. A painting by Jean Michelin, 1656 (*left*), shows a baker's cart apparently associated with a form of spirits. *Above:* spinning by candlelight in 18th-century Germany. *Below:* making straw hats in Baden, 1823. Even the children are profitably employed. (2, 3, 4)

**Textiles** were by far the most important cottage industry. Wool, flax and, in eastern Europe, hemp provided the basis. The making of linen was widespread in the rural areas of the north-west and centre. *Above:* two examples surviving into the 20th century. The old lady selling coarse cloth in the market at Morbihan, Brittany, was photographed in 1913. The three lace-makers at Speen, Buckinghamshire, are probably somewhat later. Both pictures show the elaborate but durable fashion of country clothes. *Below:* a German weaver in his cottage, late 19th century. Like Silas Marner in George Eliot's novel, he lives, works and sleeps in a single room. (5, 6, 7)

# Poverty and endurance

The security of village life was a fragile one; at the lower end of the social scale there was virtually no escape from a poverty that could end in complete destitution.

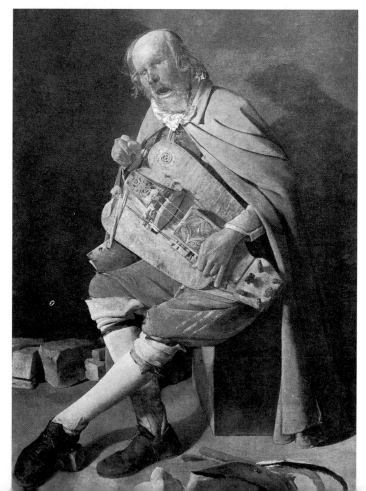

**Sharing with animals** was normal in most parts of Europe, lasting in remoter districts until the 19th century. *Above:* a Polish interior by Aleksander Kotsis. (10)

**'Hard Times',** by Hubert Herkomer (*above centre*): the out-of-work labourer rests with his family by a country lane. The late 1870s, just before this picture was painted, were indeed 'hard' years in Britain. (11)

**'A Blind Hurdy-gurdy Player',** (*right*) painted by Georges de la Tour in the mid-17th century. (12)

**Two views of toil.** Giacomo Ceruti's labourer (*left*), 18th century, is portrayed with dignity and respect; Millet's (*above*) has been crushed and brutalized. (13, 14)

**The spectre of famine** had been exorcised in most
European countries by the late 19th century, but it still
haunted Russia, where a harvest failure could mean
starvation for millions. *The Death of the Settler,* by the
painter Sergei Ivanov, shows a poor farmer who has gone
east with his family in search of better land and has died
on the road. His wife, prostrate and hopeless, has covered
his face with a cloth and placed a holy icon upon him. The
date is 1889. (15)

# 6 RURAL UNREST

YVES-MARIE BERCÉ

# Rural unrest

Today civil wars are rare; by and large society settles its differences by peaceful means; and violence in most Western countries is outlawed and controlled. All these are only comparatively recent achievements. At least until the end of the 17th century, a sense of insecurity was inseparable from the world of the countryside. Self-defence was only too obvious a necessity. One had to be in a position to defend oneself against the brutality and encroachments of quarrelsome neighbours. One had to protect one's sheep from the threat of stray dogs or wild animals. Until the middle of the 19th century, packs of wolves could emerge at any moment from the surrounding woods to attack sheep or poultry or even, in very severe winters, men. When labourers set off for the fields, they always carried an iron-shod stick; together with their rough boots, it was the very sign and symbol of a countryman.

During the years of war, with soldiers marching to and fro across the land, the chronicles tell us that the peasants ploughed with their swords at their sides. Indeed, it was normal to carry something more lethal than a mere stick, although laws were always being passed in most countries regulating the bearing of arms and, in the course of the 16th century, restricting this privilege to the nobility.

In point of fact, these laws were not enforced before the first decades of the 18th century, a change that coincided with restrictions on hunting rights, the building of walls around the royal forests and the enclosure of the big estates. So, until the 18th century and even later, the peasants held on to their arms practically without let or hindrance, illegally but very generally. Some of the countrymen had been soldiers, either for several years or for a single campaign; they had brought home old-fashioned arms, such as halberds or pikes; arquebuses, after these had been replaced in the armies by muskets; and in due course old muskets, when the regiments had been armed with rifles. They hid these arms behind barrels or in wood piles and looked them out when they were needed.

Skill at handling arms was even more indispensable when man was surrounded by natural forces he did not fully understand and beleaguered by an environment he could not properly control. Villages which today stand empty and settlements now deserted were once inhabited. The plots of cleared land went very high up into the mountains and very far over the moorland. None of these country people had any pleasant thoughts

of 'returning to the soil'; they were at the mercy of the seasons, the hazards of bad weather and the uncertainties of isolation at the end of seemingly interminable roads, often impassable in winter. They were born and they died in the shadow of their church tower; they knew nothing of distant towns and could not imagine them. News circulated very slowly and unreliably; the rare echoes from the outside world were picked up in the numerous fairs and markets, where the peasants liked to do their bartering, and even more to see people and to hear the news. Beset as they were by threats and anxieties, their feeling of local solidarity was extremely strong. However they lived and whatever the political and social conditions, the village community was an essential component in the structure of social relationships. It was the centre of religious practice, the background of economic life, the basis of the various systems of taxation – seigniorial, ecclesiastical and royal – and,

*A German woodcut from the time of the Peasants' War of 1524–25. Patient, conservative and religious, the countryman was roused to revolt only when it seemed that his natural and traditional rights were being taken away from him.*

not least important, the unit of defence. There was no lack of occasions for calling the community to arms. Then the tocsin would be heard ringing furiously in the church belfries or the rustic horn sounding afar. The villagers assembled in the village street, which they could barricade with upturned carts or barrels – or else they locked themselves in the parish church. The women and children, with their most valuable possessions, were placed in the nave, while the best marksmen took up positions at the windows or in the belfry. In this way the village became a fortress, capable of resisting a small hostile force, such a group of deserters or a band of brigands. The country people did not let themselves be plundered without putting up a fight and were capable of driving off any but the strongest adversary.

The villagers' right of self-defence was sanctioned by official decrees. In fact, there was nothing like a police force to protect them; that came only in the course of the 19th century. Law and order in the lowlands was in theory maintained by the nobility, who were commanded by royal decree to leave their castles and ride out to challenge any intruders. These companies of the nobility were to be supported by peasant auxiliaries; that is, the village communities had themselves to provide military contingents to repel an invasion. In every kingdom there were provisions for 'raising the people'; the obligation was imposed on them to take up arms and attack the invaders on their soil.

One can easily see how the military capacity of the communes and the legal sanction for their mobilization must have appeared to validate the later spontaneous recourse to arms. A mustering of villages could then slide unconsciously into revolt. This transition could occur every time the peasants felt that their rights as they saw them were under attack.

### The consciousness of popular rights

The village communities' ready recourse to violence was part and parcel of a body of repeated collective practices, sanctioned over many generations. It may seem improper to speak of 'rights' here, for it was a system very different from written, learned, prescriptive laws, enacted by the state. It was more a question of feeling – feeling about justice in the abstract, something unwritten and passed on by tradition. The consciousness of common purpose that came with a common dwelling place may have been at first only a matter of habit; but with time and with confirmation of experience, it took on the obligatory character of custom. The basis of this popular law was the tacit consent of each and every one to certain essential prerogatives and principles of action. Most of life's rules, the practices of cultivation and husbandry, everyday acts, the kinds of behaviour appropriate to the various stages of man's existence – all were regulated by customs that flourished more or less widely, from a small village to a whole province. A number of these customs had been collected by learned jurists in the 16th century and codified by the ruling authorities. They thus became in one sense charged with a more compelling force but at the same time they were made rigid and lost the adaptability that had characterized them during their slow evolution.

What is called popular law was much wider than the simple collection of local customs; it embraced a very vague and very general conception of society, of the relations of sovereigns to their subjects and of the relations of men to the soil. This order, which was thought to be as old as time, seemed to be identical with nature, that is, it was believed to derive from the will of God. In this ordinance, the benevolence of the sovereign's authority was taken for granted, since the sovereign had been placed there by God to dispense justice to his subjects. This justice presupposed equitable limits to the burden of dues to which the peasants were liable; it assumed that they had definite rights over the land they farmed, and certain freedoms in managing it; at the very least, it assumed that the peasant farmer, by careful cultivation and the retention of a reasonable proportion of his harvest, should be able to assure the survival of his family and household.

Set out in terms of rights, such a proposition might appear too bold and anachronistic or, on the contrary, too imprecise, considering the extreme diversity of the peasant's status throughout Europe. Yet it expresses a feeling common to all peasant revolts in modern times, the certainty of a fundamental natural law, threatened by the disgraceful innovations of upstart ministers or by rapacious lords usurping the authority of a just king.

Having considered the firm belief in an original law of the people, we must now consider two other themes of capital importance in connection with peasant uprisings: faith in the virtue of tradition and faith in the justice of the monarch.

The conservatism of the peasantry and their obstinate attachment to the past are generally explained in terms of ignorance and backwardness. In fact, the virtues of experience make better sense in the old agrarian society than in any other period of history. They correspond to the rhythm of the seasons and the bringing in of the harvest, to the unchanging techniques and the routines of a subsistence economy. Indeed, the novelties introduced in the 16th and 17th centuries actually brought nothing but unhappiness to the countryside. The population explosion around 1500 and the increase in the number of poor people, the irreversible schism in Christianity and the wars of religion, the climatic upsets of the 17th century, the succession of years of high prices and of years of epidemics, the spread of wars throughout the continent and the brutal rise in state taxation – all these unprecedented events were fraught with misery for the peasants and seemed to them to stigmatize the new times and consign the happiness they had lost to an irrecoverable past.

Innovation came from the towns; it seemed to benefit only the town dwellers, the land-grabbers, usurers, lawyers, financiers. Village traditions and customs offered a defence or a refuge against the political and social onslaughts to which the community was exposed. The manifestoes of the revolts spoke of 'good customs' and demanded a return to the old ways. Revolt was meant to bring back a vanished golden age. The model was in the past, not in the future: revolt sought restoration, not innovation. It is only in the 18th century that the emergence of the idea of progress comes to give a sense of direction to history and to steer political aspirations towards not only a rejection of the past, but towards radical change and a new future. For the rural communities, doomed to break up with the introduction of intensive and commercialized agriculture, the equilibrium to which they were accustomed was irretrievably lost. Until their disappearance in the course of the 19th century, they could not but remain despairingly attached to the maintenance of institutions and systems which economic evolution had condemned to perish.

The peasants believed they would find a remedy against the heavy demands of seigniorial or state taxation in an appeal to the sovereign. The Christian view of the world presented the idea of a king who was a father to his subjects and whose first and most solemn function was to give them justice. It was impossible that the king could wish his subjects to be unhappy; he was by definition innocent, and the wretched innovations were only the result of his ministers' abuses. The peasants believed that the king did not know what his subjects were suffering and that he was deceived by evil courtiers. Happiness and harmony would be restored if they could only succeed in bringing their complaints to his ears. The risings were, therefore, always peripheral, breaking out in the provinces that were farthest from the king's court and were seldom reached by his authority. Risings always moved in the same direction – towards the centre of power, towards the nearest town, then towards the capital, where the king's palace stood. Periods of minority – when legitimacy was in doubt, when a child monarch's will seemed to be captive and led astray by usurpers – these were the most propitious times for disturbances to break out, as in the reign of Edward VI in England, or the Time of Troubles in Russia or the Fronde in France. By rising in revolt, the peasants thought they were merely anticipating the sovereign's will. They were quite convinced that the king, the emperor or the tsar would very soon support their cause against devious ministers, grasping seigniors or wicked boyars and voivodes.

### Rural crime

Whether the social tensions revealed by the court records are the same as those that lie behind the revolts, is still a matter of controversy. The record of the lowest order of criminal courts – those closest to ordinary people – provide a simple catalogue of offences. Their degree of frequency in any particular region can tell us whether they were deeply rooted in that region or sprang up suddenly at a particular moment in history. Certain types of rural offence have thus been correlated with certain types of countryside or cultivation. Among the specific offences of the old agrarian world are disputes arising from various customary rights. These offences and disputes could arise from the right of gleaning, permitted to the village poor at the end of the harvest, in the fields or in the vineyards; also from the regulations concerning water (use of wells or springs, upkeep of ditches and earthbanks, diversion of streams) or roads (upkeep of highways and bridges, encroachment of fields onto roads, rights of way). Wood, for heating and for the peasants' buildings, was a source of dispute with the foresters, carpenters and charcoal burners, who used to buy parts of the forest and attempted to carry out an intensive and planned exploitation of the trees; this was to the detriment of the estover of the peasants living near by, who defended their right to collect dead branches and copsewood from spinneys. The exercise of the peasant's estover, which prevented the growth of timber trees, competed at first with the royal commissioners seeking timber for ship-building and then, at the beginning of the 19th century, with the industrialists, who utilized the wood as a source of energy, before coal came into general use.

The most disputed custom of all was the free grazing of livestock. Commonage was generally allowed on fallow and waste land, whether it belonged to individual owners or to the commune, but the regulations were severe and disputes were frequent over the time and space allowed for the grazing of those animals – goats, sheep and pigs – that did the most harm to the crops. The owners, with varying degrees of patience, put up with the damage and the hindrance to their work arising from these communal customs. On the other hand, many small peasants could not have survived without the mediocre extra grazing that the commonage allowed them.

In English agrarian society, disputes over the enclosures of the great estates were widespread and provoked serious outbreaks from the 16th century onwards. Peasants knocked down fences and drove out the owners' servants, and these riotous assemblies often finished in open revolt. This was the case in the rising of the Norfolk parishes under Robert Kett during the summer of 1549. In France, the peasant phase of the Revolution (1789–92) was preceded and accompanied by the smashing of fences and walls, the filling up of ditches, the tearing down of hedges and the occupation of land that the insurgents thought had been wrongly appropriated, to the detriment of the community.

The great cornfields and the cereal growing regions saw the firing of mills and barns. The difficulties of the farm labourer, with the fall in wages following the end of the Napoleonic wars, were marked by a great increase in the incidence of fire-raising (*podzog*, in Russian). Fire, the 'red cock', as it was ominously called, was an easy and spectacular act of vengeance. When the perpetrator

*A rare illustration of 1705, showing a meeting in Bavaria to draw up a list of grievances, a common prelude to revolt, satirically entitled the 'Bavarian Parliament'. Seated round the table are the village notables – magistrate, curé, miller, schoolmaster and tailor. The cock at the window represents France, the supposed instigator of revolt. The massacre of Sendling (see plate 9) was the tragic result of one such insurrection.*

was found, he often proved to be an unhappy young day labourer who had been beaten or victimized by his master.

The extensive grazing areas were ideal for cattle stealing. The age-long antagonism between the settled cereal growers of the plains and the nomadic shepherds of the hills steeped the Mediterranean countries in blood over a long period. Raids and vendettas setting the people of the high valleys against the inhabitants of the plains flared up again when the lowlanders, driven by want or encouraged by the state, tried to bring into cultivation land that until then had been left to the shepherds. Rural brigandage, which attracted novelists and painters in the Romantic age, was a social phenomenon characteristic of regions with a pastoral economy. It expressed the fierce defiance of shepherds rejecting the authority of the state as alien to their country, their customs and their murderous sense of honour. They were never more than one per cent of the population, nor can their actions be classified as revolt, as they did not seek to involve the whole community. They could not be other than exceptional and parasitic, settled as they were on the far boundaries of the village lands; they were the reckless and fascinating counterpart of that community, but still inseparable from it.

The majority of crimes were isolated acts. They expressed not so much a general protest as individual acts of defiance, personal vengeance or responses to life.

They cannot be translated into collective terms without losing their raison d'être. We cannot reduce crime to simply an embryonic form of social struggle without depriving it of its primary motivation, which is an individual response to intolerable pressures. But while criminal activity is not to be equated with the phenomena of social conflict, one must also be careful not to assume that all matters dealt with by the courts were crimes. The court's role was not merely punitive, it also regulated social relationships. Indeed, there are probably as many examples of potential causes of revolt being peaceably translated into lawsuits as there are of interminable lawsuits which finally sparked off revolts. This later development tended to take place in cases where a whole village appeared as party to an action in the court. With the exception of countries in eastern Europe, where the downtrodden communities had lost their juridical personality in the course of the 17th century, the majority of states recognized the right of communities to go to law. It is true that the peasant's recourse to law was restricted by his mistrust of the townsman's system, which he could not understand and which seemed dominated by those in power; nonetheless, this right of appeal was important, increasingly so as time went by. In 19th-century France the petty rural lawsuits, formerly dealt with in most cases by the lord of the manor, were taken to the justices of the peace. This increasing recourse to the courts does not necessarily

137

point to a greater number of disputes, but rather to a growing tendency to settle them peacefully, a change from brute force to low cunning, as the peasants gradually became familiar with the juridical customs of educated people. Quarrels were no longer settled with blows but with sheets of stamped paper.

It could happen that a long-standing peasant claim, based on immemorial custom, supported by the conviction and good faith of the plaintiffs, would run up against an adverse decision and that the whole legal process would finally go against the community – a conflict between the idealized unwritten law of the peasants and the critical examination to which this was subjected from the standpoint of officially recognized law. In the Germanic countries, for example in the high desolate plateaus of Swabia, one finds cases of conflict between the ecclesiastical princes and their peasant subjects, which lasted for several centuries, with alternating periods of lawsuits and outbreaks of violence.

In these communal lawsuits, the peasants' claims to freedom from dues – or to exemptions or limitations – often foundered on the lack of title-deeds or of documents to which ignorant tradition had, probably quite wrongly, ascribed such liberating qualities. It was thus that in the kingdom of Valencia, the Spanish *colons*, who settled there after 1609 on territory left vacant by the expulsion of the Moors, finished by believing themselves to be the owners of the land. They hoped that the king of Spain would help them to recover their (imaginary) title-deeds. In 1693 and 1705, bands of peasants (*Eixercit dels Agermenats*) set off to seek justice from the king's officials. In the sad reality of the law, these Valencian peasants were only lessees, and liable for the payment of dues. In the spring of 1789, French peasants asked their curé to show them the king's order, abolishing their dues. The Russian serfs, emancipated by the statute of 1861, became angry over the delays and limitations of official action. Believing that the authentic text was being withheld from them or that it was not being correctly interpreted, they tried to find an honest, educated man who could read it to them in the version they expected to hear. Zapata, leader of the Mexican peasants who revolted in 1910, declared that he held in an underground cave the Spanish parchments which proved that the Indian peasants had the right of ownership to their fields.

In the countries of eastern Europe, where the sovereign authority was weak and distant, as was the case with the king of Poland or the emperor of Germany, the peasants were subject to the nobles, not only in the latter's capacity as landowners and overlords but also in that as local magistrates. They were thus cut off from the sovereign, deprived of resort to a supreme jurisdiction which would, in the event, prove impartial and compassionate.

The malcontents who went so far as to try to take their complaints to the emperor, as in Lower Austria in 1596 or in Upper Austria in 1626, or the Russian peasants who thought they could take their grievances to the tsarina in 1767, were punished cruelly for an audacity which seigniorial 'justice' stigmatized as seditious. 'God is in heaven and the Emperor is in Vienna', ran a German proverb, expressing the peasantry's feelings of abandonment and frustration.

Setbacks and denials suffered by the village communities in the courts lay behind the great peasant rising in 1846 in Polish Galicia, at that time a province of Austria. The peasants turned their arms against the Polish nationalists, country nobility or townspeople. They were led by a small tenant farmer called Jakub Szela who was the head man of his village. Since 1802, his community had been fighting a lawsuit with the local Polish overlord for reimbursement of the cost of excessive corvées (forced labour). Szela, elected head man in 1822, had won his case many times but each time procedural contrivances had enabled the seignior to prolong the suit. In 1846, he had on several occasions taken the opportunity of victimizing the village head man and the rights of the peasant community remained a dead letter.

In the more or less conscious view of many of the completely illiterate peasants, the oppression they suffered rested on documents and these documents were the source of their misfortune. Documents concealed the titles of those in possession, the bases of corvées and dues, the records of offences committed in woods and fishing preserves and of unpaid fines, the total amounts of their accumulated debts. Documents were the object of detestation and unanimous suspicion to simple people. Almost all the risings from the 16th to the 19th century were thus also opportunities to burn archives; charter-rooms were pillaged and set ablaze, documents and parchments hurled into the bonfire. The burning of a seigniorial manor in 16th-century Germany or 18th-century Russia meant not only the satisfaction of a feeling of hatred but also the deliberate destruction of proofs of seigniorial rights. During the (French) Revolution, several official decisions of the Assemblies from March 1790 to July 1793 prescribed the destruction of feudal title-deeds. These Parisian decisions merely confirm a popular practice, illustrated by numerous scenes of vandalism, which had spread since 1789 throughout the provinces. In Switzerland, in the canton of Vaud in 1802, a peasant movement, demanding the immediate abolition of feudal rights, even gained the significant nickname of 'bourla papey' (i.e. *brule papier* – burn the paper). In Poland in 1863, a general commanding the nationalist rebels took pains to win over the peasants to his cause with a similar gesture; he publicly burned the gamekeepers' registers containing particulars of minor acts of poaching or firewood cutting.

The sudden transformation of an interminable but still peaceful lawsuit into a savage revolt marked an important behavioural turning point, the crossing of a threshold. Of course, every instance of social tension did not necessarily express itself in revolt. The history of uprisings does not correspond necessarily and exactly to the historical course of society's evolution. Revolt is primarily a cultural act and has its own history. It is, therefore, necessary to define this threshold which leads to revolt and which is obviously psychological, emotional, that is, it varies with ideas and opinions held at different times and places.

## Causes of peasant revolt

The threshold of violence is crossed when an event is interpreted as an act of aggression or of provocation – the aggression of innovation or the provocation of disappointed hopes.

Innovation appeared to the country people as a break in the body of just and proven tradition, as the destruction of an ancestral and benevolent equilibrium. The demand for regular taxes constituted such an innovation. Indeed, the real burden of a tax mattered less than the way it was thought of. We shall see that resistance to new fiscal demands arose less from the actual sums of money involved than from their outrageous novelty.

The rising prices of foodstuffs and the increased volume of trade in Europe in the course of the 16th century proved remunerative for those landed proprietors who were able to market their harvests. The nobility of eastern Europe, who, unlike the French or Spanish nobility, could engage in trade without losing caste, even demanded more rents or labour dues from their tenants; many of those tenants migrated, drawn by the vast open spaces and their nomadic traditions. Until then, peasants had moved away merely to find virgin lands; now they did so to get away from the estates, where their dues were becoming increasingly crushing. To stem this great exodus, which at the beginning of the 17th century in Russia was amounting to a drain of thousands of peasants per year, the nobles pushed through harsh laws that restricted the movement of peasants, laws of obligatory residence, binding them to the soil. The increase in the number of days of labour and registration on a particular estate were forms of servitude and were clearly innovations in breach of age-old customs; they were felt as acts of aggression and violations of the ancestral liberties of the village communities.

In western Europe at the end of the 18th century, the seigniorial proprietors attempted to integrate the seigniorial system with the market economy and to adapt it to intensive agriculture. This movement, launched in France around 1770, involved the revival of ancient seigniorial rights, a revision of jurisprudence and an erosion of some long-standing customs and usages. These measures, known by the name of 'feudal reaction' were actually, again, innovations which broke down a very ancient body of custom.

Such developments as the 'second serfdom' in eastern Europe in the 16th century or the 'feudal reaction' in western Europe in the 18th often began – or were accelerated – when there was a change of overlord, whether by disinheritance, purchase or confiscation. The arrival of a new seignior and of new stewards or seigniorial tax farmers destroyed ancestral loyalties, bonds of protection and corporate solidarity, which very often existed between the peasants and the seignior's family. The dues now required did not have the sanction of communal custom or of the memories of the village elders.

All the old dues, which had become customary through immemorial usage, were accepted without argument because they appeared perpetual, unavoidable and so, it was thought, part of the natural order. The new demands, on the other hand, were easily dissociable from the body of custom. The revolts did not generally challenge the whole seigniorial system but confined themselves to attacking specific and recent innovations.

Like the extension of seigniorial taxation, the institution of state taxes in the 16th and 17th centuries formed part of the process of innovation. The requirements of the wars of religion and then of the Thirty Years' War obliged the most ancient monarchies and those most advanced in the process of centralization – particularly France and also Spain and the empire – to increase their revenues considerably. The state at that time relied heavily on indirect taxes on corn, wine and salt, commodities that were not only essential to life but were also held sacred through their association with the Christian liturgy. Townspeople angrily rioted against these taxes; the peasants, being more or less self-sufficient, were less affected by them. The state then increased direct taxes. These had to be either completely new levies or greatly increased old ones; and although they were announced as provisional and exceptional, they soon became permanent and regular. 'Tailles' (tallage) in France, the principal royal revenue, were based almost entirely on the income of the peasants. Increases in tallage were so savage around 1630 as to give it the dimension of an entirely new levy. It was at this time that the most serious peasant revolts in early modern France took place.

In other kingdoms, where the power of the sovereign to institute regular taxes was not clearly established, the rulers had recourse to levies in kind, collected by the armies. Regiments were formed and armed at the communities' expense, and the soldiers were sent to live on the country. This practice of 'billeting the troops' often came very close to organized looting. Billeting was feared, indeed, loathed, for even under the most respected generals and on the estates of the most powerful seigniors, the soldiers behaved as if they were on conquered territory. The great Catalan revolt in 1640 began with the refusal by the mountain villages on the route to France, over which troops were continually passing, to provide billets for them. On the French side, the provision for the soldiers was probably the cause of a great number of riots. The struggles between the soldiers, extorting and pillaging, and the peasants, defending their villages or setting ambushes for the looters, became a commonplace in the realist paintings of the 17th century. The two stages of this struggle can be seen in the subject of 'the scourge of the peasants', which shows the pillage of a hamlet by the soldiery, and in 'the peasants' revenge', the massacre of the soldiers cut off by the peasants. Cruel genre scenes of this sort were illustrated by the Flemish artists David Vinckeboons (1576–1629), Sebastian Vrancx (1573–1647) and, above all, by the native of Lorraine, Jacques Callot (1592–1635).

Among the multiplicity of taxes rejected by popular indignation, the mythical tax on births played a particularly provocative role. The rumour spread in many countries that a tax was to be levied on every child born. It seems to have arisen from the general confusion regarding the notaries, the parish registry office and the onerous requirements of written documents in various social transactions. The poorest people, those whose only wealth consisted in their family, the 'proletarians' in the etymological sense of the word, would thus have been struck at through their most treasured possessions. This myth, recurring regularly in the 16th and 17th centuries, was, to take one example, the cause of the revolt of the Tard Avisés who rose in Quercy in May 1707.

The idea of a tax on births was a paradigm case of provocation. It struck at the ineradicable, inextinguishable hope of the poor people: for better things and the ultimate recognition of their sufferings by a just king. They waited patiently for the king or tsar to abolish slavery, to liberate the peasants, cancel their debts, make them masters of their own fields. Their ignorance of city politics, their credulity and the slow circulation of news among simple people all gave wings to rumours, false news or half truths. The wildest hopes, the cruellest disappointments and the most terrible provocations to violence, therefore, all come in the years of political change, when power appeared to falter, and when there were promises of great reforms. The greatest hopes engendered the most cruel frustrations, the most violent outbursts and revolts. Particularly crucial periods are the Reformation, which saw the great revolts of the peasants in Germany in 1525; in France, the summoning of the States General by Louis XVI in 1789, which set off the revolt in the countryside; and the abolition of serfdom in Russia in 1861, which was followed by an immense increase in agrarian disorders.

So we can imagine groups of angry peasants, determined to get a hearing for their wrongs, coming out of church one Sunday or meeting together on a market day. There they would compare grievances and draw up lists of complaints: the curé – or a notary or an educated villager capable of putting into writing and in some sort of order – would write down the charges enumerated by those present. Such peasant manifestoes could then be copied, passed around, read in public, commented on, transformed and spread abroad.

The Cossack leader Pugachev. In 1773 he raised the standard of revolt against Catherine the Great, and for a year spread terror throughout the whole of Russia, capturing and destroying the city of Kazan. In 1774 he was defeated, captured, brought in an iron cage to Moscow and excuted.

## Forms of peasant revolt

A group of parishes has decided to take up arms in defence of their rights. The tocsin sounds: the peasants line up in military order with musket, pitchforks and spades, scythes with the blades reversed, cutting edge outwards, or just iron-shod sticks. They raise their banner and choose a captain. The news of the revolt spreads round the neighbourhood. The tocsin rings out from one belfry to another. The messengers go round the hamlets, calling the people together. Orders signed by the captain threaten reprisals to any who are unwilling to take part. Small groups go from farm to farm, seeking everybody out, bringing in willy-nilly the young men capable of bearing arms. By degrees, willing or unwilling, the gathering takes on the dimension of a small army.

The contingents of several parishes, assembled at a rendezvous, elect or acclaim a colonel or a general. In the crowd, each parish maintains its cohesion, with its own captain, its few musketeers and leaders on horseback. They are not at all hopeless or depressed, but on the contrary are joyful and enthusiastic, each and every one certain of the justice of their cause and of a quick and easy victory. Musical instruments accompany the beginnings of the revolt; bagpipes and fiddles and hurdy-gurdies having been brought along from the villages. The military strains of fifes and drums beat out the steps as they march along.

Peasant armies could number several thousand. The captains attempted to control the disorderly crowds and form them into regiments, sending the useless ones home. The biggest armies, like those brought together by the extraordinary popular revolts in Russia, did not exceed twenty thousand men at any one time, even under Pugachev in 1774. This strength represented the military nucleus of the revolt. The total number involved in an uprising or vaguely supporting it could be several hundreds of thousands. As they moved around, the peasant armies were continually renewed. Peasants from the same parish would accompany the army for several days and then go home, either because they felt they had moved too far out of their own district, or because they thought that the aims of the revolt had been successfully achieved or because, as farmers, they felt the urgent call of their seasonal tasks. Those who left could be replaced by new arrivals, hastening to join the approaching peasant army, but it could also happen that the whole assembly would drift away into the countryside and that the captains would find themselves left on their own with a few loyal horsemen. This coming and going might throw whole provinces into confusion but it meant that the total effective strength of the insurgents was never brought together at the same time. In the short run that was often an advantage, since it would have been impossible to maintain and command such a vast undisciplined multitude. But, just as surely, it brought the certainty of defeat and disillusion at the end of the day. The human tide led by Pugachev renewed itself each day, bringing in Cossacks, peasants and foreigners of six different races. The armies of the Vendée of 1793 were mobilized for only a few days or a few weeks. Cardinal Ruffo, who led the Calabrian peasants' rising against the French invasion, said afterwards that he never knew from one day to another how many men he could count on or whether the villages he would come to on the morrow would join him or not.

The leaders were chosen solely for their military prowess, and were often far from representative of the causes for which they fought; they were supporters, friends of peasants, but rarely peasants themselves. Their adherence was sometimes a matter of coercion, the villagers having sought them out and compelled them with threats to take command. This was often the case with the smaller gentry whom their neighbours or tenants called on to join them, to contribute their social standing, their personal aptitude for military command. Old soldiers, retired after many years in the field, took up active service again, leading their insurgent fellow countrymen.

The Croquants, who rose in France against the taxes of the Thirty Years' War, were led by obscure gentlemen, who were styled generals, colonels and captains of the communes. Among them, the Baron of Madaillan, who gave himself the title of 'Brigadier of the Communes of Perigord' in 1637, was of the ancient but impoverished nobility. He had commanded a Swedish regiment in Germany and had campaigned for a long period against the imperial troops or the Spanish. A marginal and precarious social and economic situation, a taste for adventure and intrigue, or pressure from the

peasants, such were the conditions which in 17th-century France made a gentleman the leader of a peasant rising.

In the countries of eastern Europe, the typical leader would be a veteran of the fighting against the Turks, a captain of frontier garrisons or a Cossack chief. One of the most celebrated of such men was Giorgy Dosza, styled 'the king of the peasants'; he commanded the great uprising of the Hungarian peasants in 1514. Dosza was a captain of the forts on the borders of the Turkish domains, fighting off enemy raids and himself leading expeditions into Muslim-occupied territories. Matija Gubec, leader of the Croatian revolt in 1572, had distinguished himself in the war against the Turks. In Russian history, the Cossacks, free horsemen of the southern Steppes, played a decisive role. They served as frontier guards to the domains of the rulers of Poland and of Russia, resisting incursions led during the summer by Tatar and Turkish horsemen and at the same time winning the admiration of the subjugated peasants, thousands of whom tried to join them. Their influence on events was ambivalent, at times serving the crown, at others acting as subversive models of peasant emancipation. The leaders of the greatest revolts – Khmelnitski in 1648, Razin in 1671, Boulavin in 1707 and Pugachev in 1773 – were all Cossack hetmans.

Village notables also appear at the head of insurrections. They, too, were chosen for their qualities as leaders of men. Such were Stefan Fadinger, leader of the peasants of Upper Austria in 1626, and Hans Emmenegger, leader of the Swiss peasants in 1633. Emmenegger, called 'the handsome Banneret' or 'the peasants' jewel', was a prosperous landowner, highly thought of in his valley, sufficiently educated to act as schoolmaster and church organist. Antoni Soler, who

*Stenka Razin was another Cossack rebel of the century before Pugachev. Between 1661 and 1671 his revolt spread across the immense regions of the lower Volga and represented a serious threat to the developing modern state of Russia.*

commanded the Catalan insurgents in 1689, was the richest landowner in his mountain region.

Certain trades which were important in the social life of the countryside appear frequently in these chronicles: tavern-keepers and landlords of the inns, where people went to drink, meet each other and gossip, and village tradespeople and pedlars, who knew everybody. They moved around several cantons, bought and sold everything, always had ready money, spread the news and acted as money-lenders. Jacques Cathelineau (1759–93) was a carter and pedlar, visiting all the inns in the west of France. From this village, he did the carters' regular rounds, stopping at all the great fairs of the region. He bought wool and flax from the farms and resold it to the cloth and fabric-makers in the small weaving villages. He held forth in the taverns and had a fine voice; he was in demand as a singer in church or at weddings. He was the most respected of the popular leaders in the war of the Vendée and was called 'the Saint of Anjou'.

Andreas Hofer (1767–1810) was an innkeeper in the valley of Passeyr in Tirol, one of the rich men of the canton, handsome, very strong and very devout. He was involved in trade and bought grain, wine and horses in Italy and resold them in the valleys. This remarkable highlander had commanded a troop of Tyrolese chasseurs in the resistance to the French invasion in 1796. In 1809, he was the leader of the Tyrolese revolt, drove out the French and, virtually alone, governed his rebellious province for several months.

The picture one has of these leaders is bound to vary as one goes down to the level of those who are just leaders of riots and instigators of scenes of violence, but the essential traits remain the same, a rural background and the gift of command. Social tensions within the rural community relaxed when it was threatened from outside. Local animosities were silenced by hatred for a new overlord, for profiteers from the towns or for plundering soldiers, and at such times the endangered community presented an apparently united front, a bond of solidarity, which was unshakeable, at least for the first days of the revolt. We are not suggesting that there were no conflicts between the old landowners and landless peasants, between farmers and day labourers, village artisans and smallholders, between families engaged in hereditary disputes or between neighbouring villages; but these internal conflicts had to give way when it came to presenting a solid front against outsiders, that is, against townspeople. These people, whether purchasers of land, tax officials, money-lenders, tax farmers or bailiffs, were intruders and enemies.

The wealthy townspeople knew only too well how to turn to advantage the cyclical crises of high prices which marked the 16th and 17th centuries. We have seen in a previous chapter how the growth of population and production had clearly got under way from the second half of the 15th century; it came to a halt throughout Europe between 1560 and 1620; bad harvests accumu-

lated while tax demands continued to increase. From that time, the peasantry were doomed to an inexorable plunge into debt; they saw the townspeople moving onto their lands, invading and controlling them. The ascendancy of the towns, through land purchases and through the farming out of seigniorial rents and state taxes, became the major social fact in the period from the 16th to the 19th century. It disappeared only when the owners found in industry a better means of increasing their capital. The domination exercised by the towns was not only economic, based on land ownership, it was also social and cultural. Fashion, opinions, ideas, behaviour and clothes came from the towns and the peasant elite longed to escape from the village yoke and to identify themselves with urban models. The peasant, confronted with urban manners, seemed clumsy, uncouth, ignorant and stupid; he felt himself exploited, laughed at, ridiculed and rejected. Peasant revolts always fed on this feeling of resentment, and retained, regardless of time and place, the distinctive character of a war against the towns.

Once assembled under arms, the peasants set off on their march to the nearest town. This they needed in order to have the tactical strongpoint provided by its ramparts and cannons and to use it as a publicity medium from which they could publish their manifestoes and gain the ear of the magistrates. They also had to slake their hatred of the urban enemies whose houses would be pillaged and who would be killed if they had not already escaped. Antagonism between town and country was not just one-way; there are well proven examples of ferocious animosity by townspeople towards peasants. In the repression of defeated risings, the bourgeois militias, emerging from their defences, and later the *gardes nationales* in the 18th and 19th centuries, were all guilty of massacring routed peasant armies.

In fact, the outcome of peasant revolts was almost always an unhappy one. After their initial successes, the insurgents soon dispersed. Confident in their numbers and carefree after an easy skirmish, some celebrated by getting drunk among the broken winecasks. Others thought they would take a chance in the open country, where troops of well trained horsemen, far fewer in number, easily routed the crowds of peasants. The chronicles are full of accounts of bloody defeats where thousands of peasants are cut to pieces by military detachments, mounted nobles, regular regiments and armed bourgeois, who found no difficulty in breaking the yokels resistance.

## Everyday violence

Besides the great revolts remembered by history, there were thousands of forgotten outbreaks of rural violence. One of the commonest causes was the simple fear of hunger, a fear which periodically swept through the ranks of the very poor and which was inseparable from the old subsistence economy, in both country and town.

*Bread riots in England, 1830. To those living on the edge of subsistence, a bad harvest meant the threat of starvation. Riots were provoked by the knowledge that prices were being kept artificially high, both by private speculators and by duties preventing the import of foreign corn.*

After a bad harvest, the approach of the months between crops sent up prices and aroused dread of scarcity to come, which would claim the lives of the poorest and weakest, the little children and the old people. Angry crowds then set out to raid the merchants' barns and bakers' shops. In the country, where scarcity was relatively less feared, years of high prices led to the blocking of high-roads to prevent the movement of the cartloads of corn and to halt the convoys and steal the sacks of grain. These activities were not the work of miserable people dying of starvation, but of villagers haunted by the fear of famine. Terrifying stories spread around of starving people eating the grass in the ditches or even devouring their own children.

In the end food riots resulted only in the breakdown of the transport of grain in periods of high prices. They may have succeeded in upsetting the speculations of merchants gambling on prices falling in the following months; but if the harvest was really insufficient, the riots did not produce a single grain more, and only served to hinder the bringing of help from the productive regions to the needy ones.

This type of disturbance was to continue as long as the subsistence economy lasted, that is, it only disappeared with the ease of transport provided by the railway. In 19th-century France, the years 1812, 1816 and 1847, especially, and again 1868 saw corn riots with the same scenes and the same slogans as in the 17th century. The year 1874 saw the definite decline of the price of cereals; this irreversible fall was the result of the arrival in the European market of shiploads from the New World, from Canada, the United States and the Argentine. It meant the end of famines, but also the ruin of a large number of the cereal growers of the Old World. The last great famine of the 19th century was in Russia in 1891; it was said to have cost 700,000 lives and reduced thirty million people to indigence. The horrifying recollection of it gave rise to the pillaging of barns

on some of the great rural estates in 1898 and 1902, recurrences which brought back images of violence from a distant past.

The riots against the billeting of troops and the exactions of the soldiers also belong to this obscure register of unknown tragedies. They were numberless, as long as no special provision was made by the military to accommodate troops at their halting-places or in permanent garrisons, or to control and repress the soldiers' brutalities. The construction of barracks and depots, the proper organization of supply columns, the introduction of military uniforms, the precise ordering of ranks and the regularizing of promotions and, finally, the establishing of a system of pay, all these elements of military administration had been put in hand with difficulty from the end of the 17th century. Building of barracks, which was to put an end to the intolerable burden of billeting and was decided in France by the minister Louvois around 1680, was carried out only very slowly in the course of the 18th century and finally systematized only in the time of Napoleon.

'Little war' – guerrilla warfare – of peasants against enemy armies makes its appearance in every century: during the wars of Louis XIV, the war of the Austrian succession and of course the wars of the Revolution and the empire. Its frequency at the beginning of the 19th century made people think it was something new; the Romantic historians seized on it, exalted it and were keen to identify it with the awakening of national feelings. The rising of Andreas Hofer in Tyrol against the French and the Bavarians in 1809 and the rising of the Spanish peasantry against the French occupation from 1808 to 1812 were saluted as patriotic struggles and claimed as precursors by the liberal movements of the following decades. In reality, these acts of resistance followed traditional patterns; they consisted not of a single unified insurrection but of many popular isolated outbreaks, unco-ordinated and spontaneous. Without the assistance of regular armies and outside intervention, they would not have had the least chance of success. The English landing in Portugal was more effective than the actions of the *guerilleros*, and the guns of the English and Russian fleets had more effect in struggles for independence in the Balkans than popular insurrections, however glorious and romantic these may have appeared. In the same way the insurrection of the peasants of Calabria, the Basilicata and the Abruzzi against the French, was victorious in 1799, thanks mainly to the support of their allies. When renewed during the second French invasion, in the years 1806–11, at the height of the empire's power, peasant resistance was crushed. Finally, the same regions rose against the Piedmontese troops at the time of the integration of the kingdom of Naples into a united Italy; totally defeated, they suffered brutal terrorist repression from 1861 to 1866, while European public opinion stood by unconcerned or scornfully indifferent. At all times, invasion and enemy occupation bear hard upon the country-folk, penetrating the byways and hiding places of their territory, generating countless acts of petty persecution and unsung heroism.

### The great revolts
### from the Reformation to the Revolution

There can be no question of covering all the outbreaks of peasant wars in Europe over four centuries, but one can at least mention the most serious and try to place them in their historical context.

The first decades of the 16th century were dominated in the Germanic and eastern countries of Europe by the explosions of the Reformation and the advance of Turkish conquests. The Ottoman threat, coinciding with the effects of the 'second serfdom', led to the revolt of the peasants in Hungary in 1514. Beginning as a crusade against the infidel invader, the peasants turned their arms against the overlords. It was crushed in one of the most horrible repressions in history.

Of all the popular revolts, the German Peasants' War covered the widest geographical area. The strengthening of princely prerogatives and seigniorial jurisdiction struck at old customs and ancient Germanic liberties. The peasants' growing unrest over these changes came at a time when the Lutheran reformers were active in the towns and the countryside, preaching individual inspiration and the end of ecclesiastical authority. Reformation propaganda seemed to authorize the affirmation of the peasants' liberty, an issue which had already set off a string of revolts in the German lands from about 1480. The 'Twelve Articles' of protest, drawn up by the Swabian peasantry, demanded the abolition of restrictions which were beginning to affect their freedom to marry and to pass on their property. They also vigorously affirmed their customary rights to hunt, fish and gather firewood. Starting in Swabia in June 1524, the revolt had spread, by the spring of 1525,

*Dürer's strange imaginary monument to the collapse of the peasant movement in 1525, known as 'Peasant Melancholy'. The sheep and cattle at the base seem to share in the resignation of their master. The farmer's humble possessions – his wooden coffer for linen and valuables, his dairy utensils, a sheaf of corn bound in with hoes and forks (rustic fasces), and a basket containing a chicken – rise precariously in bitter parody of a classical trophy to support the peasant himself, his clothes in rags, his shoes worn and over his shoulder an old two-handed sword, sad relic of his impotent revolt.*

to cover the whole of the southern and western territories of the empire. In the first days of June, the peasant forces were crushed in five different battles by armies drawn from the nobility and the Lutheran towns. The bloodiest routs were at Weinsberg in Franconia, at Frankenhausen in Saxony and at Saverne in Alsace. These defeats of 1525 have generally been regarded as leading to the loss of all political power. Present-day scholars however point to the maintenance of peasant status and of customary rights in south-west Germany and see in their survival an indirect victory for the revolt.

Among the many uprisings provoked by the slowly increasing pressure of the 'second serfdom', one may instance the revolts in Croatia in 1573 and in Lower Austria in 1597, and, above all, the 17th-century civil wars in Russia, where the peasants, lately reduced to serfdom, and the recently conquered outlying peoples rallied in tens of thousands to Cossack leaders from the southern Steppes and the free lands of the Don and the Lower Volga. The dynastic crisis in the early years of the 17th century was followed by a whole series of uprisings: Bogdan Khmelnitski, rebelling in the Ukraine against the Polish overlords (1648), and especially Stenka Razin (1668–71), who threatened the equilibrium of the whole tsarist state.

In the west, the expansion of modern states was only made possible through the increase of taxes, which fell for the most part on the peasants. The first peasant revolt against taxation in the western monarchies was in Aquitaine, where they refused to pay the *gabelle*, the tax on salt, in 1548. The later risings of the Croquants and of the Tard Avisés covered more or less the same geographical area. Their dates correspond to various tax increases, in 1594 at the end of the wars of religion, and in 1637, on France's declaration of war against Spain and the empire. The revolt of the Nu-Pieds of Normandy in 1639 took place at the same political juncture. Insurrections in Catalonia in 1640 and in the kingdom of Naples in 1647 correspond exactly with the war-efforts demanded by the king of Spain from his different dominions. The rising of the Swiss peasants in 1653 was also an after-effect of the Thirty Years' War, from which the cantons, which were not involved, had managed to profit. The conclusion of peace in 1648 led to the calling up of debts which had accumulated through the easy terms of the previous decades. The excessive issue of debased copper coins caused inflation in the monetary dead-end of the rural areas; this and resentment under the yoke of the town officials, who were their overlords, led the peasants of the mountain valleys to demand the end of their dues and of their vassalage. The troops from Berne and Lucerne suppressed the revolt in a few weeks.

During the war of the Spanish Succession, the peasants of Catalonia, Valencia and Aragon rose in 1705 against the Franco-Castilians, while the highlanders of the Bavarian Oberland, resisting the Austrian invaders, were bloodily crushed in January 1706.

In the 18th century, the expectation of the end of serfdom set off upheavals which no longer harked back to the past but looked with impatience towards the future. In Russia, the tremendous rising under Pugachev was only the most serious of a whole sequence of rural disturbances. At the summons of this simple Cossack, who claimed to be the surviving Tsar Peter III, Cossacks, peasants and peoples of other races joined together in a conquering army. In the Urals, where the beginnings of the metallurgical industry tied the worker to his bench, just as the peasants were bound to the soil,

the serfs in the factories helped the revolt to spread over great areas. But in spite of the taking of Kazan (July 1774), Pugachev was unable to prevent the progressive dispersal of his troops.

In the west, the seigniorial system was no more than a parasitic survival, which had lost all its real values and was detested by all those subjected to it. The French Revolution was preceded and then accompanied, in its initial stages, by peasant disturbances, which were occasionally linked with the events in Paris, but whose demands proved completely independent of the opnions of the political assemblies. From 1789 to 1792, one can distinguish several waves of disturbances in the countryside. First, in the spring of 1789, hopes aroused by the meeting of the States General resulted in July in the scenes of panic known under the name of the 'Grande Peur' (the Great Fear). These often turned into anti-seigniorial riots. The night of 4 August, when the abolition of privileges was decreed, was in fact a disappointment to the peasants, who wanted an immediate and complete abolition of their dues. From the winter of 1789 to the summer of 1792, demonstrations in the countryside of varying degrees of violence intimated the absolute refusal to pay any seigniorial rents or tithes which might still be in existence.

The abolition of the seigniorial system, now obligatory under French law, was to be carried abroad by the

*During the unrest that accompanied the Reformation in Germany many peasant movements looked back to a primitive Christianity which they believed would vindicate their claims to liberty and land rights. In this woodcut they carry a banner showing the crucifixion, while in the background is the sacrifice of Isaac by Abraham.*

victorious revolutionary armies. These authorized emancipations were sometimes preceded or accompanied by popular risings. They bore witness to the peasants' hopes and to the ambiguities in the abrogative measures, which were spread out over a period and were subject to redemption payments. In the event, the collapse of the 'feudal' structures turned out to be final and the later withdrawal of the revolutionary armies and the restoration of Anciens Régimes did not entail the return of any forms of subjection for the peasants.

## The new masters

The chronicle of peasant insurrections does not of course end with the victory of bourgeois ideologies. In central Europe, the bonds of economic servitude remained unchanged and the bonds of personal servitude lingered on in the Russian Empire; while, in the west, the agrarian communities, relieved of the rents due to the nobles, faced much tougher adversaries with the ascendancy of the prosperous bourgeoisie and the development of intensive agriculture.

It was conscription, more than any other institution, that disturbed and angered the country people and it was its exactions that turned the peasants of the west of France overwhelmingly against the revolutionary regime set up in Paris. The levies of men, voted by the Convention, took effect in the spring of 1793. Never before had the state assumed the power to call upon all the young men of a country. If they were snatched away from their homes and from their villages, the work in the fields would be short of hands. Family undertakings could only prosper with the help of sons and sons-in-law; the result of their departure for long periods – perhaps to meet a wretched death, far from their ancestral church – was the ruin of many farms. The call-up of young peasants was the more disgraceful in that conscription obviously passed over numerous sons of bourgeois families. Moreover, it followed several other measures that were hurtful to the communities. Some parishes had fallen into decay as a result of administrative reorganization and were impoverished by the sale of church property. The Ancien Régimes' taxes, which had been abolished, were replaced by even heavier ones. Both the final recourse to royal authority and the benevolent protection of the curé were condemned and persecuted. The Revolution proved a tantalizing and agonizing disappointment.

The first call-up of conscripts in March 1793 was the signal for the uprising that, in a few days, swept through lower Poitou and parts of Anjou, Maine, Lower Brittany and Lower Normandy. The war of the Vendée (as this area is known) was clearly a social war; all the inhabitants of the countryside were on one side, all the bourgeois and townspeople were on the other, with very few exceptions. From 1793 to 1833, there were, on a simple count, five separate Vendéan wars. We can distinguish three types of action: first, the initial village riots, spontaneous and soon dispersed; then the regular war, known as the 'Vendée Militaire', which finished with the defeats of the royalists and the ravage of the countryside by the 'infernal columns'; and, finally, the chouannerie, a small war of ambushes and brigandage, carried on by those who still held out. The extent of these wars has been systematically underestimated or even completely ignored by professional scholars, and still is. The repression undertaken by the revolutionary authorities in Paris was in the form of deliberate and conscious terrorist extermination. Estimates of the number of dead are uncertain; some are as high as 600,000. But whatever the true figure, this rising was the most long-drawn-out and the most bloody in the whole history of the European peasantry.

Insofar as French conquests created the same revolutionary situation abroad, peasant outbursts repeated the episodes of the Vendéan insurrection on a smaller scale. There was the 'cudgel war' (Klöppelkrieg) in Luxemburg (October 1798), the 'peasant war' (Boerenkrijg) in Limburg (December 1798), the 'war of shepherds' smocks' (Hirtenhemdlikrieg) in the old mountain cantons of Switzerland (April 1799), the great march of the Calabrians from Reggio up to Naples under the leadership of Cardinal Ruffo (February–June 1799) and the rising of the Tuscan Apennines (Viva Maria) in the neighbourhood of Arezzo (May 1799). The triumph of the empire did not put a stop to this succession of armed struggles directed against a foreign and innovating power, which claimed the right to snatch the young men away from the soil. The Tyrol, the kingdom of Naples and Spain were the scenes of the most famous of these resistance movements, but no region under the sway of French expansion was exempt from them. A rising of the Dalmatian highlanders against the French in June 1807 broke out, significantly, on the day of the drawing of lots for conscripts. Even in France, the rural areas harboured a great number of deserters, who were hunted down by columns of gendarmerie.

For those who were unable to revolt or to flee, there still remained the possibility of self-destruction, by suicide or by nostalgie. Doctors became very interested in this illness which was carefully described and declared to be completely new. It fell into a precise nosological category with recognizable symptoms – fever and emaciation, delirium, marasmus (wasting away) and not infrequently death. It was said to be as widespread as scurvy and as serious as typhus. It was very clearly linked with the enforcement of conscription. 'In no period were cases of nostalgie more widespread than in the French Revolution', wrote Percy, surgeon of the Grande Armée. It began to spread from 1794 onwards, filling military hospitals up to 1814. Snatched away from their families and their villages, uprooted from their customs and isolated because of their patois, the young peasants, on their hospital palliasses, just turned their faces to the wall. It was not until around 1830 that nostalgie ceased to be a specific malady and passed into the common language of the emotions.

In the aftermath of the Napoleonic Wars, the wages of day labourers dropped steeply because from that time on there was no shortage of labour, and the competition of machinery began to make itself felt (power-looms, which ruined the female cottage weaver, threshing-machines, which threw agricultural labourers out of work). Even the boom years were harsh for the masses of landless peasants, since high prices, between the wars, had led the landowners to pay wages in cash to their servants and workers rather than lodging and feeding them and paying in kind, as in the past. The hired hand on the northern plains of northern France or in the corn growing areas of England was no longer sheltered from price fluctuations, and shared with the urban masses the anguish and violence of the times of high prices. In England, the solution was to apply Poor Laws, going back to the reign of Elizabeth, in France, to fix the price of bread by official regulation. After 1815, rural violence resumed its tumultuous course, accompanied by the destruction of threshing machines (e.g. the riots of 'Captain Swing' in England, Autumn 1830).

In Ireland, the acts of rural violence were the work of small farmers, resisting the evictions with which the extension of the great estates were threatening them. Secret agrarian societies had existed since around 1760: they struck through cold-blooded murders at rapacious landlords or at those who were reorganizing their property to make more profit. The 'Troubles' – which had elements of both brigandage and religious war – raged most fiercely from 1812 to 1822, then again from 1830 to 1834 with the refusal of Catholic peasants to pay Anglican tithes: the Irish Tithe War. In the end, the establishment of a rural police force – the Irish Constabulary – in 1835 and then the disastrous famine of 1847 broke down the stubborn resistance of the smaller farmers and forced them to emigrate.

Political struggles and the passions of the cities sometimes dragged peasants in their wake, but the peasants' demands were always specific, unconnected with the concerns of governments and oppositions. In 1846, when the Polish patriots were ready to shake off the Austrian yoke, the Galician peasants attacked these rebels, who were also their overlords, and inside a week drowned in the blood of the nationalist insurrection. The Galician uprising of February 1846 sacked four hundred of the nobles' mansions and killed about twelve hundred of them and their servants. In 1848, a number of peasants in the départements of the Midi revolted against the so called '45 centimes tax', which the republican government, the product of a bourgeois revolution, wanted to impose on hereditary landholdings. In 1851, the peasants voted massively for the Second Empire.

In Russia, where serfdom was still flourishing, there were incessant peasant disturbances. From 1825 to 1855, from the accession of Nicholas I to the Crimean War, one can count a yearly average of twenty-three cases of rural violence requiring the intervention of the army. On most occasions it was only a question of the refusal

During the 1830s rural England was terrorized by outbreaks of rural violence, rick burning and the smashing of machinery in protest against the introduction of mechanical threshing, which caused unemployment, and the high price of bread. Bloodthirsty letters inciting rebellion began to circulate, signed 'Captain Swing'. This contemporary print turns the affair to a joke, but the danger was real and the subsequent repression savage. A few rioters were executed and hundreds transported for life.

of forced labour and the confused hope of coming liberation. It was believed that first the enlistments at the time of the Crimean War and then the resettlement of the devastated zones after it would lead to the granting of emancipation. Both times, in 1854 and in 1856, thousands of peasants left their estates, fleeing southwards, and troops had to be used to bring them back. The authorities were still terrified by the idea of a widespread rising, by the 'ghost of Pugachev'. The proclamation of the abolition of serfdom in 1861 was hedged about with considerable precautions for the maintenance of order. In fact, the troubles were limited; the bloodiest outbreak, at Bezdna, in the province of Kazan, cost about a hundred lives.

Nearer to us in time, the great revolt of the Romanian peasants in 1907 represents perhaps the last outburst on the communal pattern. The interests of the small tenant farmers of Moldavia clashed with the tax-farmers (arendasi) of the great estates, who since around 1890 were often Austrian Jews, and at the same time with the projects of agrarian reform, initiated by liberal politicians to speed the process of industrialization. The revolt was sparked off by the refusal of the tax-farmer of the vast estates of Prince Sturdza, at the time of renewal of leases, which customarily took place in February, to agree to the reductions which the tenants had been promised. On 5 February 1907, the peasants began to expel the bailiffs, to refuse forced labour and to seize town houses. On the eve of the spring sowing, said the peasants, we still have no assurance on agreements in the future. 'We want land', ran a slogan of a populist party which favoured the tenant farmers, 'proper agreements, commonage, universal suffrage and schools in the villages.' The peasants' occupation of Botosani, north of Jassi, a medium-sized town and seat of the prefecture, enabled the movement to spread to other provinces. Even large towns were threatened. The indulgent conservative government was overthrown and replaced by the liberal party, who decided to mobilize 140,000 men and to send the army against the rebels. In a week, the peasant forces were scattered. The number of peasants killed in this speedy repression is reckoned at not less than 11,000.

The dissolution of the old political and social order in Europe and the organization of agriculture along commercial lines resulted in a considerable increase in levels of production but, as we shall see in the final chapter, sounded the death-knell for the old communal structures and those customary rights that had enabled a large body of peasants somehow to survive. Big estates had supported small marginal peasant holdings, which had the advantage of providing the necessary labour for seasonal work. Peasants with very little land or none at all, village artisans, day labourers and seasonal labourers, were able to continue one way or another as part of the village community.

The replacement of the old orders of nobility, the breaking up of many estates, the secularization of church property, the sale of the common lands – all these measures for which Revolutionary France set the pattern, were in general to the advantage not of the peasantry but of the rural bourgeoisie. These bourgeois landowners succeeded the noble families and had more firmly based juridical titles and also plans for farming on a rationalized and profitable basis. Thus, for example, after the abolition of the vestiges of the feudal system in the kingdom of Naples in 1806 or again in Spain in 1837, one sees the emergence of a new social type of the landed bourgeois, the Neapolitan *galantuomo* or the Andalusian *señorito*. Against them, the mountain communes, which, in the remoter areas, retained their old way of life much longer, continued to affirm their former ancient rights on lands that had long since been alienated to individual owners. With each political upheaval, these communes hoped to regain their customary rights and noisily occupied the areas in dispute, as in the French Pyrenees in 1848 or in Andalusia in 1854, 1868 and 1871. Law suits over the liquidation of seigniorial rights and easements continued well into the 20th century.

The final word was not of violence nor of litigation but of the drift from the villages, of the tearing up of roots, of the move to the towns – and of emigration to new horizons, to new worlds.

---

**The violence** that lay not far beneath the surface of rural life could erupt in a variety of ways, some of them difficult to recognize for what they really were. Religious wars, national liberation movements, banditry – all could be disguised forms of rural protest. What tended to spark them off was change. Peasants accepted a social order in which there was inequality, but they resented and feared change. Revolts were usually attempts to return to a state of affairs that had existed, or was believed to have existed, in the past. Sometimes they became caught up in larger struggles with different aims – the Reformation, the French Revolution or the Napoleonic Wars – and later historians have been tempted to see in them wider issues than were actually present. During the Reformation, for instance, probably few peasants felt strongly about papal authority, salvation by faith or freedom of the will. What did concern them was the way that seigniorial powers were being increased, striking at their right to marry, to pass on property, to hunt, fish and gather firewood. In 1524 the abbot of Weissenau, in Switzerland, compiled a pictorial record of the revolt in his district. A typical page from it (*opposite*) shows the peasants gathering into an army. They came from the villages of Rappertsweil (at the top), where they are joined by a party from Weissenau, from Obereschach (in the centre) and from Untereschach (at the bottom). Here they are addressed by Stefan Rahl, one of the richest farmers of the area and a natural leader in such a situation. Behind him are three horsemen who have come from the abbey of Weingarten to try to persuade the peasants to lay down their arms. The peasants themselves wear armour and carry halberds and hunting spears. Later pictures in the same chronicle record the peasants' excesses, their desecration and plunder of monasteries and their final catastrophic defeat. (1)

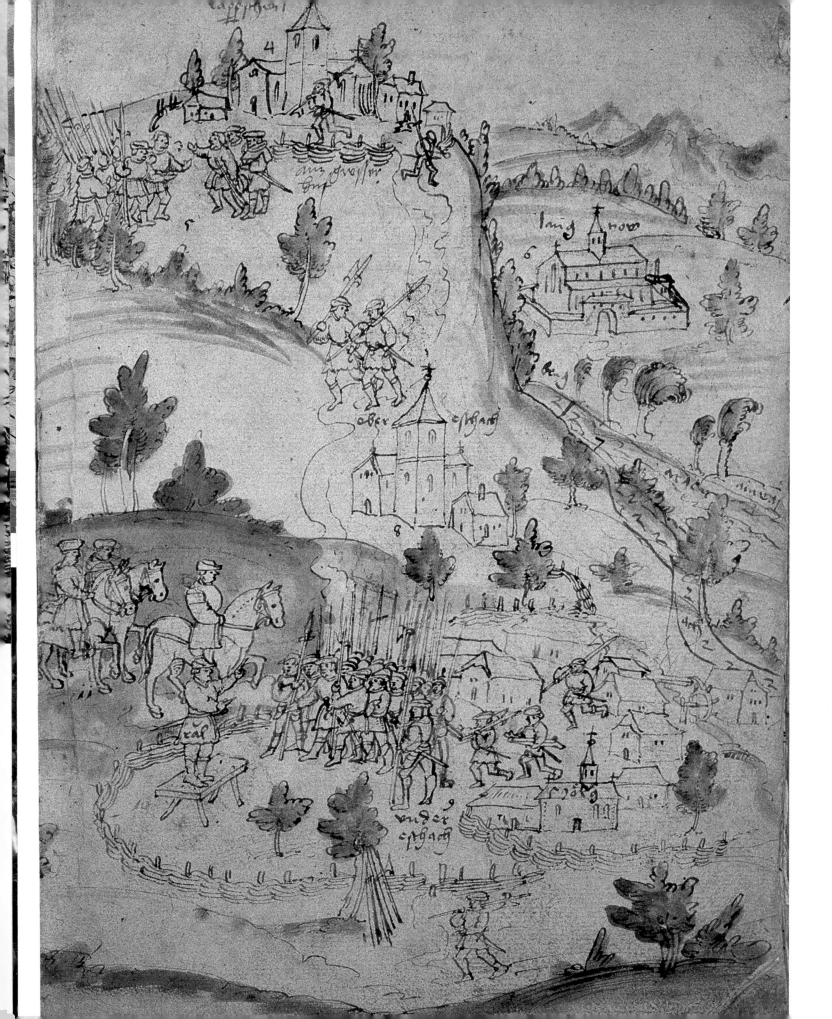

**After their defeat,** the Vendéan peasants kept up sporadic resistance for many years – a lingering, small-scale war that claimed more victims than many, more publicized, struggles. 'Les Chouans' lived as outlaws, protected by the country people at their own peril, ready to ambush, to kill and to flee again. They were only crushed by a ruthless campaign of terrorism, of which even the memory has until recently been suppressed. (16)

# 7 RURAL FOLKLORE

## JACQUELINE SIMPSON

# Rural folklore

The countryman was surrounded by forces that he had no way of understanding. The church gave him a picture of the world that made sense to some extent, but this remained remote and generalized. What we call folklore is a system of beliefs that explained events and accounted for phenomena, both natural and man-made, in terms that the peasant could assimilate and which seemed to offer him some measure of control. We misunderstand the nature of these beliefs if we treat them as fairy tales or merely picturesque legends. They were deeply serious. To be able to identify the sources of misfortune, to carry out appropriate rituals correctly, to avoid the pitfalls that lay all around and make use of powers friendly to man – all these were matters of the most earnest and urgent concern.

The systematic study of folklore began in the 19th century, and from the start attention was focused almost exclusively on rural rather than urban material. Many factors accounted for this preference. One, already noted in a previous chapter, was the tendency of educated and aristocratic elites to idealize country life; influenced by the long tradition of pastoral poetry and painting, they readily responded to a charmingly picturesque vision of sturdy, merry country folk dancing round maypoles, celebrating harvest suppers or wedding feasts or expressing their simple piety in pilgrimages and wayside shrines. Literature and art testify to the widespread appeal which this idealization of country life held for the educated 19th-century public.

Nationalist fervour, too, often stimulated the collection of folk songs, fairy tales, folk music and local customs, and the study of material folk culture – regional costumes, for example, and crafts such as woodcarving, lace-making, or embroidery. If, as was often the case, the use of one language rather than another was an issue with nationalist implications, this would direct attention to the rich rural store of dialect words, proverbs, rhymes and so forth. The tenacious conservatism of village communities was prized as the guarantor of their fidelity to the true national ethos.

The same rural conservatism also appealed to the many folklorists whose prime concern was to trace cultural traits back to their origins, and who therefore sought out the most archaic elements they could find, whether in beliefs, customs or folk tales. Some wished to recover information about the fairly recent historical past, as did Jacob Grimm when he compared folklore about giants, dwarfs and wood-nymphs in order to reconstruct 'Germanic mythology' as it existed before the conversion to Christianity. Others envisaged the study of folklore as a kind of psychological archaeology for penetrating the thought-processes and recovering the world view of primitive prehistoric man. They set the highest value on items that could be interpreted as survivals from this prehistoric stage, especially if they could be parallelled among the beliefs and customs of 'primitive' non-European peoples. Probably the most monumental and influential work based on these principles is Sir James Frazer's *The Golden Bough*.

Though this approach inspired many works of great value, it did have limitations. It tended to pick out and over-emphasize striking beliefs and practices, isolating them from their total sociological context; it devalued items of more recent origin, even where they were functionally equivalent to the more archaic ones, and automatically equated change and development with loss or corruption of 'true' meaning. There was a frequent regrettable failure to record the personal histories and social background of the primary informants, and the circumstances of transmission of the lore. In short, the focus of interest was not on the contemporary countryman himself but upon his ancestors; scholars rarely investigated the question of why the 'survivals' had survived so long, and what currently useful function was preserving their existence.

## The concealed functions of folklore

Another problem which roused, and still rouses, great debate was set by the remarkable similarity of folklore in widely separated parts of Europe, and indeed often beyond Europe, despite differences of language, religion and cultural history. One theory holds that similar beliefs, tales and customs have spread by slow diffusion over many centuries from one remote source; the alternative theory suggests that some, at least, have independently arisen at different times and places in response to similar needs and stimuli.

There are indeed some instances where similarity of function is a wholly satisfying explanation. One such is the belief that dangerous supernatural beings lurk in lakes and rivers to drown the unwary, for it is obviously advantageous to a mother if she can ensure that her children are too frightened of the water-bogy to play near some dangerous spot. Similarities in the descriptions of these beings can be explained as reflections of their supposed habits and their habitats among dark waters, trailing weeds and floating scum. Thus the English bogies Jenny Greenteeth and Peg Powler are said to have greenish skin, green eyes and teeth, long slimy green hair and long arms with which to snatch their victims. In Russia the Vodyanoi, a male spirit haunting millponds, is sometimes described as an old man with green hair and beard, sometimes as a huge frog, sometimes as transformed into a moss-covered floating log. In 13th-century France, there were said to be dangerous creatures called Dracs in the Rhône, who would seize and drown any woman who waded in too far while washing her linen. The usefulness of such cautionary tales is obvious, and explains their basic similarity and survival through the centuries. They need not necessarily be always survivals from the animistic stage in human thought (when natural objects such as rivers and trees were identified with a spirit), for they are simple concepts which could readily be reinvented.

But some resemblances are too odd to be explained away as logical developments from recurrent similar conditions. It is, for example, quite natural that every heavily wooded area, whether in Scandinavia, Germany or the Slav countries, should have tales about forest elves who frighten and bewilder travellers, making them lose their way. What is more remarkable is that the counterspell to break their power is the same almost everywhere: the victim must turn his cap or coat inside out, or put his shoes on the wrong feet. Even in the gentler English countryside pixies and fairies were credited with this same power, and repelled by this same counterspell. Again, there is a practically universal belief that fairies steal babies and leave as a substitute one of their own race, who remains sickly, ugly, mute and fretful. This belief, it is generally accepted, must have arisen to 'explain' the existence of mentally defective babies; putting the blame on the fairies comforts the parents by assuring them they are not responsible for the calamity. This idea might recur independently in different areas; but when, as is often the case, the belief is embedded in a story which goes on to prescribe exactly the same odd and elaborate magical procedure for unmasking and expelling the changeling, this must surely imply that the story has been diffused from end to end of Europe by the slow process of oral transmission.

Folklore is not merely the product of a stable, conservative society, but often serves to reinforce that stability by upholding ethical norms and justifying social assumptions. Often its implied lessons are closely allied to those of religion, so that stories pass freely from pulpit to market place and back again, and popular belief reinforces clerical precept. Examples abound, both in the Middle Ages and in more recent times, for instance in tales turning on supernatural punishments for blasphemy, ingratitude, inhospitality and other breaches of the moral code. One common

motif is the story of a sunken city, once proud and prosperous, which was engulfed by the sea or by a lake because of its sins – the Breton legend of Keris is a well known example. Another is a legend attached to groups of standing stones in over thirty places in England, Ireland and France; it tells of how a group of dancers, often said to be a wedding party, were turned to stone for wickedly persisting in dancing on a Sunday, or (in France) while a priest was passing by carrying the Blessed Sacrament.

Ghost stories are a very common vehicle for conveying moral lessons. It is axiomatic everywhere that those who die in great sin will not rest peacefully – suicides and murderers, for example. Often the ghosts of babies who died unbaptized were regarded with extreme dread, possibly because they were denied burial in holy ground and so remained permanently outcast from the community, and presumably hostile to it. In many countries they were said to become will-o'-the-wisps, haunting waste land and luring travellers to their doom. In Brittany, women who had murdered their illegitimate babies, or had had abortions, became gruesome ghosts called Night Washerwomen; they haunted rivers and ponds, eternally wringing out filthy, bloodstained linen, which sometimes took on the form of the murdered infants, and they would waylay anyone who came near them by night, and break his arms, or drown him. Misers, too, figure frequently in traditional ghost-lore, for by hiding their money and thus depriving their natural heirs of their rights, they have offended against the primary duty of providing for one's family. Other types of ghost story serve to teach surviving relatives to follow correct procedures at funerals and to carry out the wishes of the dead; if they fail in these respects, they risk the ghost's anger.

Births, like deaths, offer opportunity for grimly moralizing tales on the theme of supernatural retribution. For example: a pregnant woman callously refused alms to a beggar woman and her ragged children, exclaiming, 'Be off, you and your little frogs!'; when her own child was born, it had deformed legs, and could only hop like a frog (Wales, 1871). In a recently collected Irish tale, a wealthy childless woman mocks her poorer sister for having more children than she can afford to feed, ignoring the proverb, 'When God creates a mouth, he creates food to put in it'; later, she herself has a child, but it is born without a mouth. A third story, known since the 16th century in both England and Germany, combines the idea that it is wicked to try to avoid having children with the theme, common in folk tales, that it is impossible to evade one's fate. A certain man, thinking he had already enough children to rear, left his wife and travelled abroad for seven years; as soon as he returned home his wife became pregnant, and bore seven children at one birth. Such stories grow out of, express and reinforce the ethical values of the communities in which they circulate.

Another extremely common and widespread class of folk tale has an aetiological function – that is, it supplies an 'explanation' or 'origin' for some notable material feature of the local environment, or for a placename, or for a traditional custom or event. A typical example would be the story, already quoted for its moralizing element, which explains a circle of standing stones as a group of petrified dancers. In this, as in many other instances, it is the exceptional and non-productive parts of the landscape that apparently demand explanation – the awkward rock or megalith interrupting the ploughed field, the prehistoric burial mound, the natural chasm, the patch of sterile or stone-covered land, rather than cultivated fields, pastures or productive woods. It seems as if, in the eyes of peasant communities, the good land could be seen as God's creation for man's use, but all that was unproductive and inconvenient needed another explanation. A taste for wild, picturesque scenery for its own sake is a late, urban, sophisticated attitude, alien to the countryman's outlook.

Therefore, large isolated rocks, tracts of stony land, abrupt clefts and the like were ascribed to the activities of the Devil, or of giants or of heroes of superhuman strength. Their actions might spring from hostility towards man (the Devil or a troll hurling a rock at a church), or from playfulness (giant and hero competing in stone-throwing games), or from stupid clumsiness (giant or Devil dropping a load of building stones). Prehistoric mounds and other mysterious earthworks, or even natural hillocks, were said to be homes of fairies, elves, dwarfs or whatever was the local term for small earth-dwelling spirits; they were often taboo areas, never to be ploughed up or used for grazing. But a valuable feature such as a spring could be attributed to a benevolent supernatural power; it might be said to have sprung up where a saint's horse pawed the ground, or where a martyr's blood fell.

Some aetiological legends can be securely dated to the Middle Ages by references in written sources, such as chronicles and saints' lives, or by the early occurrence of significant placenames encapsulating the legend. In other cases, dating remains an open question; good stories were imitated and adapted to new settings, and this process continued for many centuries. Nowadays, many topographical legends have ceased to belong exclusively to the rural communities where they originated; printed in folklore collections, children's books and guidebooks, they have become common property, and are often consciously exploited as tourist attractions.

Even so, only a tiny fraction of the total number of local legends ever passes outside the bounds of its own area. Any close local survey will reveal a wealth of traditional anecdotes (admittedly, often very brief ones) about places in the village itself or its surroundings. Not merely large-scale landscape features, but individual trees, paths, crossroads, fields and ponds are the subjects; so too are buildings, especially those that are central to community life (the church, the inn, the manor house), and those with unusual architectural features. Anything noteworthy, from an illegible tombstone to a curious weathervane or a chimneypot differing from the normal local pattern, may rouse curiosity and stimulate a legend. The stories may involve the supernatural, but equally they may embody that simplified version of national and local history that survives in the communal memory, alluding to famous or infamous kings and nobles, or to outlaws, robbers, national heroes and so on. Or they may deal plausibly with comparatively everyday matters – murders, poachers and smugglers, buried treasures, notorious local personalities.

A strange paradox can be discerned in this local lore. It is precisely because some site or object seems to those living near by to be unique that it inspires stories, yet the stories themselves, far from being unique, almost always conform to patterns that folklorists recognize as widespread ones – that, indeed, is how one knows they are legends, not factual memories orally transmitted. Individual story-tellers, however, do not realize this, and would bitterly resent being told of it. To them, not only the site or object but the legend about it is a unique focus for local pride. To this day, there is a strong tendency in any community to maintain that its own tradition about a ghost, say, or a buried treasure or a visit from King X must have some factual basis; to doubt this is to insult the reputable people of past generations who had vouched for its truth. Legends are a much valued element in that complex of traditions whereby a community establishes and maintains its sense of its own identity.

If 'folklore' is taken in its broadest sense, as whatever is passed on orally through personal contacts rather than by formal teaching, then for many centuries everything that country people knew and did in connection with their work would fall within the definition, and so would their games and entertainments, their crafts and decorative arts, their personal and communal customs and, in fact, almost every aspect of their adult lives outside the spheres of official religion and the law. To narrow this vast field, we propose to omit here those aspects of traditional knowledge and practice which correspond to the scientific or technological spheres (e.g. proverbial sayings conveying agricultural advice and weather lore, or the practical knowledge about the properties of plants). We will concentrate on three aspects: the role of supernatural forces in rural life; popular, as distinct from official, religious cults; and some of the ritually prescribed actions marking moments of special importance in the yearly round or in an individual life.

## Fairies good and bad

One universal feature was the belief in fairies. Known under a great variety of local names, they were envisaged as a race of non-human but material beings with many magic powers, often small or grotesque, who lived underground, in woods or under water. Beliefs about them reflect contradictory attitudes. On the one hand, fairies are dangerous, inflicting diseases on men and livestock, stealing babies, abducting people into fairyland and playing mischievous tricks; on the other hand, fairies may befriend humans, reward kindness and bring luck and prosperity. So complex is the concept of the fairy that it is unlikely to have one single origin: it seems to be a compound derived from old beliefs about fertility gods and nature spirits, about the dead in general and ancestors in particular, and even memories of prehistoric aboriginals, as recalled by later more highly developed invading groups.

For the farmers, the benevolent aspects of fairies were epitomized in the figure of the House Spirit – the English Brownie, Scandinavian Nesse or Tomte, German Kobold, Russian Domovoy, etc. There is never more than one of these per farmstead, and he embodies the luck of the farm; in return for small food offerings, he will work by night at threshing corn, feeding and currying horses, churning butter and other tasks. According to some tales, he makes his own farm rich at the neighbours' expense, magically transferring wheat from their barn to his master's. A house-fairy should never be spied on or mocked; he punishes lazy, dirty workers by pinching them; if the hearth is left dirty or slops are emptied near the house he will be angry. These implied lessons in hygiene and industrious work are of obvious practical value; more broadly, it could be argued that to believe in a luck-bringing spirit will bolster the farmer's self-confidence, which will increase his chances of success.

Various concrete practices reflected the belief in house-fairies. In medieval Germany, small wood-carvings, rag-dolls or wax figures were identified with the Kobold, and set up near the hearth. In Russia, peasants moving into a new house would lay a slice of bread under the stove to tempt a Domovoy to take up residence there. In Norway and the Orkneys, where the guardian fairy was thought to live inside a hillock near the farm (often an old burial mound), milk and beer would be poured over it, and there are even accounts of cocks or cattle being killed on the mound as offerings. A widespread practice was to put out a small bowl of milk or porridge at night, for the house-fairy. Vestiges of these beliefs and rituals remained here and there into the present century.

Apart from the house-fairy, most other fairies were thought of as mischievous or positively malevolent. In Scotland and Ireland, any cow which became thin and sickly was suspected of having been struck by 'elf-shot', that is, a flint arrow or a sharp splinter hurled by a fairy; she needed magical cures, such as being made to swallow salt, soot or a scrap of paper with a Bible verse on it, or having a gun fired over her back. These cures might have to be applied by a 'wise woman'. All over the British Isles, it was thought that fairies would ride horses in the stables by night, leaving them tired and

*Robin Goodfellow, a combination of good fairy, satyr and devil, shown here in a woodcut of 1628.*

sweating, and with their manes tangled in 'elf knots'; this could be prevented by hanging a stone with a natural hole in it at the stable door, or over the horses' backs. Similarly, cowsheds should be protected by holed stones, crossed twigs of rowan or (in Ireland) a 'St Brigit's Cross' made of plaited rushes. Every country has its favourite protections. Some are based on Christian practices – the use of holy water, crosses, Bibles, evergreens blessed on Palm Sunday, saints' emblems and so on. Others are simpler and presumably older – the use of salt, fire, iron, stones etc. Whatever their age and origins, they are functionally interchangeable.

The further a man strayed from home, the more supernatural perils he must face. Those who worked in solitary places, such as wood-cutters and the men and women who accompanied the cattle onto the high summer pastures in mountain regions, were exposed to attacks and sexual molestation by trolls and forest elves. Those who went outside after dark might meet all kinds of horrifying creatures – will-o'-the-wisps, the Wild Hunt, bogy-like supernatural animals and many more. Such beliefs reflected human reactions to the unpleasant experience of unfamiliar surroundings, projecting the panic of a man lost in the dark or the sexual fantasies of someone leading a solitary life in the forests onto an appropriately imagined supernatural figure. They were also a means of social control, discouraging such eccentric and possibly dangerous behaviour as roaming about after dark. In more modern times, local traditions sometimes hint that law-breakers such as smugglers, and underground political movements, exploited these beliefs as cover for their own nocturnal activities.

*Witches and demons dancing in a ring: an illustration from 'The Kingdom of Darkness', 1688.*

## Witches and witchcraft

The belief in witches, and the closely related concept of the Evil Eye, played an even greater role than that in fairies, and has survived more strongly to this day. Psychologically, this is easy to understand, since the main function here is to supply an explanation, and a scapegoat, for disease, death, crop failure and personal misfortune. Its great advantage is that it gives a permissible outlet for anger. If a misfortune comes from God, one has to bear it patiently; if from fairies, one can protect oneself by charms, but there is no way one can punish a fairy; but if it comes from a witch, a fellow-member of the community, one can identify her or him, and have the satisfaction of revenge.

The paradigm of a 'normal' witchcraft problem in a village would be somewhat as follows. A succession of misfortunes seems to need explanation. The victim's suspicions gather round someone whose marginal position in the community, or personal behaviour patterns, have already marked her or him as a suitable scapegoat. The victim consults what in English is known as a 'wise woman' or 'cunning man' – a person reputed to have paranormal powers in the detection of witches and thieves, whose role corresponds roughly to that of an African 'witch doctor.' The 'cunning man' confirms the victim's suspicions; he then suggests some magical cure or counter-action to break the evil spell and, usually, to inflict punitive pain on the witch. Normally, this should suffice to end the episode. However, if similar events recur or if many victims are involved, tension may rise to the point where the alleged witch is made to submit to ordeals and is brought to trial, if the law recognizes witchcraft as a crime; if not, she may be ostracized, assaulted or even lynched.

There is, however, a complicating factor in the history of witchcraft. From about 1450 till roughly 1700, a majority of both Catholic and Protestant religious thinkers maintained that witches belonged to a secret organization of Devil-worshippers who had made a pact with Satan. Church law and secular law combined to try to root out this alleged organization; sermons and sensational pamphlets publicized a lurid picture of murderous covens and Devil-worshipping sabbaths; panics, denunciations, brainwashing, confessions and executions abounded. Yet even at the height of the panic one can deduce from the trial reports that country people were still more concerned to stop the witch from injuring their children or their livestock than to find out if she worshipped Satan, which was what Church authorities were accusing her of. Material from the 18th and 19th centuries shows how quickly the older, simpler view of witchcraft re-emerged once the propaganda had ceased. There was still some talk of books of spells, but the coven and the sabbath faded into the background, remembered only in a notion that witches were particularly active on such dates as Walpurgis Night (30 April) and Midsummer Eve, and would hold gatherings on those nights.

Even when there was no witch-hunting panic on, a wide range of misfortunes was attributed to witchcraft. Epileptic fits, slow wasting diseases, and sudden sharp pains could be explained by assuming that a witch was stabbing or melting an image of her victim. Witches were also thought capable of controlling winds and hail; halting vehicles by magically immobilizing the horses or the wheels; causing epidemics among farm animals; withering crops; drawing a cow's milk out of her by magic, till she gave only blood; preventing butter from 'coming' in the churn. They were thought to exert their power by muttered charms, by a glance, or by sending out animal familiars, the commonest being mice, toads and flies. They were said to turn into hares or cats at will, and to be able to fly on various objects, notably broomsticks.

What types of person was suspected? Here tradition is inconsistent. One group of tales implies that it could be anyone at all, so that a man might accidentally discover that his own mother or wife was a witch; this presumably reflects the beliefs current during the great witch-hunts. Far more frequently, the suspect conformed to a stereotype – an old woman, from the lower end of the socio-economic scale, probably a widow living alone, and possibly eccentric or deformed or notably ugly. This pattern recurs frequently in the trial records of Britain, though on the continent it is often swamped by the mass accusations during major witch-hunts; it emerges very consistently from the beliefs and oral tales of more recent centuries, and is still a powerful stereotype in popular imagination. In his valuable study, *Witchcraft in Tudor and Stuart England*, Alan Macfarlane has set out one reason why this should be so. He notes that witchcraft accusations were almost always preceded by a quarrel arising because the old woman had asked for some small loan or gift from a more prosperous neighbour, and had been refused, at which she had shown anger. The people who had refused her were then quick to imagine that any misfortune they suffered was the result of her ill-wishing. This, he suggests, is an example of the common psychological process of guilt-projection, caused by their uneasy awareness that they had acted uncharitably towards her. He argues that it would have been particularly common at a period when the Catholic precepts recommending ample and frequent alms-giving had been recently replaced by the Protestant work-ethos, which forbade people to 'encourage' beggars, but were not yet wholly forgotten. In such a situation, mutual resentment between the poor and the comparatively prosperous part of the community would be at a peak, and the latter would suffer also from a divided conscience. To represent the old woman as a vengeful witch would justify one's previous harshness.

There is ample evidence of the widespread use of protective devices against witches, displayed on buildings, especially round the main doors and near the hearth. Those recorded in Britain include: carved oak posts beside the hearth; chalked patterns on the threshold; salt-glazed chimney tiles; horseshoes, crossed rowan twigs, holed stones, pieces of old iron and bunches of marigolds hung over or beside the door; hollies, bay-trees, rowans and various shrubs and flowers growing in cottage gardens; bones, bottles and old shoes built into walls or foundations. Similar lists could be made for every country; in Catholic areas, one would also find religious items used as protective charms. Besides the house itself, outbuildings housing animals needed protection, and places of work such as the dairy or the smithy. So, too, did individual animals; many things such as sheep- and cattle-bells and the

ornaments on horses' harnesses, which are now merely regarded as decorations, once had the function of repelling witches, fairies and evil spirits.

If despite all precautions a witch's spell was believed to be at work, counter-spells were used. These are often notably aggressive in symbolism. If butter would not 'come', one should plunge a red-hot poker in the churn; if a cart was stuck, flog its wheels; if animals were dying, cut the heart from a dead one, stick pins in it and roast it slowly. For human sicknesses, one should make a 'witch-bottle' by filling a bottle with the victim's urine, plus pins and/or threads, and boiling it. These rituals were supposed to cause correspondingly intense pain to the witch, thus forcing her to lift her spell. Aggression could also take more direct forms; by drawing a witch's blood 'above the breath', i.e. scratching or cutting her face, one could break all her power for ever.

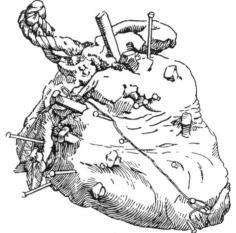

*Sticking pins in an animal's heart could be either black magic or a counter-spell: this sheep's heart is preserved in the Pitt-Rivers Museum, Oxford.*

## The Evil Eye

One of the main dangers against which country people felt that they had to protect themselves and their beasts was that of the Evil Eye. Belief in this is not quite as universal as that in witchcraft; nevertheless, it affected many parts of Europe. The Eye, like witchcraft, is regarded as a hostile magical force affecting health and fertility; it differs from witchcraft in being envisaged not as a deliberately acquired and deliberately exerted art, but as a natural, though harmful, faculty. Certain people were believed to have been born with this power, which was transmitted through their eyes to anything they glanced at; sometimes it was exerted unconsciously, but it could be greatly increased if applied in a spirit of envy and hostility. For this reason, communities where the Evil Eye is feared are usually very reluctant to utter praise of anyone or anything, or to hear others utter it: praise is likely to rouse envy, and envy will find its outlet through the Eye. To compliment a child on his good looks, health or cleverness, or to

*Holed stones had magical powers; in Cornwall sick children were passed through the hole to make them healthy.*

praise an animal, is to court danger; indeed, anyone uttering such compliments may well be suspected of being himself endowed with the Evil Eye, especially if he is a stranger.

Like other beliefs in evil supernatural forces, this idea can serve as an explanation for many natural misfortunes. In present-day Malta, for instance, a recent researcher found that 'many country people still blame the Evil Eye for the dehydrated condition of their babies following a prolonged attack of acute gastro-enteritis in the warm summer months'. Deaths and disease among domestic animals were also often attributed to it, the most vulnerable being precisely those most important to the economy, namely cattle, horses and pigs; like witchcraft, it can be the alleged cause of loss of milk in cows. In the Scottish Highlands, where a huge body of lore on this topic was collected in the 19th and early 20th century, farm life was full of taboos intended to protect the cattle. For example, they were believed to be particularly vulnerable to the Eye on certain dates, notably the first Monday of the Spring Quarter, and no stranger must be allowed to set eyes on them on that day; some farmers went so far as to keep their beasts locked up in the stalls till nightfall. In Italy, horses were thought to be especially at risk, and were bedecked with protective charms of various patterns, many of which have now found a new use as 'lucky charms' for motor vehicles. In Malta, besides cattle and pigs, young domestic rabbits were thought to be vulnerable because their natural curiosity led them to come to the front of their cages and so encounter the malevolent glance of strangers. In Greece, even nowadays, people whose plants wither unexpectedly may attribute this to some Evil-Eyed person who has praised them.

Belief in the Evil Eye has persisted in essentially the same form from classical Greece and Rome, through the Middle Ages and Renaissance, to the present day. Naturally, it has been reinterpreted from time to time; for instance, the discovery of hypnotism gave it a brief period of 'scientific' acceptability among educated people, and, even more surprisingly, an edition of the *Catholic Encyclopaedia* published in 1967 seems to endorse its objective reality: 'The evil eye causes harm through its envy, the venom of which it projects through its glance, and thus poisons its object or victim.'

Various communities have adopted an amazing variety of counter-measures to protect themselves from this peril – amulets of many different types, prayers and verbal formulas, gestures and ritual actions. A few samples will have to suffice, to show something of the variety of procedures that can be employed.

In the Gaelic-speaking Highlands and Islands of Scotland many incantations and rituals for counteracting the effects of the Eye have been recorded, most of which have a strongly religious tone. On the island of Barra, a man whose sickness is thought to be due to this cause should swallow three mouthfuls of water in which a silver coin has been placed, the first in the name

of the Father, the second of the Son, the third of the Holy Ghost. The accompanying Gaelic incantation is intended to make the evil recoil upon the sender of it, though it is addressed to the sick man:

> It is mine own eye
> It is the eye of God,
> It is the eye of God's Son,
> Which shall repel this,
> Which shall combat this.
>
> He who has made to thee the eye,
> Surely lie it on himself,
> Surely lie it on his affection,
> Surely lie it on his stock.
>
> On his wife, on his children,
> On his means, on his dear ones,
> On his cattle, on his seed,
> And on his comely kine.

The following ritual was prescribed in Inverness-shire for curing an afflicted animal: Go to a bridge over which both the living and the dead have passed (i.e. one leading to a church, used by funerals); kneeling on your right knee, scoop up a palmful of water into a clay dish, saying:

> I am lifting a little drop of water
> In the holy name of the Father.
> I am lifting a little drop of water
> In the holy name of the Son.
> I am lifting a little drop of water
> In the holy name of the Spirit.

Rub this water down the animal's spine, saying:

> Shake from thee thy harm,
> Shake from thee thy jealousy,
> Shake from thee thy illness,
> In the name of the Father,
> In the name of the Son,
> In the name of the Holy Spirit.

If any water remains, it should be poured away over a rock that is earth-fast, for fear that anyone should put its holy powers to bad use.

Another episode clearly shows how the Eye was believed to function, and also how certain people had an important social role to play in curing its effects (just as 'cunning men' and 'wise women' diagnosed and combated the effects of witchcraft). The incident took place on the island of North Uist in 1909. A man from the neighbouring island of Benbecula, who had come to North Uist to buy a horse, happened to praise a crofter's horse as he passed it. Almost at once, the horse fell to the ground and was rolling in agony. Since the Benbecula man was already known by reputation as one who had the Evil Eye, the crofter at once sent for a certain woman who had the skill to counteract it. She took three threads of different colours symbolizing the Trinity (black for the Father, red for the Son, white for the Spirit), twined them into a three-ply cord and instructed the crofter how to tie them round the root of the horse's tail in the name of the Trinity; the horse recovered at once. She had inherited her powers and knowledge from her father, a very devout man; she believed that it was revealed to her in prayer whether a particular illness was due to natural causes, in which case she prescribed ordinary cures, or to a spell, in which case she cured by invoking the Trinity in the manner described.

At the opposite end of Europe, in the Mediterranean countries, belief in the Evil Eye was equally widespread, in both Christian and Islamic cultures; this area is also notably rich in counter-charms, some of which are demonstrably very ancient. One such is the representation of a protective eye, combating the Evil Eye on the well known magical principle that 'like affects like'. One form it takes is the naturalistic painting of a pair of eyes at the prow of a fishing boat; another, more formalized, is the blue glass bead with a white circular pattern in the centre, which is one of the most popular protective devices in Arab countries and in Turkey, and is also used in Greece. This design has precedents in classical Greece and Rome, and above all in ancient Egypt. More speculatively, it has been suggested that eye patterns carved on prehistoric stone monuments also had a protective function.

The phallus was also revered in classical Greece and Rome for its protective powers; it was carved on the façades of buildings, set up as stone pillars or worn as amulets, as a symbol of good luck and fertility, and as a talisman against destructive magic, including that of the Evil Eye. Phallic representations can be found in all provinces of the Roman Empire, as well as in Italy itself. The adoption of Christianity modified public attitudes towards sexual objects, but amulets that are clearly descended from the phalloi are still popular in Italy; they are pendants shaped like a slightly twisted horn, the older examples being made of coral, silver, gold, amber or brass, and modern mass-produced ones of red plastic.

Many other amulets are used in the Mediterranean countries. Italian types include crescents, mermaids, frogs, snakes, keys, branches of rue and hands arranged in two traditional obscene gestures: the *mano cornuta* (index finger and little finger extended as horns, other fingers clenched) and *mano fica* (thumb thrust between clenched fingers). An open hand with fingers outstretched is commonly found in Arab countries, more rarely in Christian ones. All are made in glittering materials or in bright colours; the theory behind their use is that an attractive or startling object will attract the attention at once, and that since the power of someone with the Evil Eye is concentrated in his *first* glance, this will be neutralized if it falls upon an object as powerful as itself. The special efficacy of obscene pendants therefore rests both on their life-giving symbolism and on their startling nature.

Actual animal horns are also used, thus further disguising the underlying phallic symbolism. This is a common feature of farm buildings in Malta, where cattle skulls with horns attached or plaster-of-Paris heads of cattle and deer are set up on walls and roofs above doorways, or inside the buildings. This is in no way regarded as a pagan custom; the same farm that displays cattle horns may also display a statue of the Virgin or of a saint; similarly, Italian amulets are often used side by side with rosaries, crucifixes and medals.

It is probable that the use of sexual gestures and actions was once widespread in rural communities for magical purposes, but allusions to such matters are understandably rare in folklore publications of earlier generations; indeed, the informants themselves would probably have been very unwilling to speak of anything so 'primitive' to outsiders. Recent research in the Balkans has revealed a surprising amount of such practices, surviving as late as the Second World War among Albanians, Serbians and Bosnians. For example, in the 1940s, nakedness was still used as a magical protection when groups of peasants were tackling some particularly risky task, such as transporting large timbers or millstones by cart. To prevent any evil spell being put on the oxen, the cart or the load, a man would strip naked and walk beside it, ostentatiously displaying his penis and cracking jokes about it; this, it was argued, would divert the attention of any potentially evil-minded onlooker. Balkan gipsies similarly thought that if a horse could not drag its load, the driver should rub his hand first over his own genitals and then over the animal's back; an Albanian woman might safeguard her children by patting their faces with her left hand, having first rubbed it on her own genitals, before letting them leave the house, for fear they might meet someone with the Eye.

### The cycle of the seasons
The cycle of seasonal customs and annual festivals presents a complicated picture, not simply because of local variations but because such diverse factors govern their timing. Some relate to the solar year, e.g. midsummer bonfire festivals; others, to the Church calendar; others, to agricultural activities, which vary with the climate and main produce of the region – arable cultivation sets a different pattern of work and leisure from vine growing or from a pastoral economy. Work patterns influence seasonal customs both positively and negatively. Positively, by fixing the timing of ceremonies to mark the start of a major undertaking (ploughing, for instance), or its completion (harvesting, grape picking, sheep shearing); negatively, in that fairs and festivals cannot be held when work is at its peak. Finally, superimposed on the seasonal cycle, come politically inspired national celebrations – independence days, commemorations of victories, etc. When these fall close to an older seasonal or ecclesiastical feast, they may absorb some of its features, or even cause its abandonment; the

English Guy Fawkes' Night (5 November), for example, copied the Hallowe'en bonfires and in some areas superseded Hallowe'en altogether.

The interpretation of seasonal customs is equally complex. They contain innumerable local variations, and reveal different functions and significances according to the angle from which they are examined. It was in this field that scholars seeking remote origins found some of their richest material. By comparing spring festivals, harvest customs, midsummer and midwinter celebrations, certain types of folk dancing, mumming plays and customs involving animal disguise, with corresponding elements in non-European or pre-Christian religions, they discovered vestiges of various archaic cultural traits – fertility cults, sun-worship, vegetation cults, the ritual re-enactment of death-and-resurrection dramas and disguised versions of human or animal sacrifice. It was assumed that these features had existed unchanged for many centuries, thanks to the static conservatism of rural life; parallels were established across wide gaps of time, and the silence of documentary records during the intervening period could always be ascribed to a hostile clergy or to the in-difference of the literate classes towards peasant ways.

This approach has been very influential, but it can never offer more than a partial interpretation. It ignores many relevant factors from medieval or recent history, notably the pervasive effect of Catholic doctrine and ritual. Nor does it consider socio-economic and psychological functions, which are vital to the continued existence of a custom, whatever its forgotten origins may have been. Many customs, for instance, are the occasion for a *quête* – a formalized and socially permissible type of begging which can be undertaken without loss of face, for instance when a group of working men dance, sing, or act a mumming play outside the homes of wealthier members of the community, and receive food and drink, or money, to 'pay' for the luck their performance is thought to bring. Once of great practical importance, this now survives only in children's customs, or in jocular contexts. Psychological factors are also extremely important: one cannot stress too highly the value of a temporary release from social constraints – a permitted opportunity to express rowdiness, aggression, sexuality and mockery of authority, and to indulge freely in drink, good food and amusement. This spirit, supremely expressed in the Carnival, recurs on every scale from the domestic Christmas feast to the annual village fair or town pageant. Finally, most customs express and reinforce the communal bonds between the participants, whether these are the whole local community or a sub-group within it; and they are also a focus for local pride.

Anthropologists such as Mannhardt and Frazer paid particular attention to customs related to cereal cultivation as survivals of an ancient fertility cult; so it is appropriate to choose a few examples from the same area to show the complexity of seasonal agricultural practices.

Before ploughing began, the land had to be purified. In Herefordshire, a ball of hawthorn branches was burned in the field before dawn on New Year's Day, to expel evil spirits and prevent the wheat disease called 'smut'; this ball had been made one year previously, on New Year's Day, and had been hanging in the house all year for luck. This is a typical way of symbolizing, and ensuring, an unbroken sequence of prosperity; there are innumerable customs in which an object is ritually prepared and/or blessed, displayed for a year and then ritually destroyed, to be replaced at once by another. As for the burning, this is an application of the ancient and universal belief in the power of fire to expel super-natural evils, but it also reflects a now discredited scientific theory that diseases came from 'bad air' and that fire and smoke ('fumigation') would prevent them.

The ploughing itself was ceremonially begun, often just after Twelfth Night, the horses having been kept away from work and given extra food during the twelve days of Christmas; in some countries they were bled on St Stephen's Day (26 December), presumably in accordance with the medical theory that bleeding was strengthening. In eastern parts of England, there was a *quête* on Plough Monday (the Monday after Twelfth Night); farm workers dragged a decorated plough round the village, demanding money at each house and from passers-by. The last sheaf reaped at the previous year's harvest, which had been kept as a luck-bringer, might now be used to ensure similar success for the new crop; in Devon, it was ploughed into the first furrow; in Bulgaria, its ashes were strewn on the field; in parts of Scotland, it was given to the horses to eat. A Swedish ritual elaborates this into a symbolic communion between farmer, plough-horses and the plough itself: the man and the horses all shared part of a loaf made at Christmas from the grain of last year's last sheaf, and the rest of it was crumbled and mixed with the seed, after which the man drank some ale and poured the rest on the horses and on the plough.

In many parts of Europe, there was said to be a Corn Spirit living among the growing crop; it might be thought of as human (usually female), or as a goat, calf, hare, cock, cat, dog, mare or wolf. The process of reaping and/or threshing was called 'killing' this being; the last sheaf, or the slowest reaper, or both, was identified with it, and the sheaf or the reaper became the centre of various celebratory and luck-bringing rituals, which often involved rough horseplay. Here, argued Mannhardt and Frazer, was an archaic rite in which a human being or animal, incarnating the Corn Spirit, was sacrificially killed to bring fertility to the next crop.

This may indeed have been at the root of the belief, but it also had functions which kept it relevant even in the 19th century. First, the Corn Spirit served as a bogy to stop people damaging the growing crop, for it was described as a horrible and threatening being. For instance, the German Rye-Mother was a hag with black iron breasts who would crush little children if they went into the rye to pick poppies and cornflowers; the Russian Poleviki carried sickles to slash any drunkard who trampled the wheat; the Swedish Kornbock, a Goat Spirit, gradually grew taller as the summer wore on, keeping always just tall enough to peer over the barley and attack intruders; in Silesia, children were warned: 'The Wolf sits in the corn and will tear you to pieces.'

When it came to harvest time, the Corn Spirit fulfilled another function. To understand this, one must recall the anxiety and urgency of bringing in the harvest; George Ewart Evans has aptly remarked that it was 'a quasi-military operation' in which 'disciplined labour had to be brought to bear quickly and efficiently at a time chosen by the weather. It was like an attack to beat an ancient enemy.' What surer way to raise morale and turn hard toil into a competitive, aggressive sport than to personalize the enemy as a Corn Spirit whom each worker was intent on defeating? Hence the jeers at anyone who lagged behind: 'The Harvest Goat has butted him' (Prussia), 'The White Bitch has bitten him' (France). The final stages became a race, as each worker tried to avoid being the one to cut the last handful or bind up the last sheaf, for this brought disgrace and bad luck; whoever did so would be greeted with the mocking cry, 'You've got the Old Woman' (or 'caught the Cock' or 'killed the Goat', etc.). Alternatively, the rivalry could be directed outwards, against the harvesting teams of neighbouring farms. In Scotland and Wales, where the last corn was tied into a human shape known as the Old Woman or Hag, the reapers who finished first would try to throw this figure onto a neighbour's field where work was still in progress, as an insult.

The hard work once over, the reapers could indulge in outbursts of triumph and high spirits, either when the last sheaf was cut or when the last load had been carted safely to the barn. This took many forms; among the most common are ritualized cries of triumph; displays of skill in cutting the sheaf by flinging sickles at it from a distance; garlanding the last sheaf and/or the man who cut it; weaving its stalks into a human or animal form or a traditional pattern (generally now called in English the Corn Dolly); carrying the Dolly in procession, or smuggling it secretly into the farm; chasing the bearer of the Corn Dolly and drenching him with water; hurling bucketfuls of water at the cart that bore the last load. Sometimes a *quête* occurred, as when German reapers used to catch passing strangers and hold them to ransom. Everywhere there was a harvest supper; where the Corn Spirit was imagined as an edible animal, such as a cock, goose or calf, meat of this animal would probably be the main dish. The Corn Dolly was often displayed during the feast (unless, of course, it had been used to taunt a slower neighbour, as described above); thereafter it was kept for luck till the next ploughing, or the next harvesting.

Besides general farming lore, there was much lore attached to specialized skills and their practitioners; often it was thought that experts in this or that field had supernatural powers. There are traditions of this sort in Scotland and East Anglia about men in charge of farm horses who could control the animals just as they chose, for instance immobilizing them by the secret use of a particular bone taken from a dead toad or frog. In Hungary, it was said that some shepherds could leave their sticks to watch the flock and prevent it straying in their absence, because the stick contained a coffin nail, a snakeskin or a bee; in Germany, there were tales of huntsmen whose magic bullets never missed; in most countries, there were stories about men who could expel rats, mice, caterpillars or snakes. No doubt there is some wish-fulfilment in these stories where magic makes work easy; more importantly, however, they enhanced the prestige of the craft concerned and surrounded it with mystery. Attempts were undoubtedly made to turn tales into realities; as late as the 1960s, George Ewart Evans published information obtained from Suffolk farm horsemen born in the 1880s who had themselves gone through the ritual prescribed for obtaining the toad's bone, and had total faith in its powers. In fact, it was by strong-smelling substances that they controlled their horses' behaviour, but in their own minds the power lay in the bone.

## Folk Christianity

The mixture of orthodox Christian doctrine with beliefs that are pre-Christian or non-Christian in origin was virtually inevitable and was begun by the missionaries themselves, who rather than seeking to destroy an ancient custom altogether would try to Christianize it by giving it a more acceptable meaning. Stories told of pagan gods or folk heroes became associated with saints; sacred places (trees, wells, caves, etc.) were given Christian dedications; and objects connected with ceremonies of various kinds, from mistletoe to eggs and from buns to bonfires, were endowed with Christian connotations.

A supernatural figure who comes in the depths of winter and brings gifts to mankind is found in several non-Christian mythologies. This figure reappears in Christian myth in a variety of guises. In France it may be the Christ Child; in England, Holland, Germany and Scandinavia, St Nicholas – though, under the name of Santa Claus or Father Christmas, even that nominal respectability becomes rather shadowy and any connection with the actual Christian martyr, Nicholas of Myra, disappears altogether. A parallel case is St Blaise, apparently a real bishop who died about AD 316 in Asia Minor. Stories about him percolated into medieval Europe via the Crusaders, and he became the patron saint of animals, wool-combers and people suffering from throat complaints. Blaise Day (3 February) was one of the most popular rural festivals. The multiple strands of country lore making up his cult are impossible to untangle: what is significant is that they were so easily incorporated into a Christian context.

*The holy well of the Virgin at Josselin, in Brittany, was credited with the power to cure epilepsy.*

Almost all holy wells are associated with saints, though it is virtually certain that their sanctity predates the legends that are supposed to explain it. St Nonna's well, Pembrokeshire, is a good example. The area around it was probably a pre-Christian sanctuary where Nonna, the mother of St David, took refuge. Later tradition, transforming symbolism into reality, told how Nonna came to it in the middle of a raging storm and found there a tiny oasis of bright summer weather. This latter story then became the explanation of the well's holiness. Some wells are still 'dressed', that is, garlanded with flowers, a practice that goes back beyond their Christian associations, but which was encouraged by the early church, if frowned upon as idolatrous by the later. The cult of wells and springs, and the practice of making votive offerings of pins and rags at them, is particularly well attested in Celtic areas; it is probably no coincidence that there is abundant evidence of it in the same regions in pre-Christian times.

Ceremonies connected with the summer and winter solstices are found in almost all primitive cultures. They have no overt place in the Gospels, but within a very short time Christian festivals had become assimilated into the older celebrations held at these times of the year. The most obvious is Christmas, but there are others that have closer connections with the cycle of rural life, and which retained these connections more recognizably. The feast of St Lucy is celebrated on 13 December. Nothing links the historical Lucy (a Sicilian martyr of the early 4th century) with the winter solstice except her name, which means 'light'. In Sweden her feast is a sort of preliminary Christmas, with the houses brightly lit and a girl dressed in white and wearing burning candles on her head going from house to house before dawn, bringing the promise of

spring to a frozen world. It is hard to believe that this was not a rustic ceremony before St Lucy of Syracuse ever lived or died. A similar role fell to St Thomas the Apostle, whose feast takes place on 21 December. His legend, in which he rides in a chariot through grave-yards calling upon those with his own name of Thomas to rise from their graves, surely looks back to an ancient midwinter festival foretelling the rebirth of nature.

St John the Baptist inherited a parallel function relating to midsummer. The pagan bonfires that had been lit as a symbolic effort to lengthen the days of summer, repel winter, promote fertility and purify men and cattle were, in the Middle Ages and after, made to blaze in honour of St John, whose birthday was on 24 June. Customs surrounding this feast are varied and spectacular. All of them involve fire in some form or other; some use magical or medicinal plants; others became bound up with love, marriage and the hope of children. They continued well into the 19th century, and made St John's Eve a red-letter day in the peasant's calendar; this date is still a major occasion for celebra-tions in some countries, notably Scandinavia.

Just as the central mystery of Christianity, the Eucharist, can be paralleled by pre-Christian sacrifical feasts, so these more localized festivals in honour of saints often point back to ancient observances carried out by our remote rural ancestors. Bread, for instance, has always been a symbol of life, just as the egg seems to stand almost universally for the idea of rebirth and regeneration.

At Grenoble in France, on St James's Day (25 July), the statue of St James is taken out of the church and carried in procession through the streets to a certain fountain. There it is laid upon napkins filled with little bits of bread. The bread is distributed to the crowd; everyone eats a piece, and drinks several cups of water, to ensure a bountiful harvest. After this, eggs coloured red are offered up in the church.

On the Greek island of Chios, children go round from house to house on the Feast of the Raising of Lazarus, which is the Saturday before Palm Sunday. They sing songs about Lazarus's experiences in the world of the dead and the miracle of his return to life; then, as in all *quête* customs, they request a gift – in this case eggs to be used the following week as Easter eggs.

The cases mentioned hitherto are examples of customs of forgotten origin which have been given a specifically Christian connotation. Sometimes the opposite happens. For instance, the English habit of eating lamb with mint sauce at Easter is undoubtedly in memory of the paschal lamb eaten with bitter herbs. Similarly, when Bulgarians say, 'Never omit eggs at Easter, roast lamb on St George's Day or chicken on the feast day of St Peter', they are alluding to the cock which crew thrice on Peter's betrayal of Christ.

Beliefs and customs involving eggs offer a particu-larly rich example of the interweaving of Christian teaching and popular beliefs, of which some are demonstrably pre-Christian. Basically, the egg symbolizes new life and all related concepts – birth, rebirth, renewal, resurrection, creation – and already carried those meanings in the most ancient documented cultures, those of Egypt, India and China. Early Christianity adopted it as a symbol of Christ's resurrection, and so giving Easter eggs became, and has remained, a highly popular custom. There were plenty of eggs available at that date, because until recent times Lent was observed very strictly, and eggs were one of the forbidden foods; for six weeks they could be collected, hard boiled, and often decorated. The decorative techniques used are extremely varied, ranging from simple dyeing to exquisitely elaborate designs made by scratching the dyed surface, or by waxing methods or appliqué work.

In many countries, hard boiled eggs, omelettes or spicy cakes with eggs embedded in them were traditional Easter food. A 19th-century Englishman described how in Italy:

> On Easter Eve and Easter Day all the heads of families send great chargers full of hard eggs to the church to get them blessed, which the priests perform by saying several appointed prayers, and making great signs of the Cross over them, and sprinkling them with holy water. . . . These blest eggs have the virtue of sanctifying the entrails of the body, and are to be the first fat or fleshy nourishment they take after the abstinence of Lent.

These eggs, 'painted with divers colours and gilt', were piled on dishes on a flower-strewn table in the main room, and remained there all Easter week; every visitor who came to the house was given one. In Russia, Greece and the Balkans, red eggs are exchanged among the congregation at the Easter Midnight Mass when the priest cries 'Christ is risen', in some parts of Macedonia the congregation used to eat them then and there, but it is more usual to take them home. The exchange of red eggs as tokens of friendship often goes on all week.

Besides Easter eggs, eggs laid on various holy days are important in folklore; Maundy Thursday (Green Thursday in German and some other languages) is most often mentioned, but Good Friday, Ascension Day and of course Easter Sunday are also dates on which eggs acquire special powers. In many countries they were kept all year as protection against those perpetual threats to prosperity: lightning, fire, rats, mice, caterpillars and witches. In France and Germany, they had various other uses too: they prevented people from falling off ladders, helped children to learn to read and, if rubbed on the body, cured colics, fevers and hernias; their shells, hung in orchards, helped fruit to swell; if crumbled and mixed with seed-corn they ensured a good crop. Thus a Christian symbol takes on all the familiar functions of a protective, curative and fertility-inducing charm.

A more unusual aspect is the egg's link with funerary practices in Orthodox countries. In Russia, eggs were (and still are) one of the foods most commonly associated with the dead, and can be used in various ways; they may be offered to the corpse, or placed in or on top of the coffin or on top of the freshly closed grave. Eggs are brought to the cemeteries and placed on tombstones at Shrovetide and at Easter; sometimes it is not real eggs but wooden ones that are used for this, and, if so, they will be left for a year, and then replaced by new ones. Greece has similar customs. They are now unquestioningly accepted as Christian, but there is archaeological evidence that eggs were already being put into graves in classical Athens and Sparta.

The happy coexistence of Catholicism with folk practices, which had offered the countryman so many comforting rituals to protect him against supernatural perils and to give a pattern to his daily life, was roughly disrupted by the Reformation. At a stroke, the use of medals, holy water, blessed palms and so on was forbidden; most saints' festivals were abolished, and places of pilgrimage were closed down. The experience must have been deeply traumatic. The folklore collected in later centuries is full of pathetic attempts to harness what little spiritual power was still accessible to the populace, and apply it to their material needs. Anything that had been in contact with a religious ceremony was sought after for its supposed curative powers – churchyard earth, coffin nails, silver coins that had been put into the alms dish and could now be melted down into a ring. Holy days could still communicate some power; bread baked on Good Friday, for instance, would preserve a fisherman from drowning, or cure diarrhoea in man or beast. Fragments of Latin prayers and real or supposed quotations from Scripture were used in healing charms.

Above all, the figure of the cleric still retained a mysterious supernatural aura, even in Protestant lands. He had always stood apart from the village community because of his superior knowledge and 'book-learning', which might readily be equated in the popular mind with the Black Arts; many of the famous wizards in folk legend are said to have been priests. After the Reformation, this link between the clergy and magic continued,

*Two designs for painted Easter eggs from Hungary.*

and may even have increased; there are numerous legends about individual priests who could imprison dangerous ghosts in bottles or banish them to the Red Sea, exorcize demons, or command them like slaves.

## Rites of life and death

The conditions of rural life, where even survival was something that could not be taken for granted, naturally focused attention on the great turning points of life; and baptisms, weddings and funerals were made the occasion for major feasts, around which legend and ritual clustered, involving the whole village community. Weddings are a good example of the way in which such customs grew up, were elaborated, acquired and lost meanings and remain now embedded in modern life only half understood.

The custom of crowning both bride and groom with flowers has a classical ancestry. In the 16th century, one even finds metal frames being worn on the head to support elaborate floral compositions. Sometimes these included ears of wheat, an obvious allusion to fruitfulness. Vestiges of these practices survive today in the bridal bouquet and the rice thrown over the couple as they leave church.

Virtually all weddings involved a procession consisting not only of family and friends but also, more formally, of 'bridesmaids' and 'groomsmen', whose numbers might vary from two to twelve each. Their duties and privileges varied a great deal.

One of the most important elements in the wedding was the exchange of gifts, both to the newly married couple from their friends and from one to the other. Presents then, as now, were usually meant to contribute to the couple's new home; a few had symbolic meanings, for example a pair of scissors to cut 'the thread of love' if the husband proved untrue. In many country districts it was the practice, instead of each guest bringing his own gift, to make a collection of money from the assembled company. Sometimes the games played during the subsequent merrymaking were designed to raise money for the bridal pair.

The wedding banquet was the main social event of the day. Often a general invitation would be issued to the whole district; the higher up the scale of rank, the more liberal a family was expected to be. In the food served it is often possible to see a symbolic intent, though such meanings tended to be forgotten with time. In the Netherlands and elsewhere, salted cream sprinkled with sugar represented the sweet and bitter aspects of marriage. The wedding cake itself goes far back into antiquity, and innumerable customs have grown up around it: bride and groom must share the first and last piece; salt must be left out, to symbolize the absence of sorrow; parts of the cake may be given to childless women to ensure fertility; occasionally the whole cake (and the plate!) may be broken over the head of the bride. A pile of biscuits or buns is often served instead of a single cake. The diarist John Evelyn wrote: 'When I was a little boy (before the Civil Wars) I have seen, according to the custom then, the bride and bridegroom kiss over the bride-cakes at the table. It was at the latter end of dinner; and the cakes were laid upon one another like the pictures of the shew-bread in the old Bibles.'

After the banquet, the two families – or the whole village – would see the couple into the bridal chamber. Here the celebration culminated in a mixture of piety and horseplay that still seems to characterize these occasions. The priest brought a sanctified drink of sweetened wine called the Benediction Posset, after which the bridesmaids and groomsmen would sit on the bed with their backs turned and indulge in the sport of 'throwing the stocking' of the bride and groom over their shoulders in attempt to hit the couple as they sat up in bed.

Death, funerals and mourning have always been surrounded by an immense number of beliefs and customs, many of which have persisted tenaciously to the present time, despite the destructive influence of modern life. Even before death seems imminent, there are everywhere beliefs about ill-omened events that portend its coming. As it draws nearer, there are (or were) precepts as to what should be done to ease the dying man's passing. It was widely thought, for instance, that he ought to be taken out of bed and laid on the floor; this was sometimes taken as a mark of humility and penitence (St Francis of Assisi, for example, insisted on dying on a pile of ashes on the ground), but, as so often happens, there are non-Christian parallels suggesting an older layer of meaning – in this case, contact with Mother Earth. Other common beliefs are that people die more easily when the tide is ebbing, and that windows should be opened to release the spirit.

Laying out the corpse was done at home, usually by a female relative but sometimes by the village midwife; many taboos and precepts surrounded the precedure, since any slip might cause disaster – a haunting, or another death. In the Balkans, for instance, it was thought that if a cat was allowed to get near the corpse, the dead man would become a vampire. It was a rule everywhere that the body must not be left alone, nor should it be left in the dark. Neighbours visited it and prayed beside it, usually kissing it or touching the forehead; in England it is said that, if you do not touch, you will see the dead in nightmares. In some countries formal laments were sung; elsewhere, notably in Ireland, there was wordless wailing, the 'keening'. Ireland was, of course, also famous for its wakes, lively social gatherings which grew out of the simpler custom of keeping a prayer vigil by the corpse; a wake would include much drinking and smoking, singing, dancing, story-telling and games. Over 150 games have been recorded, many of them bawdy; the whole procedure constituted a vigorous reaffirmation of life in the face of death, and fulfilled an important communal function.

Local custom governed the details of the funeral procession – who should walk in it, who would be privileged to carry the coffin, what signs of mourning were worn, whether secondary rituals were also followed – for instance, deliberately taking an indirect route to the church, circling wayside crosses, building cairns at stopping places. The siting of the grave was equally traditional; an east–west orientation was usually preferred, with the face turned to the east; the north side of the churchyard was shunned. In Hungary, the layout of old graveyards reflects the structure of the community, members of one family being grouped generation by generation in a pattern radiating from the grave of their founder, whereas unattached persons were buried along the boundary wall. Occasionally, men and women were buried separately in different parts of the churchyard, or even in two separate churchyards; possibly this reflects the early medieval custom of segregating the sexes in church. Everywhere, those who had been outcasts in life were also outcasts in death; even in modern England, there are occasional instances of discreetly concealed graves in vicarage gardens – the graves of suicides, charitably laid there by former vicars because consecrated ground was forbidden to them.

Most pre-Christian religions required that the dead be given food, clothes and possessions to take to the next world. Officially, Christianity discourages this, yet in many places and periods the dead have been buried in clothing rather than in shrouds, and sometimes with rings and similar cherished possessions. Very frequently, some object indicating rank or occupation is buried with the body, or at least laid on top of the coffin.

Food customs are equally tenacious. Everywhere, it is normal for mourners to share a meal, whether this is a lavish affair or the frugal traditional Greek dish of fish, vegetables and eggs. Some customs seem to hint that the dead too should be fed, as when Cypriots lay bread, wine and nuts on the coffin. Bread, cakes or biscuits, and wine, beer or cider were sometimes handed to mourners across the coffin in 19th-century Wales and England, either before the cortège left the house or at the graveside. It is recorded that at a Protestant nobleman's funeral in Shropshire in 1671 a large pot of wine stood on the coffin, and everyone drank the health of the deceased, believing this would release him from his sins. The 17th-century antiquarian John Aubrey describes a uniquely dramatic version of this custom from Herefordshire; there, a poor man who accepted bread, beer and money handed to him across the corpse was called the 'sin-eater', for he was believed to take the guilt of the dead man's sins on himself. This exciting description of a scapegoat ritual has aroused much comment, but seems to have no parallels.

The origins of these bread-and-wine customs are probably to be sought in medieval Catholic practices (not now followed) which had become divorced from their context after the Reformation. In medieval France, for instance, mourners used to bring offerings of bread and wine to church to be blessed at the funeral mass, and would later eat them. (Food blessed in this way would not, of course, have the sacramental function of the Eucharist, but it would receive a lesser degree of sanctity, akin to that of holy water.) This custom was justified by reference to the Book of Tobias (IV: 18), 'Lay your bread and your wine on the grave of a just man.' The same quotation was also the basis for a very early Christian custom, still kept up by the Coptic and Orthodox churches, of taking a meal on tombstones on the anniversary of a death, or at the Feast of the Dead.

## Folklore today: the lost inheritance

Until recent times, folk beliefs and customs were integrally related to the whole fabric of rural life in both its material and its sociological aspects, from which they derived their functional value. They were not mere survivals of lost archaic thought-systems, however ancient they might in fact be; on the contrary, just as an archaically shaped tool still served the needs of a 19th-century craftsman, so an ancient practice or belief was still relevant to his hopes, fears or needs. But, precisely because they were so intimately linked to material conditions, they inevitably proved vulnerable to the disruptive effects of the innumerable rapid changes which have swept through Europe throughout this century, and which by now have reached even the most isolated regions.

In many cases, the arrival of a major technological change has entailed the complete and instant disappearance of any folklore associated with the older technology. There can be no place for the ritual actions and beliefs connected with ploughing and reaping once the tractor and the combine harvester have arrived. But in other cases, some attractively picturesque element will remain, divorced from its original context and given new connotations; paradoxically, it may be easier to find these transformed fragments of rural custom in the towns than in the countryside, for they have become the modern counterpart to the idealized 'pastoral image' cherished by urban elites in past centuries. Thus, horse-brasses and cow-bells decorate the suburban restaurant; Corn Dollies can be seen at Harvest Festivals in town churches as well as in the country ones, in cars as 'lucky charms' or in town shops that sell better quality bread; folk dancing, folk songs and folk costumes are immensely popular at festival entertainments where it is likely that nobody among either performers or audience has ever set foot inside a working farm. Where local pageants and folk customs survive, they are often well publicized as tourists attractions, and draw visitors from far away, rather to the irritation of local people, who feel, often with justice, that their traditional annual festival is being coarsened and cheapened. The associated publicity may also entail changes in the actual custom; it may be thought necessary, for instance, to change it to a date or a site which is more convenient for visitors, even if this means breaking (and eventually forgetting) a traditional association which was of local significance. Even in such circumstances, the festival custom often still retains its age-old function as a focus for, and a celebration of, the sense of local identity; among the inner circle of organizers and performers, there will very likely be some who are proudly aware of its local importance and its age, and who have personal ties with organizers and performers of past generations.

The supernatural beliefs once so important in country lore now survive, if at all, in an increasingly fragmented and disorganized fashion, and tend to become generalized and vague in their applications, now that the material culture with which they were linked has been disrupted. Omens and taboos that once carried quite specific meanings and associations are now simply said to be 'unlucky'; for example, sweet-smelling white flowers may still be thought unlucky even though they are not now used to disguise the smell of a corpse laid out at home; or children may be warned not to pick dandelions for fear they will wet their beds, by people quite unaware that this plant's leaves are diuretic and that its dialect name once was 'pissabed'. On the other hand, aetiological legends about landscape features and conspicuous buildings or monuments seem to be surviving well; the popularity of sightseeing in our culture, and our fondness for picturesque scenery and archaeological remains ensures that many of them get well publicized on a nationwide, rather than a purely local, scale.

It seems hard to imagine that present trends could ever be reversed, and country life become once more an isolated, sharply differentiated culture, self-contained, with only minimal mutual contact with the city dwellers. If this did happen, there would naturally soon grow up a distinctive set of customs, beliefs and tales to embody this differentiation – in short, a new exclusive rural folklore. Meanwhile, the older lore is passing through a rigorous sifting process. Much of it will be remembered only for its historical and sociological interest, but some will survive, finding new functions to fit the practical or emotional needs of a new and more broadly based society.

---

**The dragon of Tarascon** is a striking example of a local custom, possibly originating in a pre-Christian cult, which was taken over by Christianity, adapted to changing circumstance and has lasted through the centuries to fulfil a function today.

Ever since the 12th century, people in Provence have believed that soon after Christ's death his friends Martha, Mary and Lazarus arrived in that region to preach the Gospel. At the small town of Tarascon, legend claimed, St Martha found the people lamenting because they feared a dragon that lived in the Rhône; it was fatter than a bull, with a lion's face, spiked scales, six feet and a tail like a viper. St Martha found the monster in a wood, eating a man; she sprinkled it with holy water and showed it a cross, whereupon it stood as meek as a lamb, and she bound it with her girdle and led it into the town, where the townsmen killed it.

This dragon has for centuries been represented by a famous effigy, La Tarasque, first mentioned in 1465. This painting of it dates from the mid-19th century; the present-day Tarasque, kept in the local museum, was made about 1860. Its fat hollow body hides four or five men who carry it, and a little boy who squats on the framework and moves its clacking jaws. It is accompanied by young men called Tarascaires.

There are two separate celebrations, one religious and one secular. On St Martha's Day (29 July) or the nearest Sunday, La Tarasque takes part in a religious procession; she (for it is a she-dragon) is gently led on a ribbon by a little girl representing the saint, who sprinkles holy water on her whenever she tries to jerk away or snap her jaws.

But on Whit Monday, at the secular festivity, La Tarasque behaves very differently. Escorted by the Tarascaires with drums and nonsense songs, the image is carried briskly and noisily along. From time to time fireworks are let off through her nostrils, and she makes a sudden 'run' – that is, her bearers rush as fast as they can up a narrow street, swerving abruptly so that the long, rigid wooden tail knocks people flying, at which the whole crowd cheers. Nowadays, La Tarasque is set on a wheeled frame rather than being carried from inside, which has reduced both her mobility and the risk to the spectators. Between the 'runs', La Tarasque halts, and the Tarascaires dance the Farandole.

Local people still half believe that to touch the Tarasque brings good luck, especially if they can pull off one of the spikes on her body. In earlier periods, this element of magic and luck-bringing may have predominated, but in recent times the festive atmosphere, with its opportunities for drinking, rowdiness and mock agression, is mainly important as an outlet for high spirits and a rallying-point for local pride. (1)

# The wedding

A wedding was not only a high point in the personal lives of those involved; it was an occasion for the whole community to come together. The religious ceremony is a comparatively late addition to the ritual of marriage; many far older usages have been retained and incorporated in present-day customs.

**Lavish display** is an almost universal ingredient of weddings. The procession to the church, the costumes worn by bride and groom and the provision of the subsequent meal were all means of showing off the families' wealth. In Germany an elaborate cart carried the bride's dowry to her new home, together with articles symbolizing her new responsibilities. This miniature model (*far left*), made in 1905, bears a spinning-wheel, a bed with pillows, a chest and a cradle. *Left:* bride and groom in Switzerland, 1794. The bride's crown is typical of northern and central Europe; even more splendid versions held lighted candles. *Below left:* wedding banquet in Denmark, *c.* 1800, a naïve painting with the newly married couple at the end of a long table. Wedding banquets often took place in communal buildings such as town halls. (8, 9, 10)

**In Poland** the bridegroom is greeted by two friends bearing symbolic offerings (*right*). One, the head man of the village, has a banner and a wreath; the other, who acts as a fool, carries a fir branch with bells. (11)

**'Barring the way':** a custom which still exists in several countries symbolizes the 'payment' required to join a new community or leave an old one. The bridal couple are stopped on their way by a rope (in Wales the churchyard gate is tied) and not allowed through without paying a forfeit. The scene shown here is at Baden, *c.* 1835. (12)

## Unseen worlds

Folklore represents an accumulation of beliefs, going back through many layers of the past, often combining disparate or contradictory pictures of the world. Animism, magic, demons and apotropaic spells happily coexisted with Christianity.

**Sacred trees** lie behind many peasant customs (the Yule log, the Maypole, etc.), and particular examples often became associated with Christian legends. In this *ex voto* from Germany a woman prays to the Virgin (with the dead Christ in her lap and a sword piercing her heart) who appears in the branches of a tree. (13)

**'Telling the bees'.** Bees expect to be told about important family events, especially deaths, otherwise they might take offence and swarm. The woman here is fixing a black bow to the hive in sign of mourning. The key is to rap against the hive and draw their attention to the sad news. (15)

**A wayside shrine** (*left*) in Italy is enclosed within a willow, whose pollarded branches have been woven together to form a cage. (14)

**Corn Babies** or **Dollies** point back to a pre-scientific, pre-Christian world and rituals to give thanks for one harvest and secure a promise for the next. In many countries they take the form of small figures made from the last sheaf of corn to be gathered. This one (*right*) was made in the English Midlands in 1901. (16)

**Evil spirits** haunted all early communities, accounting for diseases, accidents and natural calamities. *Below* : a wooden Devil from Bessans, in France, an area with a long tradition of this expressive carving (note the puny size of the priest next to it). Although demons, bad fairies and malicious powers are a commonplace of country lore, the figure of the Devil ruling over an empire of evil is a specifically Christian idea. (17)

**At Hallowe'en,** the Eve of All Saints, the spirits walk (possibly by association with the following day, All Souls, or the Day of the Dead). As so often, what was originally an experience to be feared has turned into a game. Children dress up as ghosts, and extort a forfeit from their elders. This satanic mask (*below right*), made from vegetables and lit from behind, was photographed in England about twenty years ago. (18)

**The end of harvest.** A good harvest meant safety and survival during the winter and hope of prosperity in the succeeding year. It was therefore an occasion for rejoicing and was marked in every country by colourful symbolic ceremonies. In Poland a frame of straw was placed on the head of a village girl. On top of that the mayor put a living cock, and she led the way from the fields accompanied by musicians. If the cock crew, the future was considered good; if it refused to eat, prospects were bad. (19)

# 8 THE AMERICAN FARMER

WILLIAM N. PARKER

# The American farmer

Young Americans of the 1960s and 1970s who fled urban civilization for the hills and the woods of Maine or Colorado encountered for the first time some of the conditions faced in every region by its original settlers, nor were they much less capable of taming the wilderness. French peasants along the St Lawrence or Dutch patroons along the Hudson in the 17th century brought something of an older social structure; later, in New Jersey and Delaware, and much later in Minnesota and Wisconsin, Scandinavians brought some techniques of settlement in forested regions. Germans in Pennsylvania in the 18th century, with other central European peasant stock in the Middle West and eastern Texas in the mid-19th cenury, had been farmers in Europe before they became pioneer settlers in the new terrain. But inexperience was acute among the main body of English and Scottish settlers along the coast from Newfoundland to South Carolina in the 17th and 18th centuries. Many, if not most, of the English had been town or village dwellers, adventurers, fishermen, religious malcontents, sailors, drifters, town craftsmen. The Scots and Welsh had been herders of sheep and cattle; many bore a traditional aversion to the slow life of plough and sickle. All the Europeans, even where they migrated as small communities, had left regions where the tasks of pioneering were buried deep in a medieval, even a neolithic, past.

## Lines and tasks of settlement

In New England, the Puritan colonists kept in small bands, building villages around a common, raising stock and shooting game along the edges of forests and streams. In the southern colonies, adventurers, farmers and planters moved out from tidewater settlements to small plantations or isolated farms along the streams. In the middle colonies – New York, New Jersey, Pennsylvania – Dutch, Swedes and Germans as well as English settled rather thickly along large rivers and, by 1740, occupied the richest farming soils. Then began the penetration into the Appalachian Mountain range, from New Hampshire to North Carolina, in three directions. Movements north from Massachusetts and Connecticut began to plant new villages in northern valleys while from Pennsylvania, settlers and new immigrants – Scottish clansmen, German sectarians – moved south into western Virginia, the Carolinas and eastern Tennessee. The Westward movement – the principal fact of American agrarian history – went

through passes and gaps in the mountain-chain, or along major rivers: down the St Lawrence, along the Mohawk in New York. Through the Cumberland Gap the pioneers spread out into Kentucky and Tennessee. By 1760, the site of Pittsburgh had been established and the Ohio River reached. By 1790, the edge of the great central plain – the Midwest – began to be colonized. In the South, yeoman farmers moved into the hill country and performed the first tasks of settlement, even in the rich central areas of the 'Black belt' from western Georgia across Alabama and eastern Mississippi. Cotton began to expand strongly across the interior after the final resettlement of the Creek and Cherokee Indians in the 1820s.

Across the entire coastal plain and the Appalachian areas, as well as in the areas of French Canada, it took enormous labour to clear a few acres for a family's corn patch or pasture. The stone walls in New England, still running for miles along roads and ancient property lines, separating fields now overgrown in pine and maple, bear witness to the inhospitality of the soil and the compulsive tidiness of the settlers. Stone removal was something of a New England speciality since in no other region did settlers try to cultivate such rocky ground. Other tasks of pioneer settlement included clearing fields of timber and finally of stumps, cabin construction and fencing – whether stone, hedge, post-and-rail or the primitive 'worm' rail fence which zigzagged without posts across a field. They included also, eventually, road building as an area opened up, and the construction of farmhouse, shed, barn and community buildings – meeting house and school. These tasks were common to all regions, though pursued with slightly different styles in the South, in the middle colonies and in the West.

Land clearing was the heaviest of the tasks. The Scandinavians and Germans along the Delaware River, whose background was closest to pioneering in new heavily forested areas, may have diffused techniques and tools for land clearing and for construction of wooden buildings: in particular, the omnipresent log cabin. In the southern colonies standing trees were killed by girdling (stripping off a circle of the bark) – a method not unknown to the beaver. They could then be dismantled over some years while crops were sown in the open spaces under and around the dead branches. In the North, trees were felled by the axe and the land cleared off by controlled burning. As long as land was plentiful, the arduous task of stump removal might be delayed. Altogether it took a man as many as twenty to thirty-five days to make an acre of land reasonably free of its original cover and ready for first cultivation. A team of oxen was required to do the job well, but the very first pioneers came, like the Indians, on foot, and logs, once felled, could only be collected together by rolling. Pioneers moving in by foot or horseback spent their first weeks in a tent; those who came by waggon lived in the waggon while the first trees were felled and the cabin constructed. Log-cabin construction itself was an art, requiring the axe, and a trimming tool – the adze – to notch the logs at each end and, in some constructions, to square them off for a tighter fit. These tools and materials, with some clay or mud to daub in the chinks, and stone and clay to line the chimney, were all that two men needed to throw up a cabin within two of three days. Not even nails, glass or screening were used at first; windows might be cut later, and the whole covered with sawn boards, or replaced by a frame house of wood siding when sawmills and industrial manufactures came to the region.

Initially, the choice of crops and farming techniques was governed by a family's needs and the knowledge of what the soil could produce and how to produce it. The Indians' crops – maize and beans – were universal; wild game and hogs, penned or running wild, were the staple source of fat and animal protein. With the hog, the 17th-century settlers also brought cattle; very large and heavy oxen became common. Even more common was a smaller short-horn cow that might pull a plough as well as give milk and (eventually) meat. Just as wood was the universal structural material, the maize, or 'corn', plant was the universal food; the grain, cracked and ground in a wooden mortar, was cooked in endless puddings, meals, breads and mush; it was eaten directly from the ear in season, or dried and then soaked, or fed to hogs. Cooked, fermented and distilled, it was the source of American whiskey, Bourbon. The plant itself was animal fodder. The husks, dried, were used to stuff mattresses, and the dried cobs, light and absorbent, were replaced only in the 20th century in some rural areas by toilet-paper. Although corn was the universal food and feed grain in all sections of early United States, the mode of harvesting the corn plant soon revealed peculiarities of regional character and economic position. In the north-east, and the South, the top of the plant and the leaves below the ear were cut off (a practice known as 'topping'), tied in bundles and stored for winter feed. In the eastern Midwest the whole plant was cut down and stacked in large shocks to dry while the field was made ready for the next planting. In the South, this laborious practice was never adopted; there, the plant was left standing, topped, perhaps, for feed where livestock required it, with the ear picked at any time in the autumn. When the Midwest became the principal corn- and hog-producing region after 1830, neither shocking nor topping was adopted; in Illinois

and Iowa the stock were often turned into the field to harvest the plant for themselves.

Once land had been cleared, the agricultural tasks of pioneer settlement in the absence of commercial markets became less onerous. Wild game and fish were abundant and neither domestic animals nor children required much care. Corn yields on new lands were very high, an acre could yield first 30–50 bushels or more of corn, maintaining a steady yield of 20–30 bushels (450–800 kilos, about 1,000–1,800 pounds) after a few years, occasionally rotated with vegetables, wheat or fallow pasturage, and using little or no fertilizer. An acre or two could support a family the first year, and five acres gave an unmanageable surplus. Unlike the European cereals, corn could be sown in hills, Indian style, arranged in a checker-board pattern in the field, the soil prepared and cultivated with a hoe. The labour required varied, like a housekeeper's labour, with a settler's standard for a 'clean' corn patch, but, again unlike the other close-sown cereals, because weeds did not mix into the harvested crop weeding could be neglected without appreciable loss in yield. Even without a draught-animal and without wild game supplement, the labour of growing food for a family on a diet of rude abundance in corn meal, hog meat, vegetables and poultry could not have occupied more than thirty working days a year for a frontier family. The rest of the time was spent in the tasks of farm formation, in hunting and fishing, for the men, and food preparation and preservation, for the frontier women.

The self-sufficiency of log-cabin life, however, had one serious drawback. It meant that more time was spent in industrial activities than on farming itself. Hog slaughtering in the late autumn was followed by several weeks in which the carcasses were dressed, hides scraped, lard rendered, and hams, bacon slabs and sides salted and smoked. Apple trees meant a cider-mill, and maple trees in the north-east gave their sap for syrup-making over endless fires fed by cord-wood. Nearly every cabin had a spinning-wheel; flax and wool were

*Farm tools about 1790 – an engraving published some seventy years later to illustrate the crudity of the old techniques: rake, hoe, spade, axe and plough laboriously worked by human strength.*

*The four stages of a pioneer's progress. In the first years he clears the land of trees and builds himself a log cabin.*

*After a few seasons a greater area is cleared, the land is under cultivation and the log cabin assumes some of the comforts of home.*

the fibres, and the labour of flax preparation was particularly long and tedious. Soap-making with lye made from wood ashes was almost as widely practised as the distilling of whiskey.

When settlement reached the grassy prairies in the 1850s, in the tier of states from Illinois and Iowa to eastern Texas, a new learning experience was at hand. Wooded areas were still available as far west as Iowa and eastern Kansas, and settlers first moved along streams and into those areas despite the much higher initial clearing costs. To begin ploughing in grasslands took only a fraction – no more than 5 to 10 per cent – of the initial cost of removing a forest cover. A plough and a team were needed, and the settler, once encamped on the prairie, found a self-sufficient life impossible to sustain. The forest, after all, though an impediment, was also a resource. The pioneers after 1870 on the Nebraska and Dakota plains had only the sod as structural material and buffalo chips as fuel. In the forested areas, even on the most independent homesteads, *some* purchases were required – iron wares, plough-shares, salt, spices, the services of a saw-mill and flour-mill. Nevertheless, a forest environment offered variety in vegetation, soils and terrain, along with the resources of field and stream and water-power. A rural culture developed east of the prairies in rural neighbourhoods; the ample spare time could be used in rural crafts, and exchanges were made by barter in the absence of banks and money. On the prairies and plains, farming was the creature of railroads and the commercial market; without them, life above the level of the nomadic Indians could not be sustained. It was 1870, when the Civil War had settled the political structure of the western territories, the railroads had crossed to the Pacific and the European markets had opened wide to North American wheat and beef, rather than the official date of 1890, that marked the death of the forested frontier.

## The omnipresent market

Had it not been for its setting in a modern world of intense capitalist commerce, the movement of European and native farmers across North America would have been a primitive affair. But the period of frontier boldness, crudity and independence was brief, passing over the North American landscape like the shadow of a speeding cloud. In a commercial setting, European villagers and peasants, re-establishing themselves in new lands, emerged from the experience of settlement as individualistic American farmers. A village agrarian culture of the Old World had been broken apart and reshaped, becoming shallower, harsher, more resourceful, more aggressive, mobile and profitable.

Throughout the late 18th and the 19th century, the frontier was pushed rapidly west. One hundred years were required for a penetration from the coastal settlements to 200 to 300 miles into the Appalachian uplands; in the next century, i.e. from 1750 to 1850, the frontier moved another 500 miles to just beyond the Mississippi. After that, the surge of settlers across the prairies and plains, and the back movement east from the mineral rushes in California, had covered the 1,000 miles from Chicago to Denver and another 400 miles from the Pacific to the western slopes of the Rockies with the skin of settlement and the nerve system of the railroad and telegraph by 1900. The frontier experience lasted two or three generations in the 18th-century East. It took less than the span of a single life on the prairies and the plains. This speed-up was not caused by a mounting pressure of population. The American rural birth-rates steadily declined as population density grew. Nor was it caused by any striking changes in the techniques of pioneering – only difficult adaptations to lands that were flat, bare and dry. Canal, steamship, railroad and telegraph were essential for it, but such techniques are effective only in the presence of pressures to sell, to

*The farm grows prosperous: a roomy, two-storeyed wooden house, farm buildings, vegetable garden and fields yielding corn and hay.*

*Finally all trace of the forest has disappeared, the land is completely given to agriculture and the farmer builds himself a stately house.*

move, to communicate between the two ends of their lines. Rather, it was cumulative pressures of productivity change in the northern European and north-east industrial sector, and the thrust of commercial enterprise pushing settlement ahead at an increasing pace, that transformed the narrow but leisurely log-cabin life into the long days of driving labour and tense commercial energies of a profit-seeking agriculture. Only in the deep valleys and secluded nooks of the uplands – the Green Mountains, the Adirondaks, the Smoky Mountains, the Ozarks, the hills and poor soils of eastern Kentucky and western Virginia – did backwoods living, domestic crafts and a high degree of self-sufficiency persist, independent of the commercial economy and impoverished by that independence.

It is a supreme irony of American history that these pressures and commercial inducements were felt first in that region where their ultimate extension was least pervasive: the semi-tropical South. Sugar and tobacco in the 17th century, rice and indigo in the 18th and, at last, cotton in the 19th were exotic products grown for profit. Like spices, tea, rubber, cacao and all the rest, they offered a complement rather than a competition to the productions of European peasant farms and manorial estates. Much has been written about the intellectual history of African slavery, its morality, its legality, its ideology, its compatibility or incompatibility with church law and rationalistic Protestant conscience. But southern planters were simply northern farmers in a different economic environment. While northern farmers were performing self-imposed tasks of settlement, growing corn, wheat, and flax for trade with neighbours or coastal towns, seeking an escape from the primitive poverty of self-sufficiency and finding none except by moves deeper into the forest, their southern counterparts were taking up lands in a climate in which, in effect, hard money could be grown through the

application of labour to limitless land. In the colonial and early federal South, markets, land, techniques and enterprise all combined to offer the chance to create wealth – a chance so tangible it could be almost smelled and tasted. Only command over labour power was lacking, and human greed ensured that it could be supplied by cruelty and force. No such opportunity existed for the North until world grain and meat markets opened up in the mid-19th century. By that time the mechanical revolution had replaced slavery as a means to the accumulation of capital, and the ideology of freedom was firmly established in American law and American myth – a freedom that was bourgeois, perhaps, and certainly individualistic, Christian, and permissive of exploitation only through the workings of free markets.

By 1860, the small, free northern farmers who provided the blood and will to support Lincoln had long since turned necessity into virtue. It was the expansion of their culture, linked with the manufactures of the north-east, that precipitated the Civil War and predetermined its outcome. That war – the central and peculiar crisis of American nationhood – was a war of competing variants of capitalistic agrarian enterprise. By the standards of European serfdom, the cotton plantations were pitifully small-scale enterprises. Although most of the slaves lived on estates with workforces of between 10 and 50, and a few estates on the rich lands along the Mississippi held 100 or more, most of the slaveholders held from 1 to 10 slaves as an extension of a family enterprise and, even on very small farms, of family labour. But the slave power and its competing Black labour force had been banished by ordinance from what became the ante-bellum corn, hog, wheat and cattle kingdom, between the Ohio and the Mississippi Rivers, even as early as 1787. The farmers and other small businessmen who had penetrated those rich lands and purchased the soil by money, labour and political rhetoric were the fanatics of a free federal union, extending its free lands and labour to the Pacific. As such, in the 1850s, they found political voice with their north-eastern counterparts to form the Republican Party, under whose dominance the vast agrarian and industrial growth of the next seventy-five years was carried out.

What then were the bases of this agro-business civilization, which spread like a flood over most of the continent – in Canada as well as the American Midwest – which destroyed the slave power with an outpouring of blood and righteous enthusiasm, leaving Blacks and southern whites in a backwater for nearly a century? Underneath it all was, of course, a psychology and a mode of social organization that the settlers brought with them, and which both found expression and became sharpened as families emerged from the experiences of frontier settlement to face the opportunities of commercial agriculture. These patterns of social behaviour were made tangible and symbolic in a legal system that blended English common law and continental Roman law through the structures of federal and state constitutions, the powerful decisions of courts and the enactments of legislatures. In addition, an element of purely native, frontier law was present, a customary law affecting the behaviour of law-makers and judges and emanating from the necessities of social life in a hostile wilderness. Because it impinged first on the lives of farmers, the law appeared in the system by which the land itself was distributed.

The American land system was initially a form of tenure similar to that of the late feudal period: the king of England granted the right to hold land to companies, bands of settlers, projectors and various noble persons. The initial grants were very large and the boundaries exceedingly vague; the companies or proprietors receiving them then regranted them to subtenants and ultimately to individual settlers, usually for a price or in exchange for a nominal quit-rent. By 1789, the new federal government in the United States had become both proprietor and sovereign to all the unallocated lands outside the boundaries of the thirteen original colonies, in particular to all the lands west of the Allegheny Mountains, north of the Ohio River and south of Tennessee. This federal domain extended to the Mississippi River at that time; between 1800 and 1868, the vast acquisitions from France (the Louisiana Purchase), Mexico (Texas, the south-west and California), Great Britain (the north-west) and Russia (Alaska) were added to fulfil the republic's self-proclaimed 'manifest destiny'.

The colonial and federal land distribution system formed an important element in the environment facing the first farmers, and their effects are to be seen in American field patterns and the American landscape today. Anyone flying over the eastern United States cannot fail to note how the patchwork of irregular fields east of the mountains changes dramatically into the huge squares and rectangles, often of uniform size, with perfectly straight boundaries extending sometimes for hundreds of miles across the flatlands between the Alleghenies and the Rockies. The surveying and subdivision of the federal domain across three-quarters of the land area of the United States is an artifact directly out of French 18th-century rationalism as filtered through the mind of Thomas Jefferson. His basic plan, no doubt based on a Roman model, caused the land to be surveyed in great squares, six miles on a side, called townships. Within each township, the square miles (called 'sections') were numbered, and sold usually in units of a quarter-section (160 acres) or multiples thereof. Directing the seemingly wayward movement of pioneer settlers – the families and the waggon trains – therefore, was a perfectly regular and orderly arrangement of the land that would have delighted the heart of Jeremy Bentham. The Canadian provinces followed various methods of land distribution, but in the extensive dominion lands in the prairies and the west a rectangular survey, along the lines of the American system, laid out the plans for disposal through a system of fees and homestead settlement.

After a decade of trial in the federal republic, the 17th-century practice of making huge grants or sales to individuals or to trading or land companies was abandoned in response to popular pressure for direct access to the domain. By the Act of 1796, supplemented by numerous adjustments in the terms of sale over the following half-century, federal land offices were established, and the land, once surveyed and subdivided, was placed on auction, a few townships at a time. The land, the age-old basis of sovereignty and social order in Europe, was thus made into a commodity like any other and sold to the highest bidder. Between that date and 1863, the lands to the Mississippi River and just beyond it, north and south, were released to private ownership by thousands of small farmers and small-town land speculators and investors. After 1863, so called 'homesteaders' could acquire a quarter-section of public land simply by claiming it and settling on it. At the same time, the system of large grants was revived in order to subsidize railroad construction, particularly across the plains and arid regions, but the railroad companies essentially imitated the federal system of sales to settlers.

There were many other points at which the pioneer experience, combined with the commercial excitement offered to small farmers by abundant market opportunity, led to alterations in the legal forms and structures inherited from Europe and made of the law the instrument to a rapid development of small-scale business enterprise. Such changes occur in the law of contract, of eminent domain, of negotiable instruments. A small-town business civilization grew up around land offices, merchants, lawyers and transport and banking agencies in the farming area as the land was put under the plough. The farmer was apart from this – slightly,

*In the South wholesale business methods were applied to farming, and estates were run for profit, using slave labour. Whitney's cotton gin, shown here, separated the fibre from the seed and enormously increased productivity.*

but only slightly. He worked with his hands and muscles, he employed animal-power and the labour of a wife and children. He commanded the mysterious technology of soil, seed and rainfall, and held to familial patterns of sympathy and sociability. But he largely shared the speculator's ambition to grow wealthy. He would create a physical infrastructure of canals, roads and towns, and an organizational infrastructure of politics, markets, prices, money and even those necessary evils – banks and middlemen – in order to do it.

What then was this opportunity for wealth seen by the American farmer on his way from frontiersman or peasant to the role of little businessman? It is no part of agrarian history to detail it. Put briefly, the opportunity was two-fold. First, and most prominent, was the opportunity for large speculative gains both from appreciation in the value of land and from the chance that high yields in early years would be realized in a rising market. Second, and more steady, the opportunity existed to realize very large physical surpluses of basic food crops above what was needed for a family's own subsistence. Of course, speculative gains of the first sort were dependent on the prospects of a steady realization of gains of the latter sort. Land speculation – in which every landowner was involved to a degree – was a risky game where the productive capacity of a piece of land and the location of future towns, roads and railroads were not yet known. In land sales, many gains were made by a bidder's special access to information about the land or its prospects. But the steady growth in land values depended on growing knowledge of the land, growing density of prosperous settlement and improving markets for the crops. These required the growth in a region of a solid body of steady farmers

whose annual surpluses would make the development of transport and business services worthwhile. From the side of supply then, it can be seen how critical was that surplus above the pioneer's consumption, as already mentioned. In upstate New York and in Pennsylvania, and most of all in the new lands beyond the Ohio River, all the talk in the 1820s and 1830s was of 'internal improvements' to 'realize the surplus'. This meant a struggle by any economic, legal or political means for settlers to use their family's labour to exploit their entire holdings – ten to twenty times the effort needed by a log-cabin pioneer – and to deliver these vast quantities of produce to commercial markets. Only in such a way could land rents be generated and land values rise.

The other side of this picture was the market growth in the manufacturing and urban centres in the northeast, from Boston to Baltimore. The southern cotton plantations, like the sugar islands of the 18th century, may have taken substantial quantities of produce at certain points, but mostly from nearby farms or from the upper South. But the northern cities and towns were as eager to find markets in the countryside as the farmers were to supply them with cheap food. In a society so hungry for wealth, so obviously able to obtain it on a wide scale and so responsive to popular pressure and sentiment, the erection of a network of transport and business services was as lightning-like, as inevitable as the leaping of a spark between two oppositely charged poles. The opportunity for the northern farmer was not simply to produce large physical surpluses and get them hauled away, but to be able to use the income from these sales, and the wealth from the rise in land values, to buy a mounting array of

*The railways were a vital element in the growth of farming as a business in the trans-Mississippi West. Here beef cattle are herded aboard a waggon of the Kansas–Pacific Railway in 1871.*

manufactured goods both to beautify and to facilitate daily life, and to increase the family farm's productive capacity. To plug into this profitable circuit of exchanges, the northern farmer was ready to work himself and his family long hours in the field and barn, to borrow in order to hold more land or purchase better tools, to seek continually the best-yielding crop choice for his farm, and to exercise care in selecting the best seeds and stock. As in similar economic circumstances among the landowners and tenants in 18th-century England, there was a 'rage for improvement'; the peasant suspicion of innovation which had protected agriculturists for centuries from foolish risks was lost in the zeal to 'keep up with the times'.

Here, then, was that same tangible, almost tastable, chance that the southern planter had faced earlier in tobacco and, contemporaneously, in cotton – the chance of a lifetime to make a 'killing' in farming and land-holding – if only the obstacle of labour scarcity could be removed. Slavery was out of the question – though the fear that slave-holders might bring their slaves into the plains and prairies lay near the surface of political thinking in the 1850s. As long as labour was free and land was cheap, hired labour or even tenant farmers were nearly impossible to find. A family's own labour, stretched to the utmost, could be supplemented by animal-power but animal-power required grain and hay, and before 1840 animals could not lighten the peak labour requirement in the agricultural year, that of harvesting. But the 19th-century American agrarian settlement was occurring in the presence of an Industrial Revolution in its mechanical phase. Is it surprising then that, given the level of mechanical skills, Patent Office records begin to exhibit a bewildering array of mechanical inventions for use on the farm – and that the most successful of these mechanized the grain and hay harvest?

Outside German Pennsylvania and French Canada, the North American farmer before 1860 was not a peasant, indeed probably did not derive predominantly from peasant stock. In the South he had become a slave-master, or failing that had remained a poor, isolated, half-idle independent mountaineer. In the North he made a good frontiersman exactly because he was not steeped in the traditional lore of peasantry. The typical New England Yankee made quick adjustment to continually changing economic circumstances, to the opening of new areas, to steady and almost continuous shifts in crop combinations, to new techniques and genetic stock. He searched continually to find ways to make his labour go further, over more land, to produce an ever larger marketable surplus. And he could maintain sanity in conditions so novel, so changeable and unstable, so risky and dangerous, because beneath the improvisation, the innovations, the strangeness of daily life, there lay burning a strong hard drive towards wealth and abundance. The American farmer had a fixed star that kept him on course; it had the glitter in it of silver and gold. But it lay in a firmament across which ran the straight, rationally devised lines of a rectangular system of land survey, and the axioms of private property rights, inviolable except in the interests of a greater wealth for the community. And beneath his feet lay the solid earth of 19th-century society, the emotional support and indulgence of family, church, neighbourhood and school.

### The productive achievement

Before considering the American farmer as a full social being, it is necessary to trace out the story of his economic success and its attendant ironies over the century since the Civil War. The story is not of society and psychology, but of agricultural technology and the operation of commercial markets. These form a stratum which must be penetrated, and whose operation and mediation must be understood before we can reach the human roots out of which the whole social, technical and economic vegetation grew.

Two reaping machines shown in the American section of the Great Exhibition, London 1851. Hussey's (above) was the earliest, developed in the 1830s. McCormick's (right) improved on Hussey's and was sold in large numbers up to about 1860.

A comparative picture to the one shown earlier: 'farm tools of the present time', i.e. 1861. A far greater variety is available, though the more elaborate machines are not represented here.

By 1870 it was evident that, in improving, expanding, linking itself to industrial society, the agrarian community in North America had burned its bridges behind it. Settlement on the plains and prairies, the shift into dairying around the Great Lakes and the introduction after 1900 of specialized and perishable fruit and vegetable crops in Florida and the Pacific coastal states put farmers into commercial agriculture on a continental, indeed, a world-wide scale. In the new areas of the West and the south-west, even the limited degree of self-sufficiency that Midwest farmers had enjoyed as late as the 1880s was physically not possible except with a very sparse population. More important, the capital structure of farming itself had become fixed to produce large surpluses of specialized crops while also releasing labour to move off the farms to industrial and small-town employment. Like a tree in an ornamental orchard, American agriculture had been shaped, pruned and set, as it grew, in a design – the design of an industrial world economy.

Geographically, the design may be sketched out on the map showing the distribution of crops in the North American continent in, say, 1910. It is evident that, with one exception, the major farming regions had already assumed their present-day extent. It was, roughly, the design first observed in Europe and rationalized by the German theorist of spatial economics, Von Thünen. From the cities and ports of the Atlantic and the Great Lakes, perishable and labour-

using crops – fruits and vegetables, dairy products – came to be produced on specialized farms devoted very largely to these activities. In a great ring beyond them, from Tennessee through the old Midwest as far as Iowa and Wisconsin and into south central Canada, dairying was mixed with meat production and the production of feed grains, especially corn for hogs and farm cattle. Hay for city horses was produced near cities, since it was bulky to haul, but much hay was produced in all areas to feed draught animals. Beyond the area of mixed farming lay the belt of wheat lands – from 300 to 600 miles wide – beyond that an even wider belt of cattle ranges, and beyond them, in the mountains, sheep. On the western side of the Rockies, something of this same succession appeared in progression from the young port cities of the coast. Across the South through central Texas, it was cotton rather than wheat that spread out across a thousand miles from east to west. This pattern, not dissimilar to that in Europe, where a great market centre like London affected production as far away as Australia, New Zealand and Argentina, was the reflection on the land of an efficient transport system, of spatially concentrated markets for food and fibre, and of a natural, space-using agricultural technology. It was the creation of a responsive agricultural population, required to serve demand at lowest cost through the operation of competitive markets for produce, for land and for farm credit. It vastly reduced the cost of farm products; indeed, no other spatial arrangement could

*American farming in 1920; fruit and vegetables in the rich, well watered coastal areas, cotton in the South, wheat in the centre and North, and a huge area of unproductive desert in the West. The pattern was to remain for several decades, but in the last twenty years has changed considerably.*

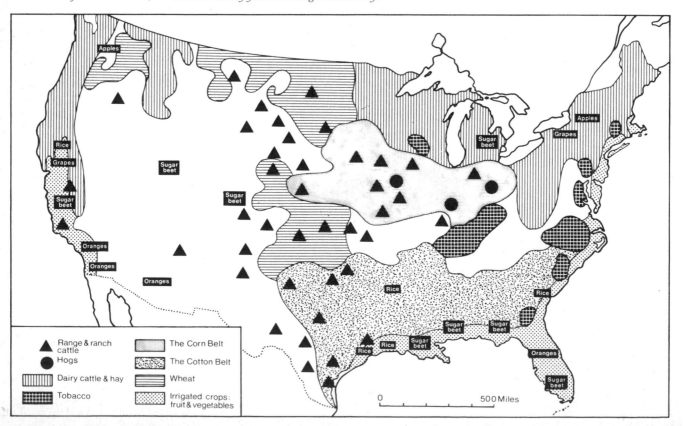

*Transporting grain by canal from the Middle West to the Atlantic, an indication of the continental scale of American commercial farming.*

have begun to feed the populations that grew up in Europe and North America in the 19th century. Between 1890 and 1950 it changed little; its logic remained intact. In North America, cotton spread to the southwest, with irrigation, partially abandoning its former home in the old slave states, and cheap shipment of perishables sent most of the vegetable industry to California and Florida. Otherwise, the main supports of the spatial pattern remained in place.

That no such pattern is proof against a changing technology is shown by another characteristic of the farm capital structure before 1920: the power technology. From the ante-bellum developments of threshing- and reaping-machines, operations in all the crops pushed towards mechanization. The goal was attained with varying lags and varying degrees of success. Harvesting of the row crops, corn and cotton, tobacco and vegetables, resisted mechanization till well into the 20th century. This meant the retention of much labour working (and overworking) during the harvest season. Family labour of share-croppers and independent farmers was strained, and in the West hired migratory labour filled the need. Particularly awkward was the failure of the steam-engine to adapt to widespread farm use. But the important substitute, where mechanical power could not be applied, was the farm animal – horse or mule. At the peak of the draught-animal population on United States farms, a quarter of the cultivated acreage was devoted to their feed. This was in 1920; by 1950, this whole arrangement had been made obsolete by the tractor. The substitution of petroleum for hay and pasture grasses as an energy source for farm-power released to the food crops or other uses about one-quarter of the land under cultivation – about ninety million acres, an area roughly equal to the arable area of north-west Europe.

The growth of specialized farming regions and the ready adoption of mechanical techniques are but two examples of the responsiveness of American farmers to the pressures and incentives of world and continental markets. Specialized regions were the geographical response to urban growth and transport improvement. 'Tractorization' was but the most spectacular demonstration of the power of the Industrial Revolution to affect farming operations. The incessant striving for mechanical improvement, characteristic of northern farming before the Civil War, continued on a vaster scale aided by thoroughly professional techniques of research and development. Where farmers themselves showed such readiness to make money, one may be sure that a farm equipment and farm service industry lost no time in producing and marketing things to sell to farmers. But modern farm productivity depends less on geography and machinery than on amazing new fertilizers, genetic research, and field and feeding techniques. These have not derived from the mere play of markets or the simple extension of industrial patents to replace human feet, arms and fingers in farm tasks. Between 1840 and 1940, agricultural science, which had received its impetus in the technical schools and landed estates of western Europe, was received into American agriculture. The European institutions were recreated, the experiments were continued, the research equipment was improved, the statistical techniques were extended, the genetic and chemical theories were modified. Most effective of all, these improvements, coming out of the commercial impulses of a democratic state, were shared and spread. The lag between discovery and application grew shorter; any delays were caused not by communications obstacles or fixed prejudice about technology but only by the need for the right set of market conditions to make new techniques profitable.

To understand this ultimate, self-extinguishing achievement of the American farmer, it is necessary to look beyond a mere responsiveness to commercial markets, abundant land, or a ready involvement in a

*Tractors, 1890 and 1924. The steam-tractor (top) provided power but was heavy and unwieldy on the land and took excessive time to set in motion. Petrol-driven tractors had none of these drawbacks and machines like the 'Farmall' tractor (bottom) revolutionized farming.*

scientific and technical development originating in industrial capitalism. Its sociology and ideology are more complex than that, and may be clarified in the concluding section of the chapter. But the assessment of the whole achievement and its costs to American rural culture cannot at this point be postponed. By 1940, geographical specialization and mechanization together had, in effect, solved the labour problem in American agriculture. Output per man since 1840 had increased two- or three-fold in cotton and corn; four- to six-fold in wheat and the grasses; in dairying and meat production, similar productivity gains were registered; yields per acre, reflecting improvements in seed and fertilizer, as well as geographical arrangement of production, had increased relatively little, but had maintained their levels in the face of the vastly increased output and shifts to new and drier areas.

It was between 1940 and 1980, that the pay-off came to the applications of science and power-driven machinery in American agriculture. Labour requirements in corn, wheat, and cotton had been cut by 1980 to between $\frac{1}{5}$ and $\frac{1}{20}$ of their 1940 levels, and yields of land had doubled or trebled. From 65 per cent of the American labour force in 1850, farm labour fell to 17 per cent in 1940 and $3\frac{1}{2}$ per cent in 1980. The farm population, which formed just over 50 per cent of the United States' population in 1850, accounted for about 3 per cent in the Census of 1980. In Canada, after 1920, agricultural productivity showed similar gains. This

growth in the productivity of the soil and of the human and capital resources working it may prove indeed to be North America's lasting and peculiar achievement in an industrializing world. But it meant – or at least was accompanied by – the disappearance, indeed, the destruction, in America as in western Europe, of the society based economically, socially and politically on farming and rural ways of life.

The story of the decline in the farm community, its independence, its social values and its weight in the national culture is not a happy one. It did not occur suddenly through brainwashing, or doctrinaire violence, such as a planned economy based on Marxian notions of class struggle might have exhibited. It occurred, rather, through the gradual and fluctuating attrition of market relationships as they acted on the hopes of succeeding generations of new farmers. From 1870 on, through decades of its greatest expansion of output and its greatest technical changes, American farming was afflicted by the disease of relative economic decline. There is no point in simple or static comparisons of farm and non-farm incomes. They show a growth in farm family income roughly equivalent to that in other sectors of the economy. But this growth occurred in the presence of a marked slow-down in the growth of the farm population, a migration of young people from the farms that was at least as great as the huge immigrations arriving from Europe between 1870 and 1920. As a major sector of economy and society, American farming died a lingering death – a fact attributable to its responsiveness to market processes in this great and inevitable transition in the national life.

Hard times on the farms occurred in two great waves, the earlier of which was a period of enormous growth in farm output. In the period 1870–96, the so

called 'Great Depression' in world price levels bore heavily on the American farmer. The specialized literature covering these decades of the farmers' discontent is vast, and inconclusive. Perhaps real incomes did not fall; perhaps the terms of trade did not shift strongly against farm products; certainly railroads and machinery companies drastically reduced the costs of transport and equipment. The record of the farm press and farm politicians of the period is, nonetheless, a litany of complaint directed at the urban–industrial society on which farming had become dependent. The complaints focused on two points: the 'unfair' pricing practices of 'monopolies' – railroads, communications services, marketing middlemen, equipment suppliers and banks – and the loss of sons and daughters to the towns and cities. The prairies and the plains became the seat of an agrarian radicalism – a revolt against a commercial system that had offered, then snatched away, a dream of prosperity, independence and continuous expansion. In the distribution of radicalism in the United States and, somewhat later, in Canada, one can read something of its nature and source. It played little part in the history of groups with the lowest incomes – share-croppers, Black and white, in the cotton areas; hill farmers, still in large part self-subsistent; hired farm labourers; scrub farmers on poor soils in the Canadian Maritime Provinces, New England or cut-over regions in New York and around Lake Superior. Nor did it make deep inroads on comfortably settled dairy and mixed corn and hog farmers east of the Mississippi. American agricultural expansion had been based partly on the successful provision of suitable commercial produce to regular markets, but much more on the dream of rising land values, farming bonanzas, high risks and overcommitment on the frontier. It was this oppor-

tunity that the American farmer saw slipping away in the 1870s and 1890s in the plains and the prairies, even as torrents of grain and meat were pouring out from the new lands.

The economic ceiling lifted again between 1896 and 1920, and again an investment boom in Midwest farming areas got under way. When finally the slow dull ache in wheat and cotton markets in the 1920s extended after 1929 to the entire farming industry, even eastern farmers and the most hidebound Midwest Republican individualists sought relief in group action, export bounty schemes and, at last, crop limitation and government price supports. For farmers of middling condition, government programmes simply eased the transition to extinction. Share-croppers, labourers and tenants were helped little, if at all. Only the continuous off-farm movement after 1940 reduced what was perceived as poverty in agriculture. Wealth in agriculture then began to reappear in the 1960s and 1970s through the management of large acreages, a heavy capital investment and the deft use of government support and tax laws.

## Farm families and rural neighbourhoods

The development of a successful commercial agriculture in North America did not come directly out of the experience of the frontier or the pioneer settlement. As I have indicated, that could have led as easily to the formation of a traditional agricultural society. Even without markets, simultaneous industrial growth and transport improvements, the colonial populations would have continued to reproduce and to spread west. A view of how that non-commercial American agrarian society might have developed is offered by the experience of the Appalachian uplands where yeoman farmers, families and clans spread across a thousand

*Threshing demanded the combined efforts of the whole farm. In a painting by Grant Wood of 1934, the men are shown arriving at the farmhouse, washing in the porch and sitting down to their midday meal (fourteen of them), while the women cook and serve food from the kitchen on the right.*

miles of hilly terrain, poor soils and isolated valleys. The link with the commercial economy was feeble, intermittent, suspect, tentative. Here, out of pioneer stock and primitive conditions, a 'hill-billy' culture developed, clannish, fertile, unschooled, independent, religious. People had large families and migrated, to form a 'southern' and mountain underlay in the lower Ohio and Missouri valleys where some transformation occurred. But enough people remained on the scrub farms at home, like a bubbling spring, to continue their culture's contribution to the national life. It was not along this path that American agriculture moved to its feats of commercial, capitalistic, scientific activity.

Instead of a native development from the frontier, one must postulate, I think, an agro-business culture, almost (though perhaps not quite) from the start. Some prerequisites for such a culture – in the land system and in the price system – working through money, banks, salesmen and lawyers, the settlers took with them in the move west. The very term 'farm' or 'farmer' in Anglo-American usage is indicative. A 'farm' means a holding from which revenue is derived. In the American case, the owner, the 'farmer' and the tiller of the soil were combined in one person, who held his tenure not from a king or a nobleman, but from the price system itself. He was always in danger of losing it, if not to a bank or mortgage-holder, then simply by yielding to the temptation to sell out to someone who could 'farm' it at a higher return, for himself and for society as a whole. Frontier democracy added to the individualism of this capitalist culture, and at the same time, by way of the democratic state, it shaped policies without regard even for private property rights, in the interests of the rapid economic development of the whole community. A small-town business culture set the standard, the values, the measures of worth and success for the rural areas, yet the rural culture was rural, after all. Had it been merely individualistic, profit-minded, competitive, shallowly commercial and unable to act at a social level beyond the individual family, its development could not have been quite so rapid nor would its achievement have been so solid.

Among the social forms in rural areas, the farm family was fundamental; yet we know very little about its internal structure and tensions, the features that distinguish these from any other set of farm families in Western culture. Its nucleus was perhaps closer knit since farmsteads were scattered across the countryside instead of being grouped in villages; perhaps it was less authoritarian since each member contributed something to the common labour. Because the farm was a joint enterprise of man and woman, it is very likely that the role and position of the woman was higher than in peasant families in northern Europe. This may be shown by looking at the birth-rates, which begin to decline in the East in the early 19th, or even late 18th, century, and fall steadily from original high levels in every region as settlement proceeds. The higher posi-

tion of women may also be indicated by the fact that even after large investment expenditures, the farm budgets still left enough to spend on goods for the household to create enormous markets for work-lightening or life-enhancing consumer goods. The family was also the principal channel by which farming techniques were passed down to the succeeding generation until schools, colleges and extension services usurped its function. A question that seems to obsess historians is whether this family, and the ethical culture of which it was a part, was 'puritanical'; that is, did it transmit a sense of sin that led to a life of endless self-justifying labour? What gave rural families the driving zeal that they showed in joining the American pursuit of wealth? Perhaps these values were absorbed from the surrounding commercial milieu; certainly no traditional rural society existed to counteract their force.

The next level of social control in Europe above the family, i.e. the village, was missing from the North American scene. Instead, the agrarian culture substituted a communications network stretching for a few tens of miles around a farmhouse: the rural neighbourhood. Neighbours met in those pioneering tasks that required joint labour: log rolling, roof raising, fence building, harvesting. The sharing of teams and equipment occurred, though evidently not on a very formal basis. Threshing, corn husking and corn shelling, especially, were tasks where the superior productivity of a work group was apparent. As the surplus produce of a region began to gain in value, labour, too, became worth something, exchanges might be made and finally a money wage paid. An incomplete drift from primitive gift-giving between families, to barter, then to hourly or daily hire occurred, but loans of labour still retained a social quality.

Similarly, the centres of group activity and communication in a rural area served both an economic and a social function. A small Protestant church met every Sunday – and usually on Wednesday evening as well – and furnished an outlet for individual souls to express and exorcise the fears and terrors of everyday life. But, as in a family, around this basic emotional experience, social communication, education, sport, courtship and the exchange of information and opinion about crops and techniques took their places. Much the same concerns and functions are manifest wherever the rural people met – at the schoolhouse, at lodges, clubs, and social circles, or at the county seat on business – legal or commercial – or at the county agricultural fair. It must be remembered that the competition among rural people, for land, good yields, high prices, was not really a rivalry such as might occur between two business firms in a restricted market. At most it was a friendly rivalry, which spurred each farmer on to greater achievement, but rewarded rather than penalized him for sharing his secrets. The market was so wide, the individual participants so small, that their gains were not made at the expense of one another. Northern

*Grain elevator, New York, 1877, with long trains arriving from the west and ships ready in the harbour to transport the grain across the world.*

farmers were a reasonably homogeneous people – the Germans a bit apart and a bit clannish among themselves. Their sociability, exaggerated as it was by the relative isolation of a family's daily life, was easily released, permitting a society to form with a certain structure of prestige, based partly on wealth, but also on a general respect for a variety of natural qualities – strength, intelligence, saintliness, eloquence. Ministers, lawyers, schoolmasters, and any with a gift and ambition for political life, were respected and listened to. Indeed, of all rural activities, perhaps politics was the most enjoyed, and election day the centre of the warmest rivalry and sentiment.

American northern rural culture, then, was a culture with an internal strength based on strong, relatively isolated families, whose homogeneity of origin and aims permitted fairly easy communication. At the same time, it was a culture that looked outward – to the state for land and local improvements, to the law for the protection of property and the advancement of development schemes, to speculators, banks, lawyers and school-teachers as a literate elite who could advance it in wealth; ultimately it looked to science and industry to organize its research, and to the federal government

to solve its economic problems and to continue to further its economic status. It is easy to see how such a society expanded geographically, adopting new techniques and arranging itself in economically rational patterns as part of a developing capitalistic world economy. Among communications techniques, the railroad was followed by the telephone and the automobile, and, like so many other industrial gadgets, these found a wide and enthusiastic market in American rural areas. Electrification, when it came in the 1930s, completed the transformation of the farm household. Such a culture had no defence against industrialization; it shared an incurable American optimism that what is new is better. The dark side of modern industrial progress was not wholly missed. The farm community of the 1890s and the 1920s and 1930s suffered a serious loss of morale – so great as to make farmers in the 1930s desert temporarily the Republican faith, to revive populism and ally themselves in the United States, to some degree, with the foreign mass of urban labour. But by that time farmers were no longer a decisive voice in the national polity, or even in the political and developmental decisions that were made at state capitals.

It cannot be said, of course, that the American South

shared in this culture to a full extent. Its existence and persistence almost makes one feel that God is a social scientist, intent on furnishing North America with a control group against which to test explanations of northern achievement by comparative study. The answer to the question of the South's relative retardation lies partly in the disaster of the Civil War, and partly in the peculiar shape of the international market for farm products. But at bottom, one feels one must seek an answer in social structure. The problem would require a chapter of its own, and indeed has furnished the topic for a vast literature by political and economic historians. But the outlines of an answer suggest themselves and seem to fall out of what has already been said. To my mind, the most satisfactory way to look at the South is to consider the southern planter as a counterpart of the northern commercial farmer, appearing as markets appeared two hundred years before the markets for northern products, and able at that time to avail himself of slave labour. Given that initial development, the southern planter class grew, as a capitalist class, maintaining good connections among its members, each of whom was set at the centre of two networks of non-capitalist economic relationships. Around the planter on his land were the slaves on whose exploitation his wealth depended. But in the surrounding area there was another network of semi-self-sufficient white farmers, with one or no slaves, who were also allied to him by kinship, debt, and a client-like dependence. The strength of this social formation, which resembles that in much of the rural world, in countries of older as well as of recent settlement, is demonstrated by the combination of forces that was required ultimately to shatter it. The boll-weevil plus mechanization moved cotton west; wartime jobs drew Blacks and poor whites into northern cities. Federal programmes – TVA, aero space, military installations – stimulated southern industry. A new footloose character to industrial location brought the Sun Belt into prominence, and new markets for mixed crops, some based on very modern agricultural technology, altered the whole nature of farming. By 1960, southern planters and northern farmers had become small-scale industrialists, commanding significant blocks of capital. Pockets of rural poverty, exploitation and ignorant self-sufficiency persisted, but North American agrarian society had transferred most of its population, its culture, its value system and its social problems to a town or an urban environment, and so had ceased to exist as a peculiar social entity.

---

**That farming should be a business,** an undertaking intended, like any other, to make a financial profit, was an idea that only gradually took root in Europe. In America it had been present from the beginning. America never had a peasant class, men who lived on the same land for generations, and whose horizons were limited to their own closed communities. If such a life were forced upon the early settlers, they accepted it merely as a means to an end. The ultimate aim was not subsistence but progress. That distrust of change that we have seen to be so characteristic of European farmers was replaced in America by enthusiasm for improvement and confidence in the future.

The naïve but expressive painting by John Gast, of 1872 (*opposite*), called *American Progress*, epitomizes this philosophy. From the coastal cities of the East, in the background, pioneers set out towards the West bringing not only agriculture but railways, the telegraph and education. For all these things were necessary to the business of successful farming. The farm was not a self-sufficient unit. Its products had to be transported to distant markets (by road, railway or canal); consumer goods from the East must be made available (shops and warehouses); there must be money for expansion (so banks were among the first institutions of a new township), as well as hotels, schools, land agencies, service industries and processing plants. These developments took place at different speeds and in different proportions in the various parts of the country. Environmental variations led to social cleavages, especially between North and South, but they had enough in common to make 'the American farmer' a distinctive breed. (1)

**The mechanics of farming,** which made such strides in the 19th and early 20th centuries, have now reached a point where in most crops little further improvement seems possible. A giant corn (i.e. maize) harvester such as this one in Iowa can deal at speed with six rows of stalks at a time, shelling the grain and spewing husks and cobs out at the back. The field seems limitless, with the farm a tiny oasis in its midst. Further progress will probably come not from mechanical but from chemical and genetic research. And, as in Europe, problems of environmental protection and of adjustment to markets loom larger than those of merely growing the food. (28)

# 9 THE PEASANT IN THE MODERN WORLD

HARVEY FRANKLIN

# The peasant in the modern world

When the peacemakers gathered at Versailles in 1919, the principal factors that were going to modify rural life in Europe over the next sixty years were already clear. Among them, technology, mass culture and central government policies were to change the countryside radically. As the rest of this book has shown, rural life has always been extremely diverse – diverse physically and diverse in its social tradition. It was not until after 1959, following two decades of international boom and slump (1919–39) and two decades of war and reconstruction (1939–59), that uniformity prevailed over diversity, and rural life began to exhibit a degree of homogeneity without precedent in the past. And even then human manipulation of the environment was already producing new diversities.

## The implications of modernity

In 1919 rural Europe could be divided into three major zones: the east, the south and the west. In the east were the agrarian states, many of them newly independent, with overwhelmingly agricultural economies; they lay to the east of a line running from Danzig to Trieste and included Greece. The leaders of these states were faced with a daunting array of tasks: to achieve not only economic growth and economic self-sufficiency for a population that was largely rural and still increasing, but also national unity and democratic participation. Until the Second World War they failed. It proved impossible for them to slip the chains that bound them to the past, and whatever progress they made was either destroyed by outside forces or wasted through the inadequacies of their own leaders. But in 1945 these states recommenced the work begun in 1919 under vastly different circumstances and finally succeeded in breaking with the past. Forced industrialization, particularly during the 1960s and 1970s, placed rural issues in a totally different context. They were no longer a mass of low-productive small farmers, but industrialized economies burdened with a substantial agricultural sector.

In the south were the Mediterranean nations of Italy, Spain and Portugal, also largely agrarian economies, beset with their own problems, but not so troubled with questions of political integration as the agrarian states of the east. Each of them displayed striking geographical divisions within their borders reflecting differing levels of economic development and living standards, differing social and economic structures of long historical standing. In general, the south suffered from the exactions of large aristocratic estates. In the end the problems of the south – southern Italy, Spain and Portugal – were not to be solved without a rural exodus on a massive scale.

In the west, agricultural progress was smoother. Political equality was secured and land ownership was not confined to a privileged class. Modernization was well under way. Rural communities had been pentrated by road and rail, state educational systems, a network of markets and agricultural extension schemes. Various forms of legislation, not always effective, had been introduced: to protect labour, to insure against bad luck such as hail damage and livestock disease. Governments recognized the need to cope with issues related to leisure in the countryside – for rural people that is – and to improve the lot of country women; issues that were recognized as being directly related to the depopulation of the countryside and the rural exodus. Many of these schemes and innovations look inadequate to modern eyes; nevertheless, by the 1920s a coherent if not concerted effort had been begun to integrate the agricultural sector and its labour force into modern industrial society.

It was difficult for the experts of the interwar period to foresee that rising yields and output would eventually mean surplus production and fewer farms. It was difficult, too, to realize that an overall secular rise in living standards would make rural society one of the great reservoirs of the under-privileged in the modern state, or to anticipate that agriculture and agriculturalists would be among the thorniest issues of the new industrial state. These long-term trends were obscured by historical accidents, such as the slump, which made industrial life uninviting for rural people and even provoked 'back to the land' movements in the towns.

Just about everywhere in Europe the traditional peasant economy had been an adaptable but stable system. Typically, the family's holding provided full-time employment for the labour force. Ideally, it combined arable and livestock farming, possibly with some degree of crop specialization (e.g. tobacco, vines, hops). It was the livestock that constituted the critical, vital element for survival, for it was in this branch of farming that the peasant farm could demonstrate its superiority. Other forms of farm organization found it difficult to match the care that family labour could lavish upon the animals. However, there had always been a hierarchy of large, middle and small peasant farmers, and on the lower rungs of the ladder there had always been family farms that found it difficult to function efficiently. With the sustained rise in living standards throughout society as a whole, more and more small farmers found themselves in this position. They were, in any case, labouring under disadvantages peculiar to the countryside. They lacked modern services; they did not use, and were not offered, credit facilities; they were often physically inaccessible.

The result was that conditions once regarded as acceptable began to appal observers. Writing of inter-war Bosnia, Doreen Warriner reported: 'The Muslim peasants live the most primitive life possible; each peasant, his family and his cows in three or four huts in a little enclosure inside a fence against bears and wolves. The house is a low hut, smoke-blackened and empty, where the family sleep on the floor around the blazing open fire. The soil is turned with a long wooden spike. The peasants walk 20 or 30 miles to market to sell a few pounds of butter or a goat.' As she noted, in Croatia and Galicia, a long historical process which had often worked in favour of the peasant class was now leading to poverty. Pressure of population had produced a chaotic subdivision of fields, and even in the best of villages the peasants were clearly living on the verge of destitution with their three acres and a cow as their only source of income.

Conditions in south-western Germany were never as bad as this, but whole districts were classed as small peasant communities. High rates of population growth and the practice of dividing inheritances had reduced holdings to very small and highly fragmented units – despite emigration to Brazil, America, the Danubian lands and local towns. The Allmende, communally owned plots of arable land, frequently reassigned, supplemented the income of some families. Seasonal work as plasterers and building workers as far afield as Alsace and Switzerland had been another source of relief. General destitution was avoided by the practice of part-time farming and commuting, until whole districts that had been classified as small peasant communities as late as 1939 had to be reclassified as commuter or worker–peasant communities by 1961.

The possibility of having two or more sources of income had been the historic solution for a number of small peasant districts, allowing them to survive. Tourism, artisanal activities, administrative duties, or petty trading were the usual possibilities. Industrialization allowed whole villages rather than individuals to increase their incomes. Some people commuted daily or weekly to work in the factories of the nearby towns. Others worked in plants established by town entrepreneurs in the villages. In some cases the small peasantry became themselves entrepreneurs. By the mid-1930s this vital element of rural life was well established in south-western Germany and Switzerland, demonstrating another possible way of solving the farm problem: not by propping up the marginal holding but by rendering rural society itself more complex.

Rural society almost invariably consisted of more than the sum of the families actually engaged in farming. In the case of many western European villages the additions necessary to complete the sum may not appear to be great, but they were, nevertheless, significant. Rural dwellers who were not farmers or farm workers included the schoolmaster, the priest, artisans and land-owners. Located in the nearby towns were the notaries, government officials, merchants who bought livestock and agricultural produce, shopkeepers and factory workers in the processing plants. These people have influenced the rate of modernization; modernization in turn has altered their composition and contributions. In southern Italy (and the southern parts of Spain too) the influence exerted upon economic development by these non-farming rural dwellers proved to be quite pernicious, even as late as the 1960s. Their strength and capacity to thwart modernization rested upon their control of land and capital and the weak position of the many landless day labourers. The term feudal inevitably springs to mind. But the relationship between the landowners and the labourers was not feudal. It was essentially a capitalistic relationship of a most one-sided and inequitable sort, arising from a market situation in which there was more labour than work. In the market squares of Calabria and Apulia during the high points of the agricultural year the crudest of labour markets could be seen operating at the break of dawn. Those

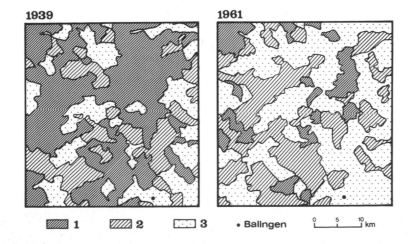

*Changing social patterns in a specific area of Germany between 1939 and 1961. The dot near the bottom of the map is the town of Balingen, in Baden-Württemberg. In twenty-two years the area inhabited by small peasant communities (1) has noticeably shrunk, while worker–peasant communities (2) and, even more, industrial and dormitory settlement (3) have increased.*

*It is only in modern times that the plight of the peasant has been portrayed in art with complete realism. A lithograph by the German Expressionist Käthe Kollwitz, of 1902, conveys all the fatigue and desperation of harsh toil.*

who could not find work just went away. No one was obliged to look after them.

The labourers of southern Europe, like those of eastern Europe, saw their salvation in obtaining access to the land. Only by escaping from the labour market could they ensure a future for themselves and their families. Land hunger became the basis of land reform movements and, ultimately, when the hunger was satisfied, of conservative political movements. This was a marked contrast to the situation further north, where the labourers, operating in a more satisfactory capitalistic relationship, wanted not land but better wages and working conditions, provided by a capitalist or, if the revolution came, socialist employer. On the capitalist estates of interwar Germany and in the Paris basin the landless wage workers were quite content to see the government protect farming.

In other words, there were many different ways for the peasantry as a class to disappear, to be transformed and to merge with other classes; and the repercussions of these processes could be many and various. With this in mind, let us look in more detail at the historical and geographical contexts.

### The succession states of eastern Europe

'The emergence of the peasant', wrote David Mitrany, 'as an active factor in the political and social life of Europe was perhaps the most telling and certainly the least expected effect of the First World War and a striking phenomenon in the social history of the continent between the two wars. It was marked enough even in the countries of the west; in the agrarian east it dominated every other aspect of the time and amounted to a social revolution.'

This social revolution took the form of a series of land reforms designed to avoid political revolution. In total it redistributed over 25 million acres of land, the equivalent of all the farmland in England and Wales. Its antecedents can be traced back to the French Revolution, but it was not a simple matter, and geography played as crucial a part as history.

The legislation that accompanied the introduction of a capitalist system in the countryside at the turn of the century enabled land to be more easily transferred, encouraged the movement of labour and increased the money supply. But all these measures naturally favoured the larger landowners rather than the smaller peasantry.

The large estates found their raison d'être in the exporting of cereals and other agricultural commodities and this gave the landowning class a strategic political position based upon their economic importance. Many landowners, particularly in Romania, Hungary and the Baltic states, had before 1914 tried to maintain their estates as single units of exploitation, employing as labourers the emancipated peasantry who had holdings quite inadequate to their needs. Growing pressure of population increased the peasants' hunger for land and so a contest arose. The peasants tried to starve the landlords of labour, pressuring them to accept other forms of organization – share-cropping, tenancy, outright sale – and the landlords, for their part, tried to starve the peasants of land. Growing land hunger among the eastern European peasantry meant that some resolution of the agrarian issue could not be staved off for ever. The bitter revolution of 1907 among the Romanian peasantry demonstrated that the day of reckoning was drawing closer, and the Romanian government proceeded to draw up plans for reform. The First World War both expanded the area where reform was demanded and quickened its pace.

Many of the new states that then arose on the ruins of the old Ottoman, Russian and Austro–Hungarian empires found themselves in the position of having either to stem or to legitimize a land-grabbing movement undertaken by returning and armed soldiers and members of the impoverished classes. In Croatia and Voivodina (Yugoslavia) and the eastern territories generally, the masses were in a state of ferment caused by the destruction of the countryside during the war and exacerbated by the proximity of Soviet Russia. The provision of independent holdings for several hundreds of thousands of peasants who could not otherwise support themselves was considered a vital factor in achieving peace.

Added strength was given to the movement by the fact that the large estates within the boundaries of the new nations often belonged to foreigners, so that expropriation took on a nationalistic coloration and continued old ethnic battles. In Poland, areas that had been acquired by the Prussian Land Settlement Commission in the west and the Russian Peasant Land Bank in the east were confiscated. In Lithuania, too, the lands acquired by the Russian Peasant Land Bank and the Bank of the Russian Nobility, in a process of Russification carried out in all the Baltic states, were also confiscated and subdivided. At the time it was the only way the land could be worked, the owners having fled eastward during the war. In southern Serbia, the last Serbian region to be freed from Ottoman rule, the land reform took on the appearance of land colonization rather than land redistribution, aiming at the 'speedy nationalization of the territory'. The obverse of this movement was the Bulgarian attempt to find land for their nationals who had been made refugees by changing boundaries. The Greeks were in a similar position.

'Peasants! The Polish landlords want to make you slaves!' One of Poland's grievances had been that foreign capitalists owned large estates. A Russian poster seeks to exploit this resentment.

In Bosnia-Herzegovina the land reform had many facets. Foremost among them was the abolition of the remnants of the Ottoman ancien régime, especially the obligation to pay one-third of the crop to the landlords who were Muslims of Slav origin. Because the tax was levied on only the arable crops, the effect of its abolition was to improve the standard of farming by encouraging the substitution of clover and fodder crops for extensive permanent pastures maintained at a maximum to keep down the proportion under plough. The effect of the reform was to establish a middle grade of peasantry long accustomed to the practice of farming and running an enterprise. These circumstances contrasted with those in southern Serbia where some of the new farms were granted to semi-nomadic people and day labourers with little experience of farming. The work was often left to the women, or the plots rented to others. In Crotia and Slavonia, efficient, productive large estates were dismembered.

The popular, insurrectionary, nationalistic character of the reforms was not to be denied. Non-economic factors had to take precedence in many instances, much to the anguish of some economists who saw the reform

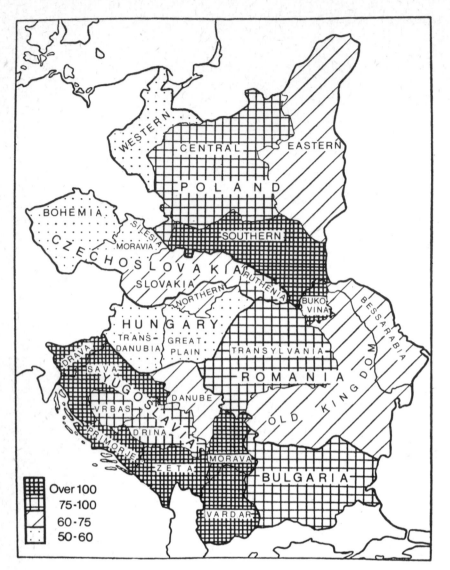

The numbers of people which the land had to support varied enormously throughout eastern Europe. This map gives a rough bird's-eye view of the situation as it was in 1930–31. Figures represent farm population per 250 acres of farmland.

as a chance to establish an agrarian structure suited to the potential of modern farming methods. The political slant acquired by the reform evoked a counter-movement led by conservative and Fascist elements once the insurrectionary danger had passed. After the brief revolutionary Bela Kun episode in 1919 the rulers of Hungary more or less ignored the whole issue, eventually putting through a token reform. Eastern Poland remained a stronghold of the big estate.

### Peasants and populists

In the eyes of their architects, however, the land reforms were not just a first step towards solving the economic problems of the new states. More importantly, the possession of the land, its redistribution, established the social basis of the new democratic nations. Agrarian, peasant parties rapidly became prominent elements of postwar political life, some leaders becoming international figures. Witos, a peasant, became premier of Poland for a short period. Stamboliski, son of a peasant,

was prime minister of Bulgaria from 1920 until 1923 when he was overthrown and tortured to death by the military. The Radić brothers and then Maćek became major political forces as leaders of the Croatian Peasant party, most often in opposition, in the new kingdom of the Serbs, Croats and Slovenes. With the exception of Czechoslovakia, however, the agrarian parties were unable to apply their parliamentary strength to solving the economic problems besetting their peasant electorates. With power in its grasp for the first time ever, the largest economic class found it difficult to influence and impossible to control its own destiny. Just about everything weighed heavily against this happening.

To begin with, the boundaries of the new nations contained enormous disparities in level of development, particularly in Poland and Yugoslavia. Policies suited to one region had adverse effects in another. National economic integration, even at the level of a common currency, a common legal code and common legislation, was delayed in some countries until the late

1920s. An administrative structure and cadre capable of implementing a policy of reform was lacking. The vast bureaucracies, along with the military, absorbed revenues from the taxes that fell with increasing burden upon the peasantry. Dispossessed of their land by the reforms, the former landowners gravitated towards the capitals, strengthening the social base for the right wing military and Fascist counter-movements that put peasant leaders under detention or in jail, where they were humiliated, or sent them into exile.

In this situation the peasant parties were powerless; they were designed for parliamentary manoeuvring, not for the creation of sustained rural movements. Where rural movements were established and maintained, the circumstances were exceptional. Czechoslovakia was the most advanced and least agrarian country of the succession states. Her rural movement, essentially a co-operative movement, was not aimed at establishing an agrarian and populist democracy, but at incorporating agriculture into the industrial state. The Croatian rural movement – again co-operative and educational in its thrust – was located in the more developed parts of Yugoslavia, and lost its political force only because its leadership became associated with a separatist movement, which the Serbian centralists would not tolerate. The events of the first postwar decade demonstrated that although the peasantry might constitute the largest social category of the new nations, and in the eyes of the populists represent their cultural foundations, the sum of the society and the nation must always be greater than the peasantry. As a consequence, peasant parties became involved in regional, religious and nationalistic disputes, which effectively diverted their attention from the rural issues that had initially drawn them into politics.

The sources of populism were numerous and its elements diverse, but there was one issue to which all populists had to address themselves at some time: the creation of an economic system suited to the needs of a largely peasant nation. Socialism and capitalism were both unacceptable to them. The first was oriented towards the interests of the proletariat. Capitalism preferred the interests of the capitalist and, like socialism, it, too, led ultimately to the proletariatization of the peasantry for monetary rather than doctrinaire reasons. The populists sought the preservation of a peasant landowning class. The Bulgarian leader Stamboliski maintained that 'the government should concentrate on economic development, since without economic progress no other advances are possible'. He saw an economic parliament, in which all the country's major occupational groups were represented according to their size, as the principal agent of reforms, aiming at a fairer distribution of both burdens and benefits. The populists interpreted the crucial economic issue as a matter primarily of redistribution: the redistribution of economic and social power in favour of the peasantry. They were not averse to the creation of

wealth via industry, but they wanted that industry ruralized. They never considered the problem as involving the creation of a sound, modernized middle peasantry with all the attendant and far-reaching changes it would produce, that is, the disappearance of thousands of marginal farms.

'One of the populists' . . . basic misconceptions of great political, economic and social import', wrote Tomasevich, 'was the view that the village as a social unit, and the peasantry as a whole, are economically and socially homogeneous. It was manifest, however, that economic and social differentiation was becoming greater from year to year.' Tomasevich goes on to provide a detailed socio-economic breakdown of the Yugoslav peasantry in the interwar period, and others did the same for other countries. In every case except that of Hungary three groups of peasants emerged. The first was a peasantry that possessed, for the times, land sufficient to employ its whole labour force and to provide its own foodstuffs and meet its own other needs. In the case of Yugoslavia this represented 30 per cent of the farming families, and controlled 49 per cent of the land in farms of 12 to 50 acres. The second group consisted of peasantry with insufficient land to employ or feed its families. It incorporated 64 per cent of the farms, 28 per cent of the land. In even more desperate circumstances was the third group, the 10 per cent of the people living from agriculture who were landless. Because 23 per cent of the land remained in holdings of more than 50 acres (13 per cent in 50–125-acre farms; 10 per cent in farms of more than about 125 acres) it was argued that the distress of the landless and the small farmer could have been relieved by a further round of redistribution. In part, this was true, and it eventually occurred under Tito. Fundamentally, however, the relief of this distress was a question of industrialization.

Agrarian reforms beyond a certain point were ineffectual. This point received increasing recognition as the war approached. As one Polish writer put it: 'the general problem of rural overpopulation can only be definitely resolved by a very rapid industrialization of Poland'.

## Problems of the middle peasantry

During the interwar years, the fact that marginal farms were suffering poverty and deprivation tended to obscure the fact that even the viable ones were in serious difficulties. It was also misleading to refer to these fairly well-to-do family units as 'subsistence farms'. They were in fact not self-sufficient. They were marketing a substantial proportion of their produce in order to obtain manufactured goods for consumption and investment, and in order to meet social and public obligations. If their profits fell and the price of these goods and obligations rose, 'subsistence' disappeared.

In eastern Europe, the initial prosperity of the postwar period led to an expansion in the consumption of such things as sugar, luxury items, town style clothing and in the desire to send children to school. With the depression of agricultural prices the peasantry became the victims of the price scissors. They responded by reducing their demand not only for consumption goods but also for farm inputs, such as fertilizers, that were essential in obtaining higher gross incomes. There were fixed costs, interest and taxes, which had to be paid out of a current income that was subject to periodic downturn. Agricultural indebtedness and agricultural credit as a consequence became vital issues.

There was firstly the old scourge of taxation, direct and indirect, made even harder to bear by the fact that even under elected popular governments little came back in the form of benefits to agriculture and the rural populace. Secondly, there were the debts, incurred among the middle peasants to service existing loans, to purchase land and for productive purposes, such as the care of buildings and the acquisition of livestock. Among the landless and the small farmers, it has been calculated that 20 per cent of the total indebtedness was incurred in order to purchase food. In Estonia it was estimated that 55 per cent of the total debts for agriculture was owed to the state, 18 per cent to private banks and 22 per cent to co-heirs and private persons. In its attempt to compete in a world increasingly governed by monetary relationships, the peasantry carried the extra burden of its social responsibilities. From Czechoslovakia and Denmark it was reported in 1937 that 'most frequently the debts arise out of the transfer of properties by succession (or at the time of payment of dowry) and are not due to loans contracted in order to enlarge properties'. Indebtedness was obviously also related to the degree of market development. The Czech correspondent of 1937 reported: 'the provinces furthest from the urban centre show a lower indebtedness'.

The international crisis of the 1930s forced observers throughout Europe to look closely at the economics of peasant farming, not only the economics of the rural destitute (a separate if related issue), but also those of the full-time family farmers – the middle peasantry – which governments in both the east and the west hoped to establish as a modernized peasantry, playing a conservative social and political role. In Weimar Germany, for instance, 47 per cent of the marketed produce came from the middle peasantry, who controlled 43 per cent of the agricultural land. The capacity of the peasant farm to survive crisis and capitalist competition was demonstrated in eastern Germany where the farms of between 12 and 50 acres produced 24 per cent of the market supply from 27 per cent of the land, and those of over about 250 acres with 45 per cent of the land produced 51 per cent of the marketed total. For Yugoslavia, Tomasevich's conservative opinion was that 'the rate of marketability, including the cottage industries, during the depression years of the early 1930s was somewhere between 35 and 45 per cent and during the later 1930s perhaps somewhere between 40 and 50 per cent of the total'. Bulgarian estimates were in the vicinity of 30 to 40 per cent.

Having realized the significance of the middle peasantry, the investigators set about listing the impediments to its efficiency. These fell into four categories: structural problems created by the dividing up of the land, leading to an enormous wastage of time and making coherent management impossible; vocational problems related to poor education and inadequate training for farm management; problems arising out of poor techniques and inefficient tools; and, finally, problems associated with poor marketing practices.

The recommended solutions to these problems included: reorganization of farms into larger units; cooperative action for the sale of produce and the purchase of capital goods and equipment; and investment in modern technology, together with the introduction of vocational education and agricultural extension schemes. Government price and fiscal policies remained the mainstay of all programmes. More revolutionary was the recommendation to adopt co-operative forms of labour organization.

The writers of the 1930s perceived a further and more fundamental problem besetting the middle peasantry. 'The family farm', Deslarges wrote, 'represents an investment rather of the work of the farmer and his family than of capital.' Munzinger expanded: 'the day's work usually begins at sunrise and goes on till nightfall. In the course of investigation it has been found that on an average 3,554 hours in the year are worked by a man and 3,933 by a woman. What then is the earned outcome of this backbreaking toil? Either the wages of a farmhand, if 2 per cent interest on the capital invested in the farm is all that is looked for, or a wage that is less than that of a farm hand, if 5 per cent interest is required.

*Another work by Käthe Kollwitz, an etching of an old man leaning exhausted on his scythe. The date is 1905.*

Moreover, the wage of the farm servant, too, is essentially below that of the factory hand.'

There was no visible end to this servitude of long hours, which persisted long after the disappearance of any feudal servitudes, except by tapping alternative sources of energy. In their search for relief, the peasants adopted the tractor as soon as it became economically feasible, which in most cases was after World War II. Motorization was the means by which the middle peasantry eventually solved their fundamental problem of hard work associated with low labour returns. In doing so they removed the raison d'être of the traditional household farm enterprise and destroyed their centuries' old way of life.

## Mediterranean Europe

Of the Italian army that returned victorious but badly mauled from the battlefields in 1918, almost half were peasants. As elsewhere in Europe, the politicians promised them a better life, and – as elsewhere – they were unable to keep their promises. Yet no major insurrectionary movement occurred in the Italian countryside. The class war was fought in the cities and factories. The struggle that went on in the rural areas was a very different one: it had a much longer history than the proletarian struggle, and its objective was not the abolition of property, but its acquisition.

Italy showed a remarkable divorce between land ownership and land farming. On the one hand were vast estates owned by the very rich, which were left largely uncultivated. On the other were smaller properties worked by men who had originally been tenant farmers but who, throughout the 19th century, came increasingly to own their holdings. At the bottom of the scale were the landless agricultural labourers, a class that was rapidly diminishing in numbers. Those in the north were able to better their condition by improved contracts and wages. In the south it was different. The class that gained least after the war and suffered most with the onset of the Depression, the ending of migration to the USA and the rising pressure of population were the *braccianti* – men without property, without a lease, without fixed labour contracts – a genuine rural proletariat. When destitution drove them to expropriate land, as happened after both world wars, they did so because the land remained uncultivated and because they were famished, not because the landowners were rich and their properties were large.

The presence of the big properties and landless labouring class has led some historians to see a resemblance between Italy and eastern Europe. In reality the situations were very different, both in the extent to which the land was farmed and in the social structure of the population. In Italy, what the bulk of the people needed was not land reform but new marketing procedures. Italian land reform when it was finally instituted dealt with issues that remained secondary to Italian agrarian development despite their great emotional appeal and propaganda value.

In Spain, the tensions that were to lead to land reform in Italy after World War II were already dangerous between the wars, manifesting themselves in insurrectionary movements in the countryside. These contributed their share to the final debacle of the Republic and the ensuing Civil War. But 20th-century Spanish rural history is distinguished, and immortalized, by a unique feature, anarcho-syndicalism, of vast interest to the observer of rural affairs, although in the final analysis it proved to be an impossible doctrine upon which to base a rural reform. Here was a movement that for a while brought together labourers, peasants, artisans, small shopkeepers and domestic servants. After World War I it was a powerful political force; in 1918, a series of strikes, at times violent and accompanied by sabotage, spread across the southern and eastern parts of Spain. But by the time of the Civil War it was already played out, partly because (once again) the peasantry wanted access to property, not its elimination.

The radicalism of anarcho-syndicalism was more apparent than real. Primarily its followers wished to return to the democratic existence of the primitive Spanish Commune, periodically repartitioning the land among families according to their needs. Although collectivist in this sense, the anarcho-syndicalists were reluctant to promote the greater well-being of the agricultural workers by advocating collectivization in the Russian sense. Most rural people abhorred that alternative. Furthermore, their philosophy gave greater prominence to the moral regeneration of man and to things that the materialistic bias of capitalism and Communism rendered apparently impossible: dignity, liberty, equality and leisure. Without any notable victories, the memories of Andalusian anarcho-syndicalism live on because it posed a question: in the modern world, what mode of economic existence permits the rural community to reap the benefits of industrial advancement (thus guaranteeing sufficient income and security to allow the attainment of a moral existence), while at the same time defending the farmer and the farm against the inroads of industrialism, in either its socialist or capitalist form? The answer to that question has been considered by many rural activists to be vital to the continuation of rural life if it is to bear some semblance to the rural life of the past.

The general level of prosperity in Estramadura and Andalusia was certainly low, for reasons that involved more than geography and economics. Geography and economics were, however, the crucial factors. Semi-arid, undeveloped socially and commercially, these regions could be helped only by massive investments of capital, and the necessary volume of investment could only be sustained by a modernized economy. The agrarian problems of this and similar zones of the Mediterranean littoral were disentangled only after the Second World War. Through a series of complex fiscal, monetary and interventionist measures, a simple but fundamental process was initiated. Organized capital in its billions flowed south. Unorganized labour in its millions migrated north. Pressure of population on the land was released for the first time since the 1920s, and the historic process of bringing more and more, increasingly marginal, land into cultivation was reversed. In the mountainous and hilly and marginal areas, empty houses, depopulated villages and abandoned farms made their appearances. Intensification, modernization, capitalization were concentrated in the lowlands, where irrigation was available or mechanization convenient. A new geography emerged, as those at the lower end of the agricultural scale – farmers still using the traditional methods, tenants working their own smallholdings and aging peasants – became the poor relations of the Common Market.

### Land reform: the Italian experience

Land reform movements after World War II were common to all Europe, though their form and details varied greatly from country to country. If we have to choose one example to illustrate the whole process, that of Italy is probably the best. The Italian land reform was conditioned and moulded by the experience of the past, and sought to avoid the mistakes that had vitiated reforms elsewhere.

The Enti di Riforma were the official bodies charged with administering the reform. Staffed with a knowledgeable cadre, some with experience gained in Mussolini's ventures in land colonization, the Enti provided a package of credit facilities, back-up services, organizations, institutions and processing plants to accompany the distribution of land. Paternalistic in its spirit, influenced by electoral considerations, the effort was enormous, the expense considerable, the final result – with all its faults – impressive. The fundamental fault was that the reform was an anachronism. By the time it was completed the premise upon which it was founded, to absorb low productivity farm labour, was hardly relevant. The industrial development of the north, the huge migration from the south and the demands of the French and German labour markets had radically altered the situation.

Throughout the Mediterranean, the effects of change accumulated. But the reading public's image of its rural people was to some extent distorted by the writings of, first, the novelists, such as Carlo Levi and Silone, then the reformers, Danilo Dolci, and then the social scientists, such as Banfield and Davis, and most recently the cineasts, Paolo Taviani with his *Padre Padroni*. All of these reported truthfully on a situation that, by the time it had been widely accepted as current, was in fact more historic than relevant. The book that gave the best insight to the future was Johan Galtung's *Members of Two Worlds*, an impressive analysis of the ambiguities of Sicilian village life. As a conclusion, Galtung assessed the forces that would make for change and resolution in this labyrinthian environment. Low in his estimation was the diffusion of ideas via the media or the school and via social mobility. High in his estimation as a strategy of change was the spread of capitalistic labour relations and the monetary economy. It was a solution that would have horrified the anarcho-syndicalists.

### The eastern alternative: collectivization

The Italian land reform had been preceded by a series of reforms throughout eastern Europe, which completed many of the unfinished tasks of the interwar period. The link between land reform and the nationalization of territory was maintained in those districts where German-speaking populations were expelled, particularly in the Voivodina in Yugoslavia and the Oder-Neisse region regained by Poland. As in the interwar years, the state-controlled sector was extended by the confiscation of foreign properties. Basically, the reforms were popular movements distributing the land to an even wider section of the population, initially engendering support in the rural areas for the new regimes. Members of the former landless classes were not reluctant to join simple co-operatives because, despite their receiving some land under the reform, they lacked the capital, animals and equipment to farm properly.

As the pressure for collectivization increased, however, that acceptance turned to resentment and opposition. In general the rural classes became opponents of the Stalinist régimes. In some instances opposition turned to short-lived revolt, but what really happened throughout the region during the course of this huge transformation we shall probably never know. At the present stage of knowledge, collectivization must be studied on the basis of its results rather than its histories.

The process of collectivization was rapid; the results were disappointing – the combined effect of peasant resistance, poor organization on the official side and the lack of material necessities. Among the reasons given by Polish peasants in 1968 for the failure of collective farming were the bad organization of the farm, the careless accomplishment of the field work, the frequent misunderstanding among members and the excessive size of administration, when compared with the insufficient number of field workers. They expressed the belief that the private farm provided a much greater sense of security and that individual improvement was possible only under a private farming system. Friction arose from the fact that family bonds often determined the informal structures of the enterprise, though such bonds were not formally admitted. The more complex the organization of the farm, the less efficient it was likely to be.

Yet with all its faults and insufficiencies, collectivization remained the official policy of all the eastern European governments, except Yugoslavia and Poland, and irrevocably collectivization changed rural life in eastern Europe. The demographic basis for any return to

No process in the whole history of life on the land has had such far-reaching effects as collectivization. Passionately endorsed as the solution to modern agricultural problems by the Communists, it aroused bitter opposition among the conservative peasantry. These two posters represent opposite sides of the debate. The first is meant to show the advantages of combining together: one man has a horse, another a plough, a third seed-corn; but until they all co-operate each one is helpless. The lower example is an anti-Bolshevik poster of about 1919, showing the Red Army requisitioning supplies from a hostile peasantry.

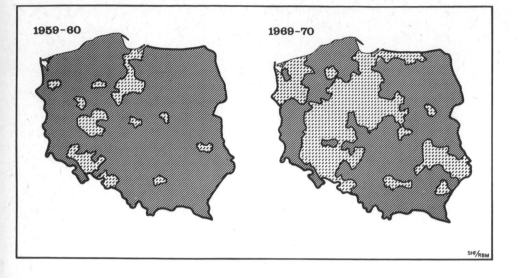

1959-60    1969-70

SHF/RBM

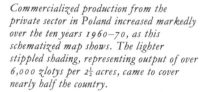

*Commercialized production from the private sector in Poland increased markedly over the ten years 1960–70, as this schematized map shows. The lighter stippled shading, representing output of over 6,000 zlotys per 2½ acres, came to cover nearly half the country.*

peasant farming has been eroded through migration, and through the social mobility and changing social aspirations associated with industrialization and the modernization of farming. The rural population, and particularly the farming population, now consists of a large section of aging people, a residual appendage to the industrial sector, supplicants to that sector's social service.

Most of the rural districts of eastern Europe are in a process of transition, and can perhaps best be understood in terms of a duality: the collectivized sector, receiving the modern inputs, mechanized, linked with the processing plants; and the private sector, still providing a remarkably high quotient of essential foodstuffs. The two sectors are quite distinct geographically. From the air, they are clearly visible within the same district as one crosses the Pannonian Plain, south and west of the Danube. They appear regionally, too, the remoter mountainous districts slackly organized in collectives, in contrast to the accessible plains, which produce a greater proportion of the marketed produce. In Yugoslavia such a geographical distinction became the basis for the formal separation of the private and public sectors. In Poland, too, socialist farming has

its own geography. The duality also manifests itself demographically, the modernized sector retaining a slightly younger, better qualified labour force than the private. But in both sectors that fundamental institution of rural life, the family, is experiencing the same sort of changes. Those harbingers of mass culture, the media, mechanization and the motor car or the motor cycle, are altering the value systems that the family once supported, and changing the needs that it once served.

### The survival of the family farm
The whole of postwar Europe has seen a huge migration from the country to the towns in search of more adequate wages and greater personal freedom. Despite cases of setback, hardship and disappointment the expansion of employment in the manufacturing and service sectors of every country has absorbed the influx. In these circumstances, what future is there for the peasant family farm? To survive, it has to be reorganized not only to meet the dictates of the industrial system but also to allow the personal aspirations of its workers some degree of satisfaction.

It was to this fundamental issue of survival that the leadership of the Centre Nationale des Jeunes Agriculteurs addressed themselves brilliantly in postwar France. As a consequence, the French experience in restructuring its agriculture occupies a significant place in any account of postwar Europe, though one has to add that this prominence is a little undeserved, for it derives in part from a laggard approach by the French to issues already tackled elsewhere. The low technical level of French farming compared with that of other west European countries had long been cause for comment. Young peasants who had served as prisoners of war on the farms of Nazi Germany remarked upon the difference in both standards and yields.

In Denmark and the Netherlands the high standards of the farmers reflected the stimulus of the export trade.

*Raising the standard of living in eastern Europe: the proportion of villages provided with electricity in the province of Cracow.*

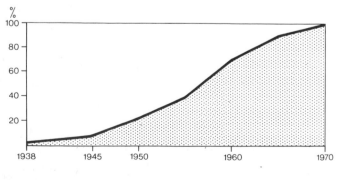

The manner in which the Danes had abandoned their protected arable system to establish an efficient livestock industry supplying the British market was a model of adaptation to modern commercial life, and like the Dutch they had been a success because specialization was supported with investment in education, research, marketing, infrastructure, and the development of the related processing industries.

The Swiss, too, in their own industrious way, prefigured the organization of peasant life in the modern nation. Like all the other peasantries of western Europe, the Swiss had suffered from the impact of falling world prices resulting from the appearance of New World grains on the home market. Between 1850 and 1905 the area under cereals declined by over a half, 750,000 acres to 335,000 acres. The state responded to the agricultural crisis with an 'arrêt fédéral concernant l'encouragement à donner à l'agriculture'. It became law in 1893. The peasantry banded together in the Union Suisse des Paysans in 1897, with a secretariat installed at Brugg. Two world wars left the Swiss wholly dependent on their own agricultural resources, and on both occasions they fed themselves adequately. But the peasants felt that their efforts during World War I had been poorly rewarded after it, when a further agricultural crisis, caused by the reappearance of cheap imported foodstuffs, drove more people from the land. The state's measures to combat the effects of this crisis proved inadequate. After World War II the response was much more comprehensive. By referendum, in 1952, the people of Switzerland approved a 'federal law for the improvement of agriculture and the maintenance of the peasant population'. This guaranteed the peasantry a place in Swiss society. For them the welfare era had arrived.

Germany's agrarian experiences were both similar and dissimilar to the experiences of the other western nations. Similar, in that land colonization continued as in Holland, Sweden, Finland and Italy during the interwar years, though in Germany's case with distinctly nationalistic overtones. Similar, too, in that the state progressively built up and assisted the construction of an infrastructure necessary to modern farming. But it was dissimilar in that the Third Reich's territory incorporated a large capitalistic sector in the east, which exerted an even greater political influence upon German life than did the capitalistic farming sectors in Italy and France. With their entailment laws, the Nazis sought to protect the middle peasantry against the inroads of capitalism. This policy also served their nationalistic and racial philosophies. After the war, the Russian dismemberment of Prussia saved the federal government the embarrassment of having to deal with the large Junker estates. With the completion of collectivization in East Germany, it is now possible to compare the operation of socialized farming in an advanced industrial state with family farming under similar conditions. The relatively poorer performance of East German farming has been attributed to the comparative inefficiency of the provision of such services as machinery, transport, marketing and the like. This indicates the degree to which farming, family or collective, is already incorporated in the general economy. It also shows the significance of these servicing sectors to the whole development of farming in the future. In West Germany the government has been preoccupied with the evolution of family farming, trying to achieve an income for the farmer equal to that of industrial workers of equivalent skill. Rising farm incomes have been achieved, but parity, except in some rare instances, has not.

In France, population in rural areas had long ceased to rise, but in comparison with other countries the proportion of countrymen to town dwellers remained high. The task of devising a policy for the modernization of farming became confused with the task of reviving the economic life of the regions that happened to contain large agrarian components. As a consequence of this confusion, the emotional appeal of any policy concerned with the peasantry was always enhanced by the additional knowledge that its protection as a class also acted to protect the vital bases of the region, or even the nation as a whole. Yet this apparent coincidence of interest obscured a fundamental contradiction.

Regional revival required the 'demographic haemorrhage', as the French put it, to be staunched. But if the people who stayed in the region remained inefficient

*Movement of people out of farming, as exemplified in France between 1962 and 1968. In limited areas, rural population is on the increase (1); in much more, it is on the decrease despite natural increase (2); while in a substantial area, rural population is on the decrease owing to migration without natural increase (3).*

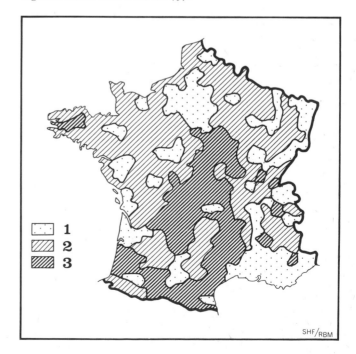

1
2
3

SHF/RBM

peasant farmers the result would be an increase, not a decrease, in regional disparities. Stronger regional economies required new structures. Only a modernized peasantry could support these new structures. So, paradoxically, a modernized peasantry required the movement of people out of farming.

It took a long time for most Frenchmen to see things this way, and some still do not. During the interwar and Vichy periods, when there was little economic growth and capitalism appeared to be on its last legs, the peasantry were regarded as the victims of inevitable monopolistic tendencies. As L. Salleron wrote: 'The truth is that a population of smallholders costs society nothing, either in food or money; on the contrary, such a population contributes enormously to society: 1, by supplying it with food as effectively as any ultra-modern, over-equipped method of cultivation; 2, by amassing its own savings; 3, by absorbing the maximum

*In postwar Hungary popular feeling – encouraged by local Communists – ran high against the old landlord class. In this poster a worker keeps back the bourgeois owners while the peasants happily take over the land.*

amount of industrial and monetary inflation; 4, by constituting a substantial market for commerce and industry.'

In the 1930s this widely held view of the peasantry produced policies aimed at their defence, not their re-organization. Protection was provided through a prices policy. Applied uniformly to an agrarian structure containing many diversities, however, this led only to growing internal disparities within the farming population. The prices policy inflated the profits of the capitalist enterprise rather than protecting the interests of the traditional peasant farm. Propagandists wrote paeans in favour of the rural idyll. But the reality was that at least a million farms had to disappear if the mechanization and re-equipment of the remainder were to be economic. The situation only revealed itself clearly after the postwar revival of the French economy.

The collapse of markets and prices in the 1950s led to growing disturbances in many parts of France. The first confrontation was in Languedoc in 1953, on 28 July. By 12 October the disturbances had moved to the Centre region. Henceforth, riots and blockades became a feature of rural politics. Commencing with a series of local meetings aimed at raising consciousness, admitting women to its membership and giving them a voice in its councils, the CNJA movement (the Centre Nationale des Jeunes Agriculteurs) made its final challenge to authority while recognizing that the rural and farming population was not homogeneous in any sense. The result was a spectacular period of legislation, which produced a structuralist policy for agriculture, as opposed to a prices policy.

The structuralists sought to preserve the traditional peasant farm by modifying some of the fundamental features that prevented its incorporation in the modern economy, or prevented its inhabitants from enjoying a life-style comparable with their urban counterparts. In addition, they wished to maintain the existing flow of funds from the treasury that were used in programmes of price support and modernization. For the aged, they sought to replace the security provided by the family farm with a state pension, on condition that the land relinquished was made available to younger men wishing to build up economic units. For the young progressive farmer wanting to remain in farming, they sought to provide more land, through regional offices that exercised a pre-emptive right over all agricultural land coming on the market. The legislation also had the effect of inhibiting urban buyers seeking to acquire farm land.

Imaginative as they were, these innovations, these policies, were of only secondary importance compared with the continuing high subsidization of farming and the continuing huge migration from farming and away from the rural districts. Debatisse gave the true measure of these reforms when he described these actions as 'holding back the train of progress in order to allow the peasantry to get aboard'.

### The vanishing peasant

In 1978 Joseph Klatzmann estimated that the 900,000 full-time farms still based upon the single family unit, in existence in 1970, would have declined to 500,000, averaging 125 acres in extent, by the end of the century. An undetermined number of part-time farms would complement the rural population. Whatever resemblance these end of the century family farms may bear to their mid-century and early century predecessors, they will differ from them in two fundamental aspects. They will have survived only on account of their complete absorption into the complex system of production and marketing; and the amount of capital utilized per unit of labour will have surpassed all historic records.

The process of mechanization and re-equipment is already well advanced: 205,000 tractors in 1955; 1,377,000 in 1975. Living standards have risen accordingly. Reading reports of 1952, for instance, we find: 'There is no bath in the whole village', or 'the bedrooms have mud floors . . . the beds contain only a heap of straw'. In 1974, by contrast, the percentage of farm households possessing a car, a television set, a refrigerator and a washing machine was either close to the national average or exceeded it. It would appear that incomes in agriculture have risen as fast as the incomes in other major occupations. But, and this is an important consideration, that same much-increased volume of gross income is now distributed among a much smaller and differently structured agrarian population than was the case in the 1950s. Between 1954 and 1975 the gross return per farmer in France may have slightly more than doubled in real terms. In the same period of time the number of independent farmers and their family aides has fallen from 4 million to $1\frac{1}{10}$ million, while the proportion of agricultural land worked in holdings of more than 125 acres has risen from 28 to 43 per cent in the period 1963–76. New structures, new systems, have emerged alongside the old in the wider rural community as opposed to the more limited farming community. Isolation has vanished, the penetration of urban values, mixed as they are, has advanced to a point never seen before. City people are now a common if seasonal element of village life. In the majority of areas rural infrastructures and rural economies are being rebuilt. Nevertheless some village communities appear to be on the point of collapse.

Many will regret the passing of the peasantry, the passing of a life-style that lasted for so long but that has been in decline for more than a century. At its best, peasant farming had much to recommend it, and included much that was worth preserving. But a curious fact cannot be overlooked. One of the best defences of peasant farming was written in 1950 by an Englishman, Phillip Oyler. Yet the very area he chose to write about, the Dordogne, was considered to be one of the more backward areas of peasant France, an area that provided the ammunition for those fighting for revival and renovation. Why is it, one must ask, that once the

*Propaganda for public ownership in postwar Romania. In the first poster: 'As far as the eye can see it is* my *farm', says the landlord in his car. In the second, the peasants on their tractor can say: 'As far as the eye can see it is* our *farm.'*

opportunity arose to migrate, an existence so engaging to present-day city dwellers was rejected by millions and millions of people? Why is it that a life that possessed so many virtues and strengths has been abandoned by so many? A French girl's comments, recorded by Michel Debatisse, reveal what so many city dwellers ignore: the rural world of the past was a world marked by insecurity, isolation and fatigue: 'Through our life there prowls a sort of permanent fear. An unspoken anxiety hovers over the house. We dread the bad luck that is sure to come along: illness, a bad harvest, hail, the death of an animal, a dealer who cheats us. We have no security. . . . We form a little cut-off world . . . enclosed in the narrow circle of our routine. . . . All my energy has been directed to one sole purpose: to complete the great sum of my daily actions – my work.'

Rural life in Europe between 1919 and 1979, for a large section of the population, could not meet the conditions that the anarcho-syndicalists of Spain sought, and many people do still seek: a mode of economic existence that allows the individual dignity, freedom and leisure enough to enjoy his intellectual, spiritual and physical endowments.

To have survived, peasant agriculture would have had to perform the impossible. Small-scale organization and traditional methods are simply irreconcilable with the requirements of a modern economy; the amount of labour demanded from the labourer is irreconcilable with the expectations of a modern citizen.

Peasant farming as we have known it is therefore disappearing. Unfortunately no one has provided a convenient term to describe what is evolving except to call it new or modern. The fortunes of the eastern European farmer are linked to the Communist governments' attempts to feed satisfactorily their own urban and industrialized masses. In the west a new system is arising, based upon the individual, well supplied with capital and knowledge, but integrated into an international complex that seeks its fortunes not only within the enlarged confines of the EEC but among the famished millions across the world.

These issues do not concern only the peasants themselves. In affecting the land they affect us all. Below a certain density of population the environment cannot be maintained. Rivers and their banks go unattended. The amelioration of an environment, so attractive to the tourist and the city dweller, which has taken place over centuries, comes to a halt, unless the peasantry are seen as mere park-keepers. In this fashion the environment of the past becomes a charge upon the treasuries of the future.

---

**The sad figure of the peasant** – puzzled, unsophisticated and honest – in Ernst Würtenberger's powerful painting *Cow dealing*, painted in 1908, epitomizes the plight of the traditional countryman in the 20th century. 'Cow dealing' is also German slang for 'sharp practice'. It is clear that the peasant is being cheated. Before these confident, fast-talking businessmen he stands irresolute; he will lose his fine cow for a fraction of her value. The new market forces have left him helpless. Caution and conservatism were once his safeguards, now they betray him. The standard of living that once satisfied him is no longer comparable to that of workers in the towns, and can anyway hardly be maintained. Only technology and organization can save him, and they will destroy his world.

The four centuries covered by this book saw many far-reaching changes in the European countryside – the replacement of the feudal system by a market economy, the emancipation of the peasants, the enclosure movement, mechanization. . . . But through all of them the rural community was able to survive in some form or other. In the last quarter of the 20th century this no longer seems possible. Neither the eastern collective nor the western commercial unit seems to have any place for the traditional village. Farming is now a national issue; crops are dictated by government, prices a matter for international committees; and the number of people who live and work on the land is constantly diminishing. The peasant is a dying species, able to exist only in small backward pockets where methods of mass cultivation are not worth employing. How much that was of value morally and culturally in his world can be kept in any future social system is an unresolved question. (1)

# The family farm

The typical well-to-do farm throughout history consisted of a single family with relatives, dependants and hired hands. This automatically set limits to the degree of specialization that could be introduced.

**Every member of the family** was expected to work, usually from sunrise to sunset. But what had been a self-sufficient way of life up to the 19th century, yields only a precarious and unsatisfactory return in the 20th. *Above*: two scenes from postwar Europe, where the traditional economy still survived – seeding potatoes in Germany and lifting beets in Poland. (2, 3)

**Spanish women** gather at the communal washing place (*left*). Such a scene already belongs to the past. The demand for higher standards of living is natural; it can only be answered by a new standard of farming in which the family unit is superseded. (4)

**The family table** remains the heart of the household. *Below left:* French farm workers and family eat together with a huge loaf, characteristic of Calvados, in the centre. French farm policy, however, is a subject of bitter dispute, and the smiling faces display a confidence which perhaps not all of them feel. *Below:* a pair of naïve paintings from Romania entitled *Yesterday and Today*. 'Yesterday' the farmer and his wife lived in a rustic cottage and wore peasant clothes. 'Today' they expect a modern house, fashionable clothes and a television. (5, 6)

**The Fascists** did in fact take the farmers' problems
seriously, and their ideology was sympathetic to
traditional ways of life. The Nazis held annual 'Peasant
Congresses' (*far right*), identifying the party with the land.
At the Nuremberg rallies farm workers with spades
paraded as the 'soldiers' of agriculture. *Right:* Italian
Fascist rallies of the thirties had similar aims. Mussolini
told them: 'The government is aware of the problems of
agriculture, and regards the peasants as a fundamental
force in the country's prosperity.' Whatever the unpleasant
aspects of his régime, it did achieve some solid gains. (8, 9)

VI CONCORSO NAZIONALE PER
LA VITTORIA DEL GRANO
BANDITO DAL CAPO DEL GOVERNO PREMI L.1.700.000 RIVOLGERSI ALLA CATTEDRA DI AGRICOLTURA

# A future for the peasant: the myth

**In the 20th century, for the first time in history, peasants and small farmers became a political force.**

**Communism puts its faith** in collectivism. A Russian poster published immediately after the Revolution (*left*) shows an idealized peasant driving his plough through the relics of capitalism and monarchy. Lenin habitually grouped 'peasants' with 'workers and soldiers', but in fact they were never consulted and had to submit to policies imposed from above. *Below:* ten years later (1930) a vigorous propaganda campaign was still in progress to persuade them to join collectives voluntarily. 'Go to the collective farm', says the slogan, as the peasant girl shakes off the grotesque little bourgeois who try to hinder her and strides towards a rosy future. (7, 10)

# A future
# for the peasant:
# the reality

Since World War II, the two blocks
of east and west have each adopted
their own solution to the
agricultural problem. Both involve
large-scale economic planning. In
the Communist countries,
production levels are set and prices
regulated by a central authority. In
the west, the same objectives are
attempted through democratic
processes and international
negotiation.

**Peasants enroll** for a collective farm
in Russia in the early thirties.
Collectivization was seen as a method
of applying industrial techniques to
agriculture. Fiercely resisted by the
wealthier farmers, and unpopular
with most of the peasantry, it was
nevertheless forced through and was
virtually complete by 1941. (11)

**In eastern Europe**, populist land
reforms were initiated after 1919 but
failed to make any decisive effect.
After World War II, under Russian
influence, experiments in co-operatives
and collectives were renewed with
varying success. This photograph
(*left*) shows a discussion between
Hungarian peasants on an early
co-operative farm. *Below:* by the
1970s almost all arable land in
Hungary was nationalized and run by
either co-operatives or state farms.
Here autumn-barley is being sown at
Boly State Farm. (12, 13)

**Mussolini at the wheel** of one of the first Fiat tractors. Party members significantly outnumber peasants. Mussolini's schemes of land colonization were in many cases practical and far-sighted. After the war, improvements achieved by the Enti di Riforma reflected Fascist experience. (14)

**The western alternative** to collectivization is the European Economic Community – an attempt to create a planned economy beneficial to all its members. This has often proved impossible, and the farmers of individual countries have found themselves penalized for the sake of the supposed common good. *Below:* thousands of French farmers at Fougères in Brittany protest against a price system that is reducing their incomes. (15)

**Farming as industry.** One of the themes running through the previous chapters has been the way in which forms of rural community have interacted with techniques of agriculture. The reasons why the peasant has to disappear are ultimately technological. A comparison between these two pictures and virtually any others in the book tells the whole story. *Top*: mass production of Parmesan cheeses. *Bottom*: automatic grading of eggs in France. (16, 17)

# Select bibliography

## 1. The village and the family

Abel, W. *Geschichte der deutschen Landwirtschaft vom frühen Mittelalter bis zum 19. Jahrhundert* (2nd ed.) Stuttgart, 1967

Agulhon, M. *La Vie sociale en Provence intérieure au lendemain de la Révolution* Paris, 1970

Babeau, A. *Le Village sous l'ancien régime* Paris, 1878

Blum, J. *Lord and Peasant in Russia from the Ninth to the Nineteenth Century* Princeton, 1961

Bonham-Carter, V. *The English Village* London, 1952

Bouchard, G. *Le Village immobile: Sennely-en-Sologne au XVIII<sup>e</sup> siècle* Paris, 1972

Braun, R. *Industrialisierung und Volksleben* Zurich and Stuttgart, 1960

Bull, E. *Vergleichende Studien über die Kulturverhältnisse des Bauerntums* Oslo, 1930

Cabourdin, G. *Terre et hommes en Lorraine (1550–1635)* Nancy, 1974

El'iashevich, V. B. *Istoriia prava pozemel'noi sobstvennosti v Rossii* Paris, 1948–51

Fussell, G. E. *Village Life in the Eighteenth Century* Worcester, 1951

Gaudemet, J. *Les Communautés familiales* Paris, 1963

Goody, J., J. Thirsk and E. P. Thompson, eds *Family and Inheritance: Rural Society in Western Europe 1200–1800* Cambridge, 1976

Gras, N. S. B. *The Economic and Social History of an English Village* Cambridge, 1930

Hoskins, W. G. *The Midlands Peasant* London, 1957

Jacquart, J. *La Crise rurale en Île-de-France 1550–1670* Paris, 1974

Laslett, P., ed. *Household and Family in Past Time* Cambridge, 1972

Le Roy Ladurie, E. *Les paysans de Languedoc* Paris, 1966

Quirin, K. H. *Herrschaft und Gemeinde nach mitteldeutschen Quellen des 12. bis 18. Jahrhundert* Göttingen, 1952

## 2. The nobility and the land

Bitton, D. *The French Nobility in Crisis 1560–1640* Stanford, 1969

Bloch, M. *La Société féodale* Paris, 1939; Eng. ed. *Feudal Society* London, 1961

Bluche, F. *La Vie quotidienne de la noblesse française au XVIII<sup>e</sup> siècle* Paris, 1973

Blum, J. *The End of the Old Order in Rural Europe* Princeton, 1978

Brunner, O. *Adeliges Landleben und europäischer Geist* Salzburg, 1949

Duby, G. *L'economie rurale et la vie des campagnes dans l'Occident Médiéval* Paris, 1962

Elias, N. *Die hofische Gesellschaft* Neuwied, 1969

Forster, R. *The House of Saulx-Tavannes* Baltimore, 1971

Girouard, M. *Life in the English Country House* London and New Haven, 1978

Goodwin, A., ed. *The European Nobility in the Eighteenth Century* London, 1953

Labatut, J. P. *Les Noblesses européenes de la fin du XV<sup>e</sup> siècle à la fin du XVIII<sup>e</sup> siècle* Paris, 1978

Martiny, F. 'Die Adelsfrage in Preussen vor 1806 als politisches und soziales Problem', *Vierteljahrschrift für Sozial- und Wirtschaftsgeschichte,* Beiheft XXXV, 1939

Meyer, J. *Noblesses et pouvoirs dans l'Europe d'ancien régime* Paris, 1973

Mousnier, R. *Les Institutions de France sous la monarchie absolue, 1598–1789* Paris, 1974

Reuter, T., ed. *The Medieval Nobility* Amsterdam, 1979

Romanovich-Slavatinskii, A. *Dvorianstvo v Rossii ot nachala XVIII veky do otmeny krepostnago prava* St Petersburg, 1870

Rosenberg, H. *Bureaucracy, Aristocracy and Autocracy* Cambridge, Mass., 1958

Spring, D., ed. *European Landed Elites in the 19th Century* Baltimore and London, 1977

Stone, L. *The Crisis of the Aristocracy 1558–1641* Oxford, 1965

Thompson, F. M. L. *English Landed Society in the Nineteenth Century* London, 1963

Vierhaus, R. *Der Adel vor der Revolution* Göttingen, 1971

Vicens Vives, J. *An Economic History of Spain* Princeton, 1969

## 3. From servitude to freedom

Bloch, M. *La Société féodale* Paris, 1939; Eng. ed. *Feudal Society* London, 1961

Blum, J. *The End of the Old Order in Rural Europe* Princeton, 1978

— *Lord and Peasant in Russia from the Ninth to the Nineteenth Century* Princeton, 1961

Chambers, J. D. and G. E. Mingay *The Agricultural Revolution 1750–1880* London, 1966

Goubert, P. *Beauvais et le Beauvaisis de 1600 à 1730* Paris, 1960

Gras, N. S. B. and E. C. *The Economic and Social History of an English Village* Cambridge, 1930

Heckscher, E. F. *An Economic History of Sweden* Cambridge, 1954

Herr, R. *The Eighteenth-century Revolution in Spain* Princeton 1958

Hilton, R. H. *The Decline of Serfdom in Medieval England* London, 1969

Huggett, F. E. *The Land Question and European Society* London, 1975

Juillard, E. *La Vie rurale dans la plaine de Basse-Alsace* Paris, 1953

Kulischer, J. *Allgemeine Wirtschaftsgeschichte des Mittelalters und der Neuzeit,* 2 vols, Vienna, 1971

Le Roy Ladurie, E. *Les Paysans de Languedoc,* 2 vols, Paris, 1966

Mousnier, R. *Les Hierarchies sociales de 1450 à nos jours* Paris, 1969

Revesz, L. *Der osteuropäische Bauer* Bern 1964

Saalfeld, D. *Bauernwirtschaft und Gutsbetrieb in der vorindustriellen Zeit* Stuttgart 1960

Saint-Jacob, P. de *Les Paysans de la Bourgogne du nord au dernier siècle de l'ancien régime* Paris, 1960

See, H. *Esquisse d'une histoire du régime agraire en Europe aux XVIII et XIX siècles* Paris, 1921

Smith, R. E. F. *The Enserfment of the Russian Peasantry* Cambridge 1968

## 4. The rural economy

Blum, J. *The End of the Old Order in Rural Europe* Princeton, 1978

Chambers, J. D. and G. E. Mungay *The Agricultural Revolution* London, 1966

Le Roy Ladurie, E. and Michel Morineau *Histoire economique et sociale de la France, 1450–1660,* vol. II (*Paysannerie et croissance*) Paris, 1977

Müller, Hans Heinrich 'Akademie und Wirtschaft im 18 Jahrhundert' in *Preisschriften der Berliner Akademie* Berlin, 1975

Thirsk, J. 'Seventeenth-century Agriculture and Social Change' in *Land, Church and People,* supplement to *Agricultural History Review* vol. 18, 1970

Van Bath, B. H. Slicher *The Agrarian History of Western Europe AD 500–1850* London, 1963

— 'Agriculture in the Vital Revolution' in *Cambridge Economic History of Europe* vol. V (*The Economic Organization of Early Modern Europe*) Cambridge, 1977

## 5. The struggle to survive

Abel, W. *Agrarkrisen und Agrarkonjunktur* (3rd ed.) Hamburg and Berlin, 1978

— *Massernarmut und Hungerkrisen im vorindustriellen Europa* Hamburg and Berlin, 1974

Armengaud, A. *Population in Europe, 1700–1900* Glasgow, 1973

Ashton, T. S. *Economic Fluctuations in England, 1700–1800* Oxford, 1959

Benecke, G. *Society and Politics in Germany, 1500–1750* London and Toronto, 1974

Braudel, Fernand *Civilisation materielle et capitalism, XV<sup>e</sup> XVIII<sup>e</sup> siècle* Paris, 1967; Eng. ed. *Capitalism and Material Life 1400–1800* trs. Miriam Kochan, London, 1973

— *La Méditerranée et le monde méditerranéen à l'époque de Philippe II* (2nd rev. ed.) Paris, 1966; Eng. ed. *The Mediterranean and the Mediterranean World in the Age of Philip II* London, 1973

*The Cambridge Economic History of Europe* vols I–V, Cambridge, 1952–77

Deslarzes, *The Capital and Income of Farms in Europe . . . 1927–28 to 1934–35* Geneva, 1930

Hartwell, R. M. *et al. The Long Debate on Poverty* London, 1972

Hill, Christopher *Reformation to Industrial Revolution. A social and economic history of Great Britain, 1530–1780* London, 1969

Hobsbawm, E. J. *Labouring Men* London, 1976

Le Play, F. *Les Ouvriers européens* (2nd ed.) Paris, 1877–79

Mathiessen, P. C. *Befolkningsprobleme* (3rd ed.) Copenhagen, 1976

Mols, R. *Population in Europe, 1500–1700* Glasgow, 1974

Thirsk, J. *Economic Policy and Projects* Oxford, 1978

Tilly, C. ed. *Historical Studies of Changing Fertility* Stanford, 1978

**6. Rural unrest**

Bensidoun, Sylvain *L'Agitation paysanne en Russie, de 1881 à 1902* Paris, 1975

Bercé, Yves-Marie *Croquants et Nu-pieds: les soulèvements paysans en France, du 16ᵉ au 19ᵉ siècle* Paris, 1974

— *Révoltes et révolutions dans l'Europe moderne, 16ᵉ – 18ᵉ siècle* Paris, 1980

Bernal, Antonio-Miguel and Michel Drain *Les Campagnes sévillannes aux 19ᵉ et 20ᵉ siècles* Paris, 1971

Blickle, Peter *Die Revolution von 1525* Munich, 1975

Broeker, Galen *Rural Disorder and Police Reform in Ireland, 1812–1836* London, 1970

Eidelberg, Philip-G. *The Great Rumanian Peasant Revolt of 1907* Leyden, 1974

Field, Daniel *The End of Serfdom: nobility and bureaucracy in Russia, 1855–61* Cambridge, Mass., 1976

— *Rebels in the Name of the Tsar* Boston, 1976

Fourquin, Guy *Les Soulèvements populaires au Moyen Age* Paris, 1972

Hobsbawm, E. J. *Bandits* London, 1969

— and G. Rudé *Captain Swing* London, 1969

Kieniewicz, Stefan *The Emancipation of the Polish Peasantry* Chicago, 1969

Landsberger, H. A., ed. *Rural Protest: Peasant Movements and Social Change* Edinburgh, 1974

Mousnier, Roland *Fureurs paysannes: les paysans dans les révoltes du 17ᵉ siècle* Paris, 1967

Soboul, Albert *Problèmes paysans de la Révolution, 1789–1848* Paris, 1976

Stevenson, John *Popular Disturbances in England, 1700–1870* London, 1979

Vucinich, Wayne S., ed. *The Peasant in 19th-century Russia* Stanford, 1968

**7. Rural folklore**

Carmichael, A. *Carmina Gadelica* Edinburgh, 1928–54

Deneke, Bernward *Hochzeit* Munich, 1971

Dumont, L. *La Tarasque* Paris, 1951

Ellworthy, F. T. *The Evil Eye, 1895*

Evans, E. E. *Irish Folk Ways* London, 1956

Evans, G. E. *The Pattern under the Plough* London, 1961

Frazer, J. G. *The Golden Bough* (abr. ed.) London, 1922

Grimm, Jacob *Deutsche Mythologie,* 1844

Gunda, Bela 'The Magical Watching of the Flock on the Great Hungarian Plain' in *Folklore* vol. 81, 1970

Hole, Christina *Saints in Folklore* London, 1966

Macfarlane, A. *Witchcraft in Tudor and Stuart England* London, 1970

Mannhardt, W. *Der Baumkultus der Germanen und ihre Nachbarstämme* Berlin, 1875

Menefee, S. 'The Merry Maidens and the Noce de Pierre' in *Folklore* vol. 85, 1974

Newall, Venetia *An Egg at Easter* London, 1971

Russell, J. B. *A History of Witchcraft: sorcerers, heretics and pagans* London, 1980

Vukanović, T. P. 'Obscene Objects in Balkan Religion and Magic, in *Folklore* vol. 92, 1981

Zammit-Maempel, G. 'The Evil Eye and Protective Cattle Horns in Malta' in *Folklore* vol. 79, 1968

Zentai, T. 'The Sign Language of Hungarian Graveyards' in *Folklore* vol. 90, 1979

**8. The American farmer**

Anonymous (? Dr John Mitchell) *American Husbandry* 2 vols, London, 1775; another ed. H. J. Carman, ed., New York, 1939

Bogue, Allen C. *From Prairie to Corn Belt* Chicago, 1963

Cather, Willa *O Pioneers!* Boston, 1913; 1962

Danhof, Clarence *Change in Agriculture: Northern United States, 1820–1880* Cambridge, Mass., 1963

Crevecoeur, J. Hector St John *Letters from An American Farmer* n.d.

Galtung, J. *Members of Two Worlds* Oslo, 1971

Gates, Paul W. *The Farmer's Age: Agriculture, 1815–1860* New York, 1960

Holmes, G. K. 'Progress of Agriculture in the US' in USDA *Yearbook,* 1899

Malin, James C. *Winter Wheat in the Golden Belt of Kansas* Kansas, 1944

Olmstead, F. L. *A Journey in the Back Country* New York, 1860

— *A Journey in the Seaboard Slave States* New York, 1856

Oyler, P. *The Generous Earth* Harmondsworth, 1961

Rasmussen, Wayne P. *Agriculture in the United States: A Documentary History* 4 vols, New York, 1975

Rolvaag, Ole E. *Giants in the Earth* New York, 1964

Sakolski, A. M. *The Great American Land Bubble* New York, 1932; repr. Johnson Reprint, 1966

Shannon, Fred N. *The Farmers' Last Frontier* New York, 1945

Washington, George *Letters on Agriculture* (to Arthur Young and Sir John Sinclair) 2 vols, Alexandria 1803 and Washington 1847

Webb, Walter P. *The Great Plains* New York, 1931

**9. The peasant in the modern world**

Bandini, M. *Cento anni di storia agraria italiana* Rome, 1957

Bell, John D. *Peasants in power* Princeton and Guildford, 1977

Dabitesse, M. *La Révolution silencieuse* Paris, 1963

Duby, G. and A. Wallon *Histoire de la France rurale* Paris, 1976

Dumont, René *Voyages en France d'un agronome* Paris, 1956

Franklin, S. H. *The European Peasantry* London, 1969

Galtung, J. *Members of Two Worlds* Oslo, 1971

Klatzmann, Joseph *L'Agriculture française* Paris, 1978

Oyler, P. *The Generous Earth* Harmondsworth, 1961

Tomasevich, J. *Peasants, Politics and Economic Change in Jugoslavia* Stanford and London, 1955

Warriner, D. *The Economics of Peasant Farming* London, 1964

# Sources of illustrations

Hofmann, 1872. Abby Aldrich Rockefeller Folk Art Center, Williamsburg, Virginia.
201 9. *Flax Scutching Bee*. Linton Park, 1885. National Gallery of Art, Washington, D.C. Gift of Edgar William and Bernice Chrysler Garbisch.
201 10. *The Barn Dance*. Grandma Moses, 1950. Courtesy of Hammer Galleries, New York.
201 11. Photo: Jonathan Cox.
202 12. Railroad across the Prairies, mid-19th century. Photo: USDA.
13. *The 9:45 Accommodation, Stratford, Connecticut*. Henry E. Samson, 1867. Metropolitan Museum of Art, New York.
202 14. Early wholesale market. Photo: USDA.
15. Construction of the National Highway, Durham County, North Carolina, *c.* 1919. Library of Congress, Washington, D.C.
203 16. *I feed you all*. American Oleographic Company, 1875. Library of Congress, Washington, D.C.
203 17. From *The Depression Years*, Dover Publications, Inc. Photo: Arthur Rothstein.
18. Marshalltown Fruit Store, 1938. From *The Depression Years*, Dover Publications, Inc. Photo: Arthur Rothstein.
204 19. Rooster weathervane. J. Howard, Massachusetts, *c.* 1800. David L. Davies Collection. From *American Weathervanes and Whirligigs*, R. Bishop and P. Coblentz, 1981. By permission of the publisher, E. P. Dutton, New York.
20. Painted wooden woolwinder. Connecticut, *c.* 1875. Howard and Jean Lipman Collection.
21. 'Thirty-Two Birds' appliqué quilt. Maryland, mid-19th century. Courtesy of the Shelburne Museum, Shelburne, Vermont.
205 22. *The old plantation*. Anonymous, late 18th century. Abby Aldrich Rockefeller Folk Art Center, Williamsburg, Virginia.
23. *The Quilting Party*. Anonymous, late 19th century. Abby Aldrich Rockefeller Folk Art Center, Williamsburg, Virginia.
206 24. Cotton pickers, 1898. Library of Congress, Washington, D.C.
25. Steam-ploughing, *c.* 1907. Library of Congress, Washington, D.C.
26. Threshing Machine. Photo: Mansell Collection.
207 27. Benjamin Holt's Combine Harvester (1887) at work near Walla Walla, Washington, 1902. Library of Congress, Washington, D.C.
208 28. Cedar Falls, Iowa. Photo: USDA.

**9. The peasant in the modern world**
211 Community Types, Baden-Württemberg, 1939–61. After P. Hesse, 'Der Strukturwandel der Siedlungskörper . . .', in *Jahrbucher für Statistik und Landeskunde von Baden Württemberg*.
212 *Ploughpuller and Woman*. Käthe Kollwitz, 1902. By courtesy of C. G. Boerner, Düsseldorf.
213 Russian Poster, *c.* 1921. British Museum.
214 The over-populated regions of eastern Europe, 1930–31. From D. Warriner, *The Economics of Peasant Farming*, 1939.
216 *Whetting the Scythe*. Käthe Kollwitz, 1905. By courtesy of C. G. Boerner, Düsseldorf.
219 *Top:* Bolshevik poster, *c.* 1920. British Museum.
219 *Bottom:* Anti-Bolshevik poster, *c.* 1919. British Museum.
220 *Top:* After P. H. Dabrowski, *Geographica Polonica* (29) pp.224–25.
220 *Bottom:* After M. Dobrowolska, *Geographica Polonica* (29) p.83.
221 After A. Fel, *Geographica Polonica* (29) p.57.
222 Poster. György Pál, 1950. National Széchényi Library, Budapest.
223 Cartoon. Gheorge Chiriac, 1960. RPR Art Museum, Bucharest.
225 1. *Cow Dealing*. Ernst Würtenberger, 1908. Kunsthaus, Zurich.
226 2. Seeding potatoes, Germany, 1959. Photo: Harvey Franklin.
226 3. Lifting beets, Poland. Photo: Harvey Franklin.
227 4. Communal washing place, Morella, Spain. Photo: Anne Bolt.
226 5. The Couteau farm, Normandy, 1940. Photo: Howell Walker, © National Geographic Society.
227 6. Poster. G. Mitrăchită. Scientific and Encyclopaedic Publishing House, Bucharest.
228 7. Russian Bolshevik poster, *c.* 1921. British Museum.
228 8. Poster by Adolfo Busi, 1928. Civica Raccolta delle Stampe Achille Bertarelli, Milan.
229 9. *4. Reichsbauerntag, Goslar*. Poster by M. Bletschacher, 1936. Bundesarchiv, Koblenz.
229 10. Russian poster, *c.* 1931. British Museum.
230 11. Russian collective farm, early 1930s.
12. Hungarian co-operative farm, 1945.
13. The Boly State Farm, Hungary.
231 14. Fototeca Servizio Informazioni, Rome.
15. Brittany, 1978. ADN-Zentralbild GDR, Camera Press.
232 16. Courtesy of EC – Photo: Pialoux–IPN.
17. Courtesy of EC – Photo: Pialoux–IPN.

# Index